The Emergence of
Industrial America

The Emergence of Industrial America

Strategic Factors in American Economic Growth Since 1870

James
Peter George
McMaster University

State University of New York Press
ALBANY

To Gwen

Published by
State University of New York Press, Albany

Printed in the United States of America

For information, address State University of New York Press, State University Plaza, Albany, N.Y., 12246

10 9 8 7 6 5 4 3 2

Contents

Tables

Preface

This book was originally conceived as a series of lectures on technological and organizational change in American manufacturing and agriculture which I delivered at the University of Cambridge, England, during the Lent Term 1974. Since then, the lectures have been greatly revised and expanded and, I hope, successfully integrated to provide a cohesive interpretation of the most dramatic elements in one of the world's great success stories — the emergence of the modern American economy. I hope the book will prove instructive and informative to students of American economic and social history, and interest the general reader as well.

In preparing this manuscript, I have incurred many debts. I wish to thank McMaster University for granting me sabbatical leave, and the chairman and members of the Faculty of Economics and Politics at the University of Cambridge and the vice-master and fellows of Trinity College for their hospitality. I am especially grateful to Dr. Brian Mitchell for helping to make my stay at Cambridge so enjoyable. Professor Ralph Gray of De Pauw University, whom I first met in Cambridge, read the manuscript at various stages. His helpful comments displayed a rare combination of keen criticism and geniune enthusiasm, and I am greatly in his debt. Some of the material in chapter 8 shows unmistakable signs of my longstanding collaboration with Professor Ernest H. Oksanen of McMaster, who has been a continual source of intellectual stimulus to me for many years. I have benefited too from countless long conversations with Professor David Gagan, also of McMaster. And last, because my dear wife has always encouraged and supported me, I dedicate this book to her with love and gratitude.

Peter George
June, 1981

1

An Overview of American Economic Growth, 1840 to 1960

Introduction

The history of the American economy since 1870 has a distinctive unifying theme. Since the end of the Civil War, the American economy has been growing primarily in response to the cumulative forces which economic historians call industrialization. However, 1870 was not the beginning of this process, for the development of manufacturing enterprise in New England and in the Middle Atlantic states and the commercialization of agriculture were initiated well before the Civil War.

As in the cases of the Canadian and Australian economies for much of their histories, discussions of the economic history of the United States in the eighteenth and early nineteenth centuries often take as a focal point the production for export markets of staple products. Staple production, which has been discussed extensively by Douglass North[1] among others, is generally associated in the antebellum American economy with the production of cotton in the South, and commercial agriculture in small grains, corn, and livestock in the Midwest. The significant difference compared with the Canadian and Australian economies is that in the United States, regional concentration on staple production seemed to give rise to diversification around the staple base, whereas in Canada and Australia the process of diversification was less noticeable. In fact, many economic historians have argued that Canadian and Australian economic development were retarded by concentration on staples. In the case of the United States, cotton and the plantation system may have adversely affected the structural composition of the southern regional economy; but, North argued, they also stimulated the development of textile manufacturing in the Northeast, especially in New England, and encouraged the production of agricultural surpluses in the Midwest. According to North, the specialization of the South in cotton was the basis of American interregional trading patterns before the Civil War.

Recent research suggests that North may have exaggerated the importance of interregional trade before 1860, by overstating the degree of regional economic specialization in the South and the Midwest and by understating each region's dependence on local or intraregional trade. Diane Lindstrom's study of the Philadelphia region is a case in point.[2] Lindstrom argues that the structure of production in Philadelphia depended primarily on local demand: Philadelphia producers rarely exported goods abroad or to distant regions of the country, exchanging their goods mainly within the immediate Philadelphia region and, by the 1840s, within the Northeast as transport costs fell. To the extent Philadelphia's experience is representative of prewar regional development, local markets appear to have been more significant than interregional trade and regional economic specialization in speeding the process of economic growth.

Manufacturing development began in earnest in the United States well before the Civil War: whether, as North asserted, in response to investment opportunities induced by staple production for interregional trade, or by a wide range of local, intraregional stimuli, need not concern us here. Whatever the source, high levels of per capita income and high rates of population growth in the first half of the nineteenth century were the common denominators upon which manufacturing production for the domestic market was based.

It was once customary among economic historians to argue that the Civil War gave great impetus to industrialization in the United States, but more recently they have learned that industrial expansion was well under way before the Civil War and, if anything, the Civil War represented an interruption of the trend rate of growth of industrial output. During the period from 1870 to 1900, the major feature of American economic history was the nation's transformation from a predominantly agrarian economy into a great industrial economy. This does not mean that agriculture ceased to be important. The continued importance of agriculture during this period is demonstrated by three facts: (i) at least one-half of the labor force was still employed in agriculture in the 1880s; (ii) agricultural productivity gains released large quantities of labor to the nonfarm sectors; and (iii) agricultural processing industries, expanding demand for farm machinery, and growing rural markets for consumers' goods constituted important linkage effects. Nevertheless, manufacturing output rose quite dramatically relative to agricultural output. And it is to the growing manufacturing sector that one looks as the main agent in the transformation of the American economy after the Civil War.

The necessary condition for continued growth in per capita income is productivity increase which results from technological and organizational changes associated with growing specialization of labor and the widening of the market. Technological and organizational changes in agriculture and manufacturing in the period from 1870 to 1930 are a primary focus in this book. It is in these two sectors that increases in productivity were to prove most important. The gains in productive efficiency resulted from several factors. First, improvements in technology promoted the adoption of mechanical equipment in manufacturing and its substitution for earlier reliance on skilled labor. In agriculture, it is possible that mechanization actually increased required skill levels because of the need to become familiar with machinery and to make on-the-spot repairs in the event of breakdown. Second, organizational innovations changed the ways in which labor, capital, and raw materials were brought together in the production process. Third, structural changes induced the transfer of labor from less productive agricultural activities to more productive sectors of the economy, especially manufacturing. Fourth, internal economies of large-scale production associated with growth facilitated both increased specialization of labor and improved organization of production and marketing. And, finally, external economies resulted from the geographical concentration of industry which greatly reduced costs of distribution and of acquiring information about market opportunities and factor supplies. In this, transportation improvements and increased population density combined to play vital roles.

Thus, the great increase in nonfarm production in the American economy after 1870 was accompanied by remarkable improvements in technology and organization which involved the increased use of complicated machinery, the exploitation of new sources of power, and the increasing concentration of production in larger and better administered enterprises. The factory became increasingly the dominant producing form in industry, and the multiplant corporation became the dominant financial and administrative form by facilitating the raising of capital to finance expansion in order to capitalize on economies of scale in production and distribution.

Increasing agricultural production in this period was brought about by geographical expansion and by analogous changes in technology and organization. The use of mechanical equipment became commonplace in many branches of agriculture, with the mechanization of small-grain farming being the most dramatic example of the technological revolution in agriculture, although cotton, tobacco, fruits and vegetables were not mechanized until well into the twentieth century. The preponderance of mixed or general farming in most regions of the country before 1870 gave way to increasing specialization in cotton, wheat, corn, hogs, cattle, and dairying in various regions and to market gardening in areas closest to urban centers. The family farm remained the basic unit of production, but lost most of its traditional independence with its integration into the market economy.

This does not mean, however, that economic growth was without its costs. Resource depletion, urban and rural slums, urban congestion, and the "quality of life" are not just contemporary problems, but also obsessed many Americans during the late nineteenth and early twentieth centuries. Not everyone shared equally in America's economic growth, for there were many conflicts within American society — blacks against whites, immigrants against organized labor, poor cotton and wheat farmers against more prosperous corn, livestock, and dairy interests, and so forth. The fear of "big" business, "big" labor, and "big" government all figured prominently, and some of these conflicts are examined later in the book.

The Dimensions of Growth: Some Economic Aggregates

Let us begin with a brief examination of the dimensions of American economic growth from 1840 to 1960, as indicated by data on selected demographic and economic variables. The necessary national accounts data have been developed for the nineteenth and early twentieth century United States economy through the researches of Richard Easterlin, Robert Gallman, Simon Kuznets, and others.[3]

These data have enabled economic historians to develop considerable insight into the nature of American economic growth in the nineteenth century, and to reinterpret many standard items in historiography. For example, once it was believed that per capita income in the South tended to be quite low relative to the national average and, in particular, to per capita incomes in the northeastern area. In fact, Easterlin's findings have demonstrated that per capita incomes in the New South were relatively high and growing in the pre-Civil War period, and this finding has cast further doubt on traditional reservations about the viability of slavery and the plantation system. A second example concerns the role of the Civil War in American industrialization. Gallman's results have prompted a substantial reconsideration of the Beard-Hacker thesis that the Civil War was an important stimulating influence in

American industrialization. It now appears that the Civil War decade was a period when the rate of growth of manufacturing output actually declined rather than accelerated.[4] An excellent post-Civil War example is provided by Kuznets. In American historiography, the decade of the 1870s has been described as a depression period on the basis of considerable evidence of unemployment, falling prices, financial panics, and incipient protest movements among farmers. Kuznets' discovery that total and per capita income grew quite rapidly during that decade — in fact more rapidly than in any other decade between the Civil War and World War II — casts doubt on this interpretation. In fact, the tendency of early historians to extrapolate the protracted recession of 1873 to 1878 backward and ahead disguised the fact that the long recession was interspersed between two periods of vigorous growth, from 1869 to 1873 and from 1878 to 1882.

The newly constructed national income and demographic data demonstrate that American economic growth was very rapid from 1870 into the twentieth century. This growth was both extensive and intensive — *extensive* in the sense that there was a substantial increase in the American population during the period which moved into large, previously vacant territories and shifted from rural to urban locations, and *intensive* as demonstrated by the significant increase in per capita output and the consequent increase in the standard of living over the period. Also significant were changes in the composition of economic activity, both regionally, between urban and rural areas, and among individual industries.

Several measures of the extent of America's growth during the past century are represented by the index numbers for population, labor, land and capital inputs, and Net National Product (with a base of 1840 = 100) in Table 1.1. These data depict rapid increases in all indicators of

Table 1.1 Indexes of Population, Labor, Land, Capital, and Net National Product, 1840-1960

Year	Population	Labor	Land	Capital	Net National Product
1840	100	100	100	100	100
1870	235	228	240	512	324
1900	447	514	566	2,343	1,037
1930	724	863	1,085	6,575	2,952
1960	1,061	1,308	1,165	10,531	5,994

SOURCE: Population index calculated from U. S. Bureau of the Census, *Historical Statistics of the United States.* (Washington, D. C.: Government Printing Office, 1957, ser. A6, p. 8; other indexes taken from Davis, Easterlin, Parker, et al., *American Economic Growth,* p. 34.

growth. Population increase from 1840 to 1960 was over tenfold. Undoubtedly, population growth alone would have led to a substantial increase in Net National Product. But, as it happened, output increased much faster than population. Between 1840 and 1960, Net National Product rose by about sixty times. Consequently, per capita output increased by a factor of almost six over the entire period. Since economists usually regard Net National Product per capita as the "best" summary indicator of the economy's performance, it is clear that the American economy was growing dramatically over the past century.

Much of the growth in output resulted from the increase in the availability of productive factors: from 1840 to 1960, labor input increased approximately thirteen times and resources input approximately eleven and one-half times, while capital input grew most substantially, increasing about a hundredfold. Not only did the supply of all inputs increase, but there was a large increase in the capital-labor ratio. In other words, the capital intensity of American production increased greatly during the period: capital-deepening is the term often applied to this growth in capital intensity of production. New technology is often embodied in new capital, and thus capital-deepening is a critical route by which technological change and productivity increase are transmitted through the economy. That part of the growth of Net National Product not accounted for by increasing factor supplies is usually ascribed to technological change, including organizational changes in the administration of business enterprise.

Regional aspects of population change are also useful summary economic indicators. As Table 1.2 shows, the spatial distribution of

Table 1.2 Percentage Distribution of Population by Region and by Urban/Rural Residence, 1840-1960

1. **By Region**	**1840**	**1870**	**1900**	**1930**	**1960**
Northeast	39.5	31.9	27.6	27.9	24.9
Northcentral	19.6	33.7	34.6	31.3	28.8
South	40.6	31.9	32.2	30.7	30.7
West	0.3	2.6	5.7	10.0	15.6
2. **By Urban/Rural Residence**					
Urban	10.8	25.7	39.7	56.2	69.9
Rural	89.2	74.3	60.3	43.8	30.1

SOURCE: *Historical Statistics of the United States,* ser. A57, A69, A172, pp. 11, 12, 22.

American population changed considerably over our period, primarily as a reflection of the westward movement of American population and growing urbanization. In 1840 the percentage of population in the northeastern United States (New England and the Middle Atlantic states) was almost forty percent and fell by 1960 to approximately twenty-five percent. Within the Northeast, New England lost ground relative to the Middle-Atlantic states. On the other hand, in 1840 the West (the Mountain and Pacific states) contained less than one percent of American population, but this percentage increased to ten percent by 1960. The South lost population relative to other areas and, within the South, the West-Southcentral region, especially Texas, gained relative to the East-Southcentral states. Finally, the Northcentral area gained population over the period, with the westernmost states gaining relative to the eastern ones.

Moreover, the American population became increasingly urbanized. In 1840, for example, only eleven percent of American population lived in urban areas. By 1900 this fraction had increased to almost two-fifths and by 1960 had reached almost seventy percent.

The spatial reallocation of American population—its westward movement and its redistribution towards urban areas—occurred mainly in response to changing employment opportunities.

A Preview

The basic lesson of economics is that the price system operates through demand and supply in competitive markets to determine what will be produced, how it will be produced, and how output and incomes will be distributed. Although the economist's perfectly competitive market is an abstraction from reality, his emphasis on the price system is an appropriate starting point for our study of modern American economic history. As Douglass North has written, "The pervasiveness of the price system in the allocation of resources . . . is central to any study in economic history, and . . . the use of price theory is an essential theoretical tool of the economic historian."[5] No economic historian would dispute this proposition.

Market prices were a dominant factor in the growth of the economy. In essence, economists believe that the individual's pursuit of self-interest leads, through competitive prices within the price system, to the growth of output. Aside from resource allocation decisions, the critical ingredients in the growth of output are investment and technological change, for technological change is embodied in new investment and brings with it productivity increases and, hence, increased incomes.

The American economy in the middle of the nineteenth century closely resembled a competitive market economy, its hallmarks being small units of production and private enterprise. Economic activity was guided by prices for the most part, although often price levels were influenced by the strength of local or regional monopolies and transportation or communications bottlenecks. Moreover, there was significant state intervention in the economy even before 1860, particularly in the promotion of transportation improvements, although it is probable that, as North claims, government's primary role in the early nineteenth century was limited to creating a stable political, legal, and social environment that enabled the market economy to operate quite efficiently.[6]

But by the end of the century, a broader framework than the competitive model is required, for within this stable environment the nature of business enterprise had changed drastically. Business firms had exploited technological and organizational innovations to greatly increase the size of establishments and to exert considerable market power. Agrarian and labor protests led to a demand for a more active government role, in particular to regulate business in the public interest. With the collapse of the economy during the Great Depression, the demand for regulation became a demand for government intervention in the economy and, after the Employment Act of 1946, its assumption of ultimate responsibility for economic stabilization policy. There is little doubt that the mid-nineteenth century economy more closely approximated the economist's competitive market framework than does today's complex economy, with its giant corporations and labor unions, and its expanded government sector. Even so, the framework of the market economy—the price system operating through the forces of demand and supply—remains an effective device for analyzing American economic growth and identifying its sources.

2

The Sources of Growth

Introduction

As economic historians, we are interested in analyzing the factors responsible for economic growth and in explaining changes in the structure of the economy.

American economic history has been portrayed as the evolution of a market economy, in which the price system serves as the prime mover in determining the allocation of goods and services and factors of production. Demand and supply analysis provides a useful framework for interpreting the growth of market economies.

Factors on the Supply Side

Viewed from the supply side, the growth of output results from growth in the quantity of factor inputs and from increases in factor productivity including technological change.[1]

Economic historians have emphasized the growth in quantity and quality of factor supplies in the nineteenth and early twentieth centuries. There were substantial increases in the amount of factor supplies as the data in Table 1.1 of chapter 1 indicate. Increased population leads, of course, to an increase in the labor force. The American labor force increased from approximately 5 1/2 million in 1840 to 49 million in 1930 and to over 70 million by 1960.[2] The importance of labor or human capital in the growth process has tended to be underestimated by economists until recently, but historians have always recognized that labor in nineteenth century America was of exceptional quality in terms of literacy and levels of formal education compared with Britain and Europe. Moreover, the American labor force probably enjoyed better health than the European. The quality of labor plus the favorable social environment of the United States contributed to the growth process. Other things being given, the more literate and more educated the labor force, the more likely it is to successfully complement increases in the capital intensity of production—that is, the more likely are increases in the capital stock to be met with the appropriate qualitative adjustments in the labor force.

A second feature of input supply is the substantial increase in the stock of capital. Data prepared by Simon Kuznets indicate that the net stock of capital in the United States increased from approximately $27 billions in 1869 to some $306 billions in 1929 and $442 billions in 1955.[3] This represents a per capita increase from about $700 to about $2,500 in 1929 and to almost $2,700 in 1955, and in per worker terms, an increase from a little over $2,000 in 1869 to $6,330 in 1929 and to $6,740 in 1955. Capital formation increased in order to provide housing for a growing population and machinery and equipment for a growing labor force. Increases in the stock of capital help to explain growth in per capita income, since new capital embodies the fruits of technological progress and facilitates increased labor productivity. This result was readily apparent with the mechanization of manufacturing and agriculture. However, the data on decadal rates of growth suggest that capital formation has slowed down from the nineteenth to the twentieth century. From 1869 to 1889, the average decadal growth in the net stock of capital was about fifty-nine percent. From 1909 to 1929 this slowed to thirty-six percent and for 1929 to 1955 slowed further to fifteen percent. Per worker decadal growth rates were approximately twenty percent through the entire period to 1929, and then slowed abruptly to 3.3 percent from 1929 to 1955, partly as a result of the growing weight of capital consumption allowances and replacements within gross capital formation and partly as a result of a decrease in the rate of population and labor force growth.

While they have acknowledged the quality of the American natural resource base and the growth of the labor force, economic historians have tended to place most emphasis on technological change as it was embodied in capital formation. They have generally inferred from impressions about the rate of technological change in nineteenth and twentieth century America that this was the root cause of rapid economic growth.

Another aspect of productivity growth indirectly related to capital formation is manifested as organizational change. In the manufacturing sector the important organizational innovation was the growing reliance on the corporate form. The increasing number of corporations reflected several influences—the increase in size of markets, the development of formal capital markets for the marketing of corporate stocks and bonds, and decreasing relative costs of incorporation with the emergence of general incorporation laws in New Jersey, Delaware, and other states which facilitated the local incorporation of broadly defined corporations. The corporate form was linked to the development of mergers and consolidations around the turn of the century and questions of the relationship of size and economies of large-scale production and marketing. Large plants could frequently make use of improved forms of organization with recourse to assembly line techniques of production. Also, there was greater possibility of specialization of functions within the firm allowing greater division of labor and a strategic deployment of plants and marketing facilities throughout the country. Finally, large firms could purchase highly indivisible capital goods which were efficient only with large outputs.

However, impressionistic accounts of the role of changes in the quantity and quality of inputs, and the role of technological change in contributing to the rise in total and per capita Gross National Product must now give way to the studies of Denison, Kendrick, and Abramovitz and David, who have measured gains in productivity—defined as the ratio of output to inputs—both for the aggregate economy and for the manufacturing and agricultural sectors.[4] Although there are some difficulties with the estimation of productivity indexes, they remain very useful summary measures of economic performance and have greatly increased our knowledge of the history of the American economy.

Abramovitz and David have argued that productivity has grown at a steady and probably an accelerating pace since the start of the nineteenth century, with most of the growth of factor productivity concentrated in the twentieth century. According to them, in the period from 1800 to 1855, total factor productivity grew at an average annual growth rate of only 0.3 percent and from 1855 to 1905 averaged only 0.5 percent, although in the latter part of this period (1890 to 1905) the rate increased to 0.8 percent. In the period 1905 to 1927, total factor productivity increased substantially, growing at an annual average rate of 1.5 percent and then from 1927 to 1967 continued to increase, growing at an average annual rate of 1.9 percent.[5]

The rates of productivity growth for the nineteenth century appear to be quite low compared with twentieth century rates. At first glance, this is a surprising finding, given the traditional emphasis on nineteenth century technological change. They admit that this result need not imply that the "progress of invention" was formerly less important to the process of growth that it is now taken to be. Rather these findings can be interpreted as demonstrating that the key role of technological change in the nineteenth century was to produce labor-saving innovations which permitted output to grow more rapidly than labor and, by implication, population.

Table 2.1 presents summary data on the growth of real product and productivity in the American economy as a whole. Tables 2.2 and 2.3 contain data on the manufacturing sector and the farm sector respectively. The data for the national economy show that real Net Product grew quite rapidly from 1869 to 1959. Output per unit of labor input grew more rapidly than output per unit of capital input, which demonstrates that the capital intensity of production was increasing. Total factor productivity grew more rapidly in the twentieth century, which confirms the findings of other studies that there was a substantial increase in the rate of productivity growth after World War I compared with the prewar period.

Kendrick found that total productivity increases over the period from 1889 to 1919 comprised about one-third of the increase in total product, the other two-thirds coming from increases in the quantities of labor and capital employed in production.[6] He observes a break in trend

Table 2.1 National Economy: Output and Productivity Ratios, 1869-1959

Year	Output (real Net Product)	Output per Unit of labor input	Output per Unit of capital input	Total factor productivity
1869	7.8	35.0	67.7	42.0
1879	15.7	54.0	90.2	62.5
1889	21.8	50.2	85.5	58.3
1899	33.9	61.2	87.6	67.8
1909	51.3	69.8	92.1	75.6
1919	70.3	79.3	91.7	82.6
1929	100.0	100.0	100.0	100.0
1939	104.8	117.2	111.5	115.9
1949	159.7	138.7	130.5	136.4
1959	233.5	179.8	134.4	169.1

NOTE: 1929 = 100. The ratio of 1929 values was employed to convert series with a 1958 base to a 1929 base

SOURCE: Kendrick, *Productivity Trends in the United States,* Table A-XXI, p. 332, and *Postwar Productivity Trends,* Table A-17b, p. 239.

Table 2.2 Manufacturing Sector: Output and Productivity Ratios, 1869-1959

Year	Output	Output per Unit of labor input	Output per Unit of capital input	Total factor productivity
1869	7.1	29.6	158.9	36.4
1879	10.2	32.7	134.6	39.7
1889	18.3	41.4	104.0	48.2
1899	27.5	47.7	93.9	53.9
1909	43.4	53.5	79.8	57.9
1919	61.0	58.0	65.7	59.6
1929	100.0	100.0	100.0	100.0
1939	102.5	123.9	120.8	122.8
1949	174.0	139.8	140.3	139.9
1959	284.3	195.6	165.3	191.1

NOTE: 1929 = 100. The ratio of 1929 values was employed to convert series with a 1958 base to a 1929 base

SOURCE: Kendrick, *Productivity Trends in the United States,* Table D-1, p. 464, and *Postwar Productivity Trends,* Table A-32, p. 274-5.

Table 2.3 Agricultural Sector: Gross Output and Productivity Ratios, 1869-1959

Year	Output	Output per manhour	Output per Unit of capital input	Total factor productivity
1869	28.9	53.9	76.7	60.8
1879	45.2	64.2	84.3	70.7
1889	57.2	69.2	87.6	75.5
1899	72.5	79.8	92.8	84.6
1909	78.8	81.4	87.6	84.0
1919	87.3	85.6	85.7	85.6
1929	100.0	100.0	100.0	100.0
1939	109.2	122.6	111.7	118.4
1949	129.9	175.3	123.5	153.8
1959	170.0	354.5	141.6	250.4

NOTE: 1929 = 100. The ratio of 1929 values was employed to convert series with a 1958 base to a 1929 base

SOURCE: Kendrick, *Productivity Trends in the United States,* Table B-II, p. 365-6, and *Postwar Productivity Trends,* Table A-23, p. 256.

at 1919. In the decade from 1919 to 1929, almost one-half the increase in output is accounted for by productivity growth, and the share increases to almost two-thirds during 1948-1966. Thus, the growth of factor supplies were certainly more important in contributing to the increase in Net National Product in the nineteenth century, and increases in total factor productivity became more important in the twentieth century.

Table 2.2 presents data for the manufacturing sector. There were very substantial increases in manufacturing output from 1869 to 1959. In fact, manufacturing output grew at approximately the same rate as national output over much of the period, and then grew more rapidly after World War Two. Output per unit of labor input grew more rapidly than for the economy as a whole. Capital input per unit of output increased as the process of capital-deepening and the substitution of capital for labor occurred. Total factor productivity growth in manufacturing was relatively rapid compared with nonmanufacturing activity until 1939; it remained substantial after the war but was eclipsed by the surge of productivity increase in agriculture in the late 1940s and 1950s.

The average annual rates of change in total factor productivity in manufacturing were 1.4 percent for the pre-1899 period, 0.7 percent for the decade 1899 to 1909, 0.3 percent for the 1909 to 1919 decade, 5.3 percent during the period 1919 to 1929, and 2.5 percent from 1948 to 1966. The post-1919 period is far and away the most significant from the point of view of annual rates of change in total productivity. The average annual rates of change in capital input per unit of labor input were also striking. In the pre-1899 decade, it was 3.5 percent, from 1889 to 1909, 2.8 percent, from 1909 to 1919, 2.8 percent, from 1919 to 1929, 1.3 percent, and from 1948 to 1966, 2.3 percent.[7] Thus, just as one would expect from the analysis of changes in total factor productivity presented above, the rate of change in capital intensity of production was most rapid in the late nineteenth century compared with the post-1900 period.

The farm sector is depicted in Table 2.3. For the period from 1840 to 1900, Robert Gallman has found that the rate of growth of Farm Gross Product averaged 2.70 percent.[8] The growth rates of labor, land, and capital inputs were 2.00, 2.33, and 2.98 percent per year respectively, and the annual average rate of growth of total factor productivity was quite low in agriculture, although some capital-labor substitution was occurring. The slow rate of growth of farm output is attributed to the slow rate of growth of demand. In turn, demand's slow growth rate can be explained by the slower growth of population in the late nineteenth century and the low income elasticity of demand for farm products taken as a group.

The growth of gross output in the farm sector from 1869 to 1929 was less rapid than the growth of manufacturing output. Output per manhour increased more slowly in agriculture than in manufacturing, and farm capital per unit of labor increased fairly slowly compared with manufacturing. In fact, many significant changes in the capital intensity of agriculture are a fairly recent phenomenon and are associated with the revival of mechanization attributable in part to rural electrification, and improved gasoline and diesel engines. The growth of total factor productivity in agriculture was considerably less rapid than it was in manufacturing until after World War Two.

The average annual rate of change in total factor productivity in the farm sector was only 0.9 percent for the pre-1899 decades, actually negative during 1899 to 1919, increased to 1.2 percent from 1919 to 1929, and to 3.3 percent from 1948 to 1966. The average annual rates of change in capital per unit of labor were slight compared to manufacturing before 1930—for pre-1899, only 0.6 percent per annum, from 1899 to 1909, 0.8 percent per annum, from 1909 to 1919, 0.7 percent per annum, and from 1919 to 1929 no change—and then averaged an astonishing 5.3 percent from 1948 to 1966.[9]

The average annual rates of change by sector indicate several things of interest to the student of American economic history. First, the rate of change in total factor productivity was substantial in the decades before 1899, and then decreased to quite low levels in both agriculture and manufacturing between 1899 and 1919, increasing rapidly again after 1919. Second, the average annual rate of change in capital per unit of labor input seems to have been substantial in manufacturing throughout the period, and much lower in agriculture for most of the period where the most significant increases in mechanization occurred in a short period around the Civil War, subsided for many decades, and then accelerated again in the 1920s and after the Second World War.

How do these measures of productivity performance relate to factor incomes and, hence, to aggregate demand? At the most basic level, productivity gains represent increases in real output per unit of factor input, and hence provide for a growth in output from which all or some factor incomes can be increased. Factor shares in the benefits of productivity increase depend on the relative quantities of the inputs and on their relative prices, and changes in factor shares over time will depend on changes in relative quantities and relative prices.

During the period from 1899 to the mid-1960s, the quantity of capital input has indeed grown relative to the quantity of labor input, and has been accompanied by an increase in the relative price of labor. Thus, there has been an inverse movement of relative factor quantities and factor prices. In the production process, producers have responded to changes in relative factor supplies by substituting capital, the factor that has become relatively cheaper, for labor which has become relatively more expensive. The net effect has been a rise in labor's share in national income from 1899 to the present.[10]

Factors on the Demand Side

In the post-Civil War period, the development of the national market is often singled out as the crucial factor in American economic growth. Two features have been emphasized: first, the role of transportation improvement, which by lowering real costs of transporting freight and passengers, extended the domestic market; second, the growth of population density and urbanization which by concentrating populations geographically reduced distribution costs still further. The domestic or national market is a function of both population size and dispersion and the level and distribution of income and, in the dynamic context, both the growth of population and the growth of income.

Following this demand or market orientation, economic historians have divided the economy into sectors depicting broad industrial classifications by the type of product produced. These sectors may be called the primary or "agricultural" sector, the secondary or "industrial" sector, and the tertiary or "services" sector.[11] Changes in the composition of national output among these sectors are designated as structural changes.

Did significant changes in the structural composition of output accompany the development of the American economy in the nineteenth and twentieth centuries? To answer this question, it is particularly useful to look at changes in commodity output, that is, at the changing shares of agriculture and industrial outputs in total commodity production. Table 2.4 summarizes the changing shares of commodity output claimed

Table 2.4 Percentage Shares of Agriculture and Industry in Value Added, 1839-1949

Year	Agriculture	Industry
1839	78	22
1869	57	43
1899	35	65
1929	17	83
1949	16	84

NOTE: The figures represent percentage shares in Gross Value Added by agriculture and industry (manufacturing and mining) in constant dollars.

SOURCE: Robert E. Gallman and Edward S. Howle, "Trends in the Structure of the American Economy Since 1840," in Fogel and Engerman, eds., *The Reinterpretation of American Economic History* (New York: Harper and Row, 1971), p. 26.

by industry and agriculture for selected years from 1839 to 1949. In 1839 only twenty-two percent of commodity output was comprised of industrial products and seventy-eight percent was made up of agricultural products. By 1899 these fractions had changed considerably; industrial outputs now represented sixty-five percent of gross value added in commodity output. This increase in the relative importance of industrial outputs was further augmented by 1929 when eighty-three percent of total commodity output consisted of industrial production. The shares have stabilized in the postwar period.

Why did the composition of commodity output change? The usual explanation is that the changing structure of commodity output reflects the changing distribution of final or consumer demand in the economy. It reflects the differing income elasticities of demand for the broad categories of agricultural and nonagricultural commodities. The agricultural sector tends to fall in relative size as per capita incomes rise because the income elasticity of demand for foodstuffs is typically inelastic, while the share of manufacturing output (and services as well) tends to increase because the income elasticities of manufactured goods are typically high (that is, greater than one). As a result, the structure of output changes from agriculture in favor of industry in order to meet the changing pattern of demand. Another factor which could influence changes in commodity output would be the emergence of new products and the development of new uses for old products. Some examples from the extractive industries are the growing nineteenth century use of coal as an industrial fuel which increased its relative importance and the development of the petroleum industry with its increased emphasis on the production of gasoline for the new automobile industry after 1900. Both contributed to an increasing relative share for mining. Finally, Robert Gallman has argued that changes in the price structure of agriculture vis-à-vis nonagricultural commodities might also explain part of the changes in commodity output shares. In the period from 1870 to 1900, a period of marked deflation, mining and manufacturing goods prices fell more rapidly than agricultural goods prices. Since the demand for agricultural goods as a whole tends to be less price elastic than mining and manufacturing outputs, the result was that the values of mining and manufacturing outputs tended to increase relative to agricultural commodities.

One of the principal factor shifts necessary to meet changing patterns of demand is reflected in figures on changes in employment. The changes in the sectoral distribution of employment have been substantial.[12] In 1840 over sixty percent of those employed were employed in the primary sector (farming, fishing, and mining). Only nine percent were employed in factory manufacturing, and about eight percent in the trade and transport sector. By 1870, the share of employed in manufacturing had increased to almost one-fifth, and trade and transport services had increased also, although by a smaller amount. By 1900 this tendency had been reinforced, and data for 1930 show that only twenty-four percent of the labor force was employed in the primary sector, and a little over twenty percent in the manufacturing sector and the trade and transport sectors respectively. The decline in primary employment was exacerbated after 1930, reaching 13.5 percent in 1950 and falling below ten perent by 1960. Meanwhile, manufacturing employment increased still further to 23.2 percent, while trade and transport stabilized at slightly more than twenty percent.

It appears that the share of commodity production in total output during the nineteenth and twentieth centuries has remained fairly constant at forty-five percent and that of noncommodity production at fifty-five to sixty percent. However, the division of the labor force between commodity and noncommodity production has changed quite dramatically. The percentage of the labor force in commodity production in 1870 was about four-fifths, but by 1930 had fallen to less than forty-five percent and to less than forty percent by 1960, with a corresponding increase in the share in noncommodity production.[13]

These changes in the relative importance of commodity production and in the share of agriculture within commodity production have contributed to sectoral income differences in the American economy. Data on income per worker are presented in Table 2.5 to demonstrate changes over time in relative incomes per worker among agriculture, manufacturing and mining, and the "other" sector which is dominated by services. In the period 1869-1879, agricultural workers received considerably less than the American average income, whereas mining and manufacturing workers received approximately an average income and the services-dominated sector had considerably more income per worker. By 1889-1899 these shares had changed somewhat, with a relative decline for

Table 2.5 Income Per Worker as a Percentage of U.S. Average, by Sector, 1869-1955

Sector	1869-1879	1889-1899	1919-1940	1950-1955
Agriculture	42	37	47	76
Manufacturing and Mining	93	128	120	123
Other	220	160	120	100

SOURCE: Davis, Easterlin, Parker, et al., *American Economic Growth: An Economist's History of the United States*, p. 53.

agriculture and the "other" sector, and a relative increase to a position above the American average for the manufacturing and mining sector. In the period 1919-1940, these tendencies were stabilized somewhat, agricultural workers remaining at fairly low incomes compared with the American average whereas mining and manufacturing and "other" workers stabilized at well above the American average. Since World War Two, however, agricultural incomes have increased dramatically relative to workers in the "other" sector.

In addition to looking at sectoral incomes, it is also useful to take a regional perspective on American incomes. Data on personal incomes per capita in the United States by geographical region for the years 1860, 1900, 1930, and 1960 are presented in Table 2.6. It is quite clear that residents of the Northeast enjoyed above-average personal incomes throughout the whole period from 1860 to 1930, and then lost ground relatively by 1960. The Northcentral area had a relatively low personal income per capita compared to the national average in 1860, essentially because much of it was pioneer agricultural area at that time. By 1900, with the development of successful commercial agriculture and manufacturing capacity, the Northcentral area had risen to a position above the national average and was able to maintain that position through 1960. Southern incomes per capita were below the national average in 1860 and, in part reflecting the long term dislocative effects of the Civil War on the structure of the southern economy, remained well below the national average in 1900 and 1930, and then rose in the postwar period with more rapid industrialization, especially in textiles and iron and steel. Western incomes per capita, which do not appear for 1860 because of the

Table 2.6 Per Capita Personal Income as a Percentage of U.S. Average, by Region,1860-1960

Region	1860	1900	1930	1960
Northeast	139	137	138	115
Northcentral	68	103	101	103
South	72	51	55	78
West		163	115	112

SOURCE: Figures for 1860, 1900, and 1930 are taken from Richard A. Easterlin, "Regional Income Trends, 1840-1950," in Fogel and Engerman, eds., *The Reinterpretation of American* Economic History, p. 40. Figures for 1960 are calculated from data on personal income and population by region contained in U. S. Bureau of Economic Analysis, *Long Term Economic Growth, 1860-1970* (Washington, D. C.: Government Printing Office, 1973), ser. C1-10, C71-80, pp. 232-234, 240-241.

sparse population of that area, by 1900 are clearly well above the national average and have remained above the national average to 1960, although losing much of their relative superiority. In part, this change reflects changes in the sex composition of population and the labor force participation rate from the pre-1900 period of very high male-to-female population ratio and high participation rates.

On the demand side, the sources of American economic growth in the late nineteenth and early twentieth centuries include the impact which rising output and income per capita together with increasing population had on the creation of a national market. Since the relative importance of exports as a stimulant to economic expansion had decreased, the growth of manufacturing output after 1870 primarily reflected increasing domestic demand for manufactured consumers' goods and producers' goods, both from the urban sector which was growing concomitantly with the development of manufacturing and the services sectors and from agriculture where increases in productivity and rising incomes also contributed a substantial market-creating effect.

Measuring the Relative Importance of Demand and Supply Factors: Case Studies

Can one assess the relative importance of supply and demand factors in explaining industrial growth? For example, our earlier discussion of supply-side phenomena suggests it is possible to measure contributions to the growth of output from the growth in the quantity and quality of factors of production (natural resources, labor, and capital) and technological progress.

In part, the answer to our question involves first the indentification, and then the measurement of elements responsible for economic growth. Market price and quantity data often provide us with some indication of the relative strength of supply and demand influences. For example, changes in income per capita, population, or the prices of substitutes all influence the demand for a particular product in predictable ways, and the growth of industry output may be unequivocally a function of factors tending to increase product demand. On the other hand, output changes may have their source in factors tending to increase supply, such as changes in the prices of inputs or technological change. In most cases, however, one does not find such clear-cut cases as an increase in demand over time with no change in supply, or an increase in supply with no change in demand. In the dynamic context, both demand and supply phenomena are shifting continuously, and changes in industry output are the product of shifts in both supply and demand. When one attempts to analyze historical markets then, one significant difficulty lies in trying to separate and assess the relative strengths of supply and demand factors. This is called the "identification problem," and its solution calls for the estimation of an economic model of the market for the product concerned.[14]

It is interesting at this juncture to look at two case studies of the growth of industry in which demand and supply factors were both important. The first is the petroleum industry between 1860 and 1914, and the second is the American iron industry between 1842 and 1858. The petroleum industry was chosen as an example of a quantitative study which is noneconometric. In other words, the demand and supply influences at work have been catalogued but there has been no attempt to apportion the relative importance of demand and supply forces in explaining the growth of output. This type of quantitative research has been quite common in economic history. The second case study represents an attempt to deduce a formal economic model of the market for iron, and to estimate the model using econometric techniques in an attempt to quantify the relative contributions of increases in demand and supply to the growth of industry output. It represents an ingenious adaptation of economic principles with a view to examining the causal determinants of industrial growth.

The Growth of the Petroleum Industry, 1860-1914[15]

Williamson, Andreano and Menezes attempted to measure the growth of output and to assess the relative importance of the petroleum industry in the American economy during 1860 to 1914. On the supply side, they identify the most significant determinants of petroleum output by examining the flow of inputs to the major output divisions. On the demand side, they examine the principal factors affecting the level and composition of sales of petroleum products.

Certainly, the output record for the petroleum industry was quite impressive. Crude oil output in the American industry increased from about 2.5 million barrels in 1865 to some 266 million barrels in 1914, a compound annual rate of growth of 9.8 percent per annum. Refined output for the same period increased from 1.3 million barrels to 189 million barrels at the end of the period.[16] Table 2.7 summarizes some indexes of physical output for crude petroleum fuels, total minerals, refinery products, and total manuacturing production. The increase in physical output of petroleum products was accompanied by a rate of increase in value added by refining which exceeded the growth of value added by all manufacturing. The value of industry output increased relative to Net

Table 2.7 Indexes of Physical Output, Selected Years, 1869-1914

Year	Crude petroleum	Refining products	Fuels	Total minerals	Total manu-facturing production
1869	11.9	11.8			37.9
1879	58.4	45.8	45.5	51.9	55.4
1889	100.0	100.0	100.0	100.0	100.0
1899	162.3	174.5	149.5	147.4	151.5
1909	520.9	388.8	278.8	261.6	251.5
1914	755.8	662.3	329.3	290.9	290.9

NOTE: 1889 = 100
SOURCE: Williamson, Andreano, and Menezes, "The American Petroleum Industry," p. 351.

National Product over the period. A summary of changes in the relative output shares of several petroleum derivative products is presented in Table 2.8.

The rapid rate of growth of output in the petroleum industry resulted from a complex of demand and supply factors. Can one separate the supply from the demand factors which account for this growth?

Several supply factors appear to have been important. First, changes in institutional factors affected production. During this period, exploration was at best pragmatic—the science of petroleum geology only emerged after the First World War. Much petroleum exploration was essentially random because of the lack of knowledge of underground geological formations. The "rule of capture" was in effect, which implies that subsurface mineral rights belonged to the property owners who brought the subsurface minerals above ground. This resulted in a

Table 2.8 Percentage Distribution of Refined Petroleum Output by Product, 1879-1914

Product	1879	1899	1914
Illuminating Oil	86.2	66.9	26.5
Gasoline and Naphtha	6.8	14.4	33.8
Lubricating Oil	7.3	12.1	16.3
Fuel Oil	0.7	6.5	23.4

SOURCE: Williamson, Andreano, and Menezes, "The American Petroleum Industry," p. 389.

tendency for a proliferation of wells drawing from a common pool when surface boundaries were involved, and probably led to a loss of petroleum reserves.

A second basic supply factor was technological change. The quality of drilling equipment improved over the period, especially with the introduction of the rotary drill in the late 1890s. The rotary drill was faster, less skill was involved on the part of the driller than in the earlier cable-tool drilling system, and it was especially suited to Gulf Coast conditions. Such changes had important implications for drilling costs. Drilling costs were comprised of equipment, labor, and materials, and tended to vary with the depth of the well, the skill of the driller, the terrain to be drilled, and so forth. It appears that there were decreasing costs per foot of putting down a well by the 1870s, and costs continued to decrease thereafter. This should not be confused with the fact that, as well depths increased, the total costs of sinking wells also increased.

In addition, major changes in the transport and storage of crude petroleum lowered marketing costs. In the early days of the industry, oil was transported and stored in barrels which were usually wooden. The cost of barrels, their weight, and their tendency to leak or permit oil to evaporate added substantially to the delivered price of oil. Consequently, when bulk handling methods were introduced after 1865, shipping and storage costs fell markedly. Bulk transfer involved several innovations: first, gathering lines enabled wells to be linked by pipelines to storage and shipping terminals; second, tank cars (wooden, and then steel generally after 1868) replaced barrels in shipping; third, long distance crude oil pipelines were developed (the first being the Tidewater Pipe Company's line in 1879 in Pennsylvania). Barrels persisted in the bulk handling of refined products somewhat longer, primarily because they were convenient for storage at retail outlets. Tank cars were used to transfer the packaging and barrelling operations from the refinery to bulk depots in retail areas, and by the 1880s tank wagon deliveries from major distribution centers to retail outlets in the growing urban markets had been introduced. Bulk handling was one of the first areas in which vertical integration was initiated by Standard Oil, both in the ownership of tank cars for the collection of crude and the distribuiton of refined petroleum, and in storage and distribution centers for refined petroleum products.

Finally, on the supply side, there were changes in refining techniques. There were two basic stages in the refining process, distillation and treating. Distillation involved the application of heat to crude petroleum, the products being drawn off in sequence. The attention of refiners seems to have been directed towards improving the distillation process by trying to reduce fuel costs and to increase control over the quality of output. Improvements in the design of stills and the introduction of vacuum distillation and, after 1900, continuous distillation were important changes. Treating involved the further processing of petroleum products before consumption in order to remove impurities and odors. Many petroleum products such as kerosene and lubricants required extensive treatment.

The refining process seems to have become more capital-intensive and plant size to have increased over the latter part of the nineteenth century. From the 1870s to late 1890s, unit manufacturing costs decreased by from twenty to twenty-five percent. Capital per worker increased over the period from $2,766 in 1880 to some $10,991 in 1909, and output per worker increased concomitantly from 282 barrels in 1880 to 6,449 barrels in 1909.[17] In part, output performance was a function of the quality of crude oil inputs; the lower yield crudes in the newer western supply areas increased unit manufacturing costs to a certain extent and prevented improvements in refining efficiency from being completely reflected in lower unit costs.

On the demand side, many considerations were important. In the first place, both domestic and export markets were of changing importance and composition over the period. In the domestic market, illuminating oil or kerosene was the most important refined product over most of the period. By 1909, fuel oil had become relatively more important and had surpassed illuminating oil after a short period of rapid growth. Sales of naphtha and gasoline grew relatively rapidly after 1904. Lubricating oil remained a small proportion of the market.

The export market in the earlier era was large. In 1869, some two-thirds of refined products were exported. This had fallen by 1889 to one-half, and by 1909 to one-third. By 1914 only one-quarter of refined petroleum products was exported.[18] One feature on the demand side, then, is the increasing relative importance of domestic demand compared with the foreign market, the relative decline of the latter being a function of increasing foreign supplies as well as the rise in domestic demand.

The demand for illuminating oil or kerosene as a petroleum derivative reflected the demand for a safe, efficient, cheap source of artificial light. Kerosene was certainly cheaper or safer than coal oil, camphene, or whale oils, the substitutes for kerosene. With increased efficiency in refining and with improvements in the handling, storage, and bulk shipment of kerosene, its wholesale price in the New York market decreased quite dramatically from 1865 to the 1880s. During 1865 to 1869, kerosene was approximately 27 cents per gallon. By 1880 to 1884, it was 8.1 cents per gallon, and by 1895 to 1899, 6.9 cents per gallon.[19] Certainly the declining relative price of kerosene was an important factor on the demand side, and undoubtedly influenced growth in the complementary manufacture of lamps and the reduction in the relative price of lamps as well.

The early improvement in the relative price of kerosene is largely attributed to supply factors, but after 1914 illuminating oil was to be adversely affected by the growing competition of electric lighting. Conversely, naphtha and gasoline were by-products in the production of kerosene, which became of increasing relative importance over the period. Before 1900 they were largely used as cleaning solvents and fuels for cook stoves and space heaters. With the development of the automobile, the demand for gasoline grew rapidly and represented twenty-five percent of refined output by 1909 and forty percent by 1914. Demand for lubricating oil grew rather slowly, even though the demand for lubricating oil was derived from the increasing use in industry of machinery and equipment with many moving parts. Finally, fuel oil increased quite significantly in relative importance after advances in refining activity by Frasch in the 1890s. It was sold increasingly in competition with coal as a boiler fuel to produce heat and energy in industry, and for marine use after 1900. Its use was geographically concentrated in the Pacific coast and southwestern areas.

Thus far, we have reviewed the various factors that influenced the supply of and demand for petroleum products from 1860 to 1914. But no attempt has been made to estimate, even impressionistically, the relative importance of supply and demand forces in the growth of petroleum output. Implicitly, both changes in supply, particularly technological change, and changes in demand appear to have been important, but a basis for quantifying their relative contributions has not been provided. We turn now to examine a study where such an attempt was made for the mid-nineteenth century iron and steel industry.

The Growth of Iron and Steel Output, 1842-1858

The second case study concerns the growth of the American iron industry from 1842 to 1858. Fogel and Engerman were concerned with identifying the factors influencing the expansion of industry generally, and reconciling the often conflicting views which have emerged in the literature. For example, in the case of the British industrial revolution, many historians have accorded great emphasis to the introduction of new machines and equipment in textiles and iron and steel as a major causal factor in industrial expansion. Other writers have argued that increases in demand were crucial; for example, Rostow has emphasized the demand for rails as the major factor influencing the rise of the American iron and steel industry in the mid-nineteenth century. And a third group of writers have stressed factors such as population growth, the economies of large scale enterprise, and reductions in raw materials costs.

Fogel and Engerman began with the premise that economic historians have lacked a theory to analyze industrial growth and have had problems with insufficient data. They proposed to build a general model for explaining the expansion of industry, using the traditional analytical tools of supply and demand in order to assess the relative impact of increases in population, income per capita, the introduction of new machinery, reductions in input prices, and so forth. The case study which they chose to examine was the growth of pig iron output in the United States in the pre-Civil War era.

Table 2.9 presents annual data on the gross output of pig iron in the United States from 1842 to 1858. Output grew quite dramatically from 1841 to about 1847, and then appears to have leveled off between 1847 and 1859. This period was one of rapid technological change in blast furnaces, featuring the replacement of charcoal by mineral fuels in more than half of blast furnace capacity. Moreover, there was a substantial contrast between the performance of the 1840s and the 1850s. The considerable growth in output in the early and mid-1840s was followed by little change in output from 1847 to 1857 coincident with a decrease in the average real price of pig iron of approximately 3.5 percent per year. An increase in the abandonment rate of blast furnaces in the late 1840s coincided with the increase in capacity over the period.

The major explanation in American historiography for the behavior of iron and steel output concerned the role of the American tariff. The "protectionist" view was that high duties on imported iron established in 1842 had stimulated the growth of pig iron output, and that the lowering of duties in 1846 had contributed to the levelling off of pig iron produc-

Table 2.9 United States Pig Iron Output, 1840-1860

Year (3 year averages)	Pig Iron (000 gross tons)
1841	285
1844	473
1847	716
1850	507
1853	640
1856	734
1859	734

SOURCE: Calculated from data contained in Fogel, and Engerman, eds., *The Reinterpretation of American Economic History,* p. 154.

tion thereafter. The "free trade" view challenged this focus on the tariff and argued that there were factors in the American economy promoting growth of the industry independent of the tariff -- in particular, the growth of capital formation associated with railroad construction and the increase in manufacturing capacity. Finally, there was an intermediate position which, while acknowledging the importance of the tariff, held that technological innovations were crucial. The tariff affected the less efficient charcoal-using sector of the industry, and the mineral fuel-using sector was relatively efficient and competitive regardless of tariff levels.

In an attempt to resolve this debate, and to cast light on the procedure for explaining industrial growth, Fogel and Engerman developed a theoretical model to explain industrial expansion and proceeded to estimate the model with data for the iron industry in the pre-Civil War period.[21] Among the variables affecting demand, Fogel and Engerman include gross domestic investment, the price of imported pig iron (the chief substitute for domestic pig), the investment elasticity of demand for pig iron, and the cross elasticity of demand for domestic pig with respect to imported iron. The supply variables include such key factors as changes in technical efficiency and input prices.

Their results were quite interesting. Shifts in supply account for all of the observed increase in total pig iron production over the period. In fact, the contribution of shifts in demand for domestic pig iron is negative, although only slightly so. This latter result does not reflect a lack of growth in the domestic market. In fact, there was a significant positive impact on demand associated with the increase in gross domestic investment over the period, but this was more than offset by the reduction in the relative price of imported iron from the United Kingdom, which was related to the tariff change.

The results differ for the two subsectors within the iron industry. The demand for domestic pig iron produced with mineral or anthracite fuel seems to have been more sensitive to the price of imported iron than was the demand for charcoal iron. Anthracite coal was used to produce rails and low grade iron. Imports from the United Kingdom were largely similar to this anthracite product. But at the same time, the increase in investment demand had a much larger effect on anthracite iron because of growing demand for low grade iron in railroad construction and other uses. Consequently, the tariff was especially important in the anthracite sector. With respect to the charcoal-using sector of the industry, output was comprised of slower growing items such as malleable castings, hand tools, and wagon axles. Consequently, there was a relatively slow growth of demand for the output of this sector. The continuation of the high 1842 tariff would have given a boost to demand, but would not have prevented the relative decline of the charcoal iron sector. In fact, high tariffs would have given even greater stimulus to anthracite iron. The irony was that anthracite iron did not need the high tariff in order to survive because the increasing demand for its product offset the increased competitiveness of imports.

Supply shifts were also estimated separately for the two subsectors. For the charcoal sector, technological progress seems to have been very important. For the anthracite sector, the growth of the capital stock was even more important than the growth in efficiency. Here is an interesting case where the growth in total factor productivity was more rapid in the "older" branch of the industry, and undoubtedly is a major reason why the charcoal sector persisted in the face of the "modern" anthracite sector.[22]

What purports to be a general model of industrial expansion is predicated, in the interests of tractability, on assumptions of a perfectly competitive industry and constant returns to scale in production. One question that immediately arises is whether or not Fogel and Engerman's use of perfect competition and the Cobb-Douglas production function lead very far in the historical analysis of this industry. Most writers have been interested in the exploitation by firms of economies of scale leading to increased size of industrial establishment and changes in levels of concentration in nineteenth century industry. In spite of this, Fogel and Engerman have indeed combined economic theory with historical information in the form of an interesting model of the behavior of the antebellum American iron industry for the period 1842 to 1858. One hopes that the future completion of data series will permit the estimation of more complex specifications of their model for the iron and steel industry and for other industries in the nineteenth century American economy.

Conclusion

The increased productivity of the economy was the result of a number of factors. It was the result of structural changes which involved the transfer of labor from less productive to more productive sectors of the economy. It was the result of firms in agriculture and manufacturing exploiting internal economies of scale which permitted the increased specialization of labor and improved organizational procedures, both of which contributed to increased productivity. It was the result of the obvious benefits of localization of industry wherein external economies were generated by some firms and internalized by others.

The traditional emphasis of economic historians in their analyses of American industrialization has been changes in technology and organization in the agricultural and manufacturing sectors. Increases in production were accompanied by a veritable revolution in technology and organization—by the use of complicated machine technologies in manufacturing, by the exploitation of new sources of power, by the increasing concentration of production in larger and better organized economic units with the factory becoming increasingly the dominant producing unit and the corporation the dominant financial and administrative form. To these developments we now turn.

3

Technological Change in Manufacturing

Introduction

From a position in manufacturing output rather behind those of Great Britain and Germany in 1870, the United States emerged by 1900 as the world's leading industrial power, and increased that lead to one of commanding dimensions by the mid-twentieth century.

If we examine the growth of American manufacturing output more closely, several features of the pattern of industrial change become apparent. In the first place, notwithstanding the obvious replacement of brute labor by machines, the substitution of machinery for handicraft skills in production was the most notable development, and commended itself to British and European observers of the American scene early in the century. In keeping with the increased use of machinery, the producers' goods industries expanded and were especially important for generating and institutionalizing the mechanical focus of technological change. Again, the emergence of new power sources was significant; first coal and the steam engine and, after 1900, hydroelectric power and the electric motor were introduced on a wide scale into industry. These three elements in the growth of manufacturing output were embodied in the products of the rapidly expanding iron and steel industry.

Some of the most obvious novelties in American industry involved organizational changes in the way in which work patterns were laid out in the business firm. In 1850, for example, at the Crystal Palace Exhibition in London, public attention was focused on a uniquely "American System of Manufacturing," whose principal ingredient was the use of interchangeable parts. Standardization of the product and, consequently, in the components of the product, and greater precision in the manufacture of components permitted American manufacturers to substitute assembling activities for highly labor-intensive fitting operations. Here, organizational change—a reevaluation of labor's role in production—was combined with an important role for machinery in providing sufficient precision to permit the fine tolerances required for interchangeability of parts.

Another notable organizational change followed logically from the "American System." The assembly line technique had been introduced as part of the "System," but the early concept of the assembly line involved one stationary assembler with all parts being carried to him. Later, first in meat-packing, then subsequently in many industries, perhaps most notably in the automobile industry, the assembly line became progressive, with mechanical conveyors moving components from worker to worker, each of whom performed a small, specialized task, until the completed product emerged at the end.

These elements in the growth of manufacturing output all embodied technological change. The development of new products, new machinery and equipment, and new organizational processes in the manufacturing sector were, in many ways, the most dramatic ingredients in American economic growth in the last century.

Components of Technological Change

The development of new technology passes through three main stages: invention, innovation, and diffusion.

Invention

Inventive activity involves the development of new devices with certain technical features. An invention may be a new product to be produced, a new instrument to be used in production or an organizational change. Disregarded for now will be organizational changes, which are frequently labelled "social" inventions and include new methods of competition or cooperation either within the firm or among firms. Examples of "social" inventions involving the arrangement of work within the firm are the assembly line and the departmentalization of management. Examples which cross firm boundaries are the development of the corporate form, and the mergers and consolidations which characterized much of the industrial sector towards the end of the nineteeth century. Organizational changes will be considered separately in chapter 5.

Inventive activity is defined in terms of novelty. What are the requirements for successful inventive activity? Jacob Schmookler,[1] for example, believed that demand forces through their influence on the size of the market for particular inventions are the major determinant of variations in inventive activity. The purchase of capital goods by an industry signals the increased profitability of inventions in that industry and inventors respond accordingly.

On the supply side, the characteristics of a population undoubtedly play a role. The American population of the nineteenth and early twentieth centuries was, in a world context, among the healthiest and best educated, and operated within a social framework which was strongly materialistic and conducive to economic mobility. The common cultural heritage with England and fairly close contact between the two countries were also instrumental in the flow of knowledge from the industrial pioneer to America. From humble beginnings in the workshop, American technology underwent a "scientific revolution" in the ninteenth century and, as inventive activity has become even more science-based in the twentieth century, the supply of new knowledge in the form of scientific discoveries has had widespread spill-over effects to various kinds of technical change.[2]

Finally, after Joseph Schumpeter, many economic historians have interpreted inventive activity as representing discontinuities or breakthroughs in the state of knowledge. In fact, Nathan Rosenberg has convincingly stated the inadequacy of conceiving of invention as an intermittent and discontinuous process, because this tends to underestimate the technological and economic importance of "improvements" to initial inventions.[3] Rather, while some inventions may be more important or more "lumpy" than others, inventive activity is essentially a continuous process—the continuity aspect is critical—in which the accumulation of improvements and modifications of the original design are essential to establishing the commercial feasibility of the invention.

Innovation

After the development of a new process or product in the inventor's workshop or laboratory comes the problem of introducing it into the actual production process. This activity -- called innovation -- involves applying or developing an invention to the point where it can meet the test of the market or give reliable service, and generate profits. In other words, innovation is crucial to establishing the commercial viability of an invention as it is incorporated in and adapted for production.

The requirements for successful innovative activity are related to expected profitablility, and to the supply of managerial abilities and highly motivated entrepreneurship. The time lag between invention and innovation has varied with different products and processes, as can be seen in Table 3.1. Mechanical innovations appear to have the shortest time lag, followed by chemical innovations. Electronic innovations tend to take a longer period to innovate. Moreover, the table also suggests that the time lag between invention and innovation has been less when the inventor himself undertook the innovation compared with those instances when he simply invented the concept and stopped at that point. On the other hand, there may be some difficulties in dating these lags. For example, to be consistent, the date of invention should be that by which all technical problems have been solved. Part of the observed time lag may be accounted for by the necessity of undertaking further inventive activity before innovation can be comtemplated. There is a danger, then, of misdating lags between invention and innovation.

Diffusion

The diffusion of an invention is the process by which the new technique is adopted and incorporated into the production process throughout an entire industry or industries. It follows logically after the innovation of the technique. The old methods or capital equipment are scrapped when rendered obsolete, and the new methods or equipment adopted. To cross industry lines, additional adaptive modifications may be necessary. The rate of diffusion depends partly on the extent to which the new technique is part of the public domain or is closely held secret knowledge. Patent laws were introduced for their incentive effects—in order to offer the inventor and innovator some degree of property rights in new techniques—but the number of patent infringement suits lodged in the nineteenth century attests to the difficulty of protecting patent rights. The rate at which the new technique is diffused—that is, displaces the old—is a function of the degree of the superiority of the new technique and the difficulties encountered in developing ancillary devices and techniques.[4] In effect, then, the rate of diffusion is explained primarily by the expected profitability of producing the new product or adopting new production methods.

Factors Influencing Technological Change

Economic historians have conveyed the impression of a rapid rate of technological change in the American economy during the nineteenth and

Table 3.1 Time Interval Between Invention and Innovation for Thirty-five Different Products and Processes

Invention			Innovation		Interval between Invention and Innovation (years)
Product	**Inventor**	**Date**	**Firm**	**Date**	
Safety Razor	Gillette	1895	Gillette Safety Razor Company	1904	9
Fluorescent lamp	Bacquerel	1859	General Electric, Westinghouse	1938	79
Television	Zworykin	1919	Westinghouse	1941	22
Wireless telegraph	Hertz	1889	Marconi	1897	8
Wireless Telephone	Fessenden	1900	National Electric Signaling Company	1908	8
Triode vacuum tube	de Forest	1907	The Radio Telephone and Telegraph Co.	1914	7
Radio (oscillator)	de Forest	1912	Westinghouse	1920	8
Spinning jenny	Hargreaves	1765	Hargreaves'	1770	5
Spinning machine (water frame)	Highs	1767	Arkwright's	1773	6
Spinning mule	Crompton	1779	Textile machine manufacturers	1783	4
Steam engine	Newcomen	1705	English firm	1711	6
Steam engine	Watt	1764	Boulton and Watt	1775	11
Ball-point pen	I. J. Biro	1938	Argentine firm	1944	6
Cotton picker	A. Campbell	1889	International Harvester	1942	53
Crease-resistant fabrics	Company scientists	1918	Tootal Broadhurst Lee Company, Ltd.	1932	14
DDT	Company chemists	1939	J. R. Geigy Co.	1942	3
Electric precipitation	Sir O. Lodge	1884	Cottrell's	1909	25
Freon refrigerants	T. Midgley, Jr. and A. L. Henne	1930	Kinetic Chemicals, Inc. (General Motors and Du Pont)	1931	1
Gyro-compass	Foucault	1852	Anschutz-Kaempfe	1908	56
Hardening of fats	W. Norman	1901	Crosfield's of Warrington	1909	8
Jet engine	Sir F. Whittle	1929	Rolls Royce	1943	14
Turbo-jet engine	H. von Ohain	1934	Junkers	1944	10
Long playing record	P. Goldmark	1945	Columbia Records	1948	3
Magnetic recording	V. Poulsen	1898	American Telegraphone Co.	1903	5
Plexiglas, lucite	W. Chalmers	1929	Imperial Chemical Industries	1932	3

Table 3.1 Continued

Invention			Innovation		Interval between Invention and Innovation (years)
Product	**Inventor**	**Date**	**Firm**	**Date**	
Nylon	W. H. Carothers	1928	Du Pont	1939	11
Power steering	H. Vickers	1925	Vickers, Inc.	1931	6
Radar	Marconi; A. H. Taylor and L. Young	1922	Societe Francaise Radio Electrique	1935	13
Self-winding watch	J. Harwood	1922	Harwood Self-winding Watch Co.	1928	6
Shell moulding	J. Croning	1941	Hamburg foundry	1944	3
Streptomycin	S. A. Waksman	1939	Merck and Co.	1944	5
Terylene, dacron	J. R. Whinfield, J. T. Dickson	1941	Imperial Chemical Industries, Du Pont	1953	12
Titanium reduction	W. J. Kroll	1937	U. S. Government Bureau of Mines	1944	7
Xerography	C. Carlson	1937	Haloid Corp.	1950	13
Zipper	W. L. Judson	1891	Automatic Hook and Eye Company	1918	27

NOTE: Invention is defined as "the earliest conception of the product in substantially its commercial form" and innovation as "the first commercial application or sale."

SOURCE: John L. Enos, "Invention and Innovation in the Petroleum Refining Industry," in *The Rate and Direction of Inventive Activity: Economic and Social Factors,* NBER Special Conference Series, no. 13 (Princeton: Princeton University Press, 1962), pp. 307-308.

twentieth centuries. This view has been supported, on the one hand, by reference to many "authoritative" statements by contemporary observers attesting to the propensity of Americans to invent and to adopt mechanical methods of production.[5] Support for this view is also reflected by an apparently high level of inventive activity, suggested by data on patents issued in Table 3.2, and the apparently rapid rate of innovation and diffusion of new machinery and production methods in the manufacturing sector.

Given the importance traditionally attached to the role of productivity change in American output growth, and given the impact of technological change on productivity growth, it is imperative to take a closer look at the determinants of technological change. In the following discussion, economic factors influencing technological change will be considered first, followed by a brief discussion of non-economic deter-

Table 3.2 Patents Issued, 1870-1960

Year	Inventions	Designs	Total*
1870	12,137	737	13,518
1880	12,903	514	14,203
1890	25,313	886	28,304
1900	24,644	1,754	29,881
1910	35,141	636	39,496
1920	37,060	2,481	43,303
1930	45,226	2,710	54,021
1940	42,238	6,145	48,383
1950	43,040	4,718	47,758
1960	47,170	2,543	49,713

*includes patents issued to residents of foreign countries.

SOURCE: *Historical Statistics of the United States*, ser. W99, 104, pp. 957-958.

minants. No attempt is made to consider the aspects of invention, innovation, and diffusion separately. Instead, technological change as a whole will be the focal point. Later in the chapter, the rate of diffusion of technological change is considered more thoroughly by itself.

Economic Factors

Economic factors or market forces, both on the demand and supply sides, are generally assigned the critical role in explaining the pace and pattern of technological change. The economic factors singled out for discussion here are factor endowments, changing profit expectations and the effects of uncertainty and risk, population size, and urbanization.

Factor Endowment. The arguments linking nineteenth century American factor endowments to the rate and pattern of technical change are long and convoluted, and only a brief survey is attempted here. The comments of contemporary foreign observers that Americans showed a remarkable proclivity towards the adoption of mechanical equipment in activities which were still being performed by skilled labor in Britain and France has recently erupted into a search for both theoretical and empirical justification of those remarks.

The classic argument has been that of H. J. Habakkuk,[6] who argued that labor scarcity in America was the probable causal factor. The United States was, in the words of staple theorists, a "new" country of recent settlement which in the nineteenth century was characterized by high ratios of resources to capital stock and resources to labor. This fact implied that American production would tend to be resource-intensive.[7] Thus, the distinctive feature of much American technical practice and much American invention and innovation lay in its being *directed* towards the exploitation of a large quantity of resources with relatively little labor.[8]

Habakkuk's chain of argument from resource abundance to the substitution of capital for labor in production and the development of labor-saving inventions has prompted attempts to extend and justify his position in two directions. The first has been to verify empirically that Americans actually did develop and introduce labor-saving technology during the nineteenth century. The second has been the attempt to develop a theoretical rationale for assigning a causal role to the status of factor endowments in explaining the pattern of American technological change.

There have been two recent efforts at substantiating the factor-saving bias of American technological change in the nineteenth and early twentieth centuries. One is a macrostudy of the entire domestic sector of the American economy by Moses Abramovitz and Paul David,[9] and the other a microstudy of the cotton and woolen textiles industries by Ephraim Asher,[10] which includes an interesting comparison of relative factor-saving bias in the American and British industries. Neither of these studies deals with the origins or determinants of technological change, but only with its observed factor-saving bias.

For the American economy as a whole, David and van de Klundert found that technological change during the twentieth century exhibited a substantial labor-saving bias. Abramovitz and David arrived at similar findings for the American economy in the nineteenth century.[11] Their findings lend empirical support to Habakkuk's thesis.

Asher measured factor-saving biases in technological change in the American and British textile industries during 1850 to 1900. He interpreted Habakkuk's argument to imply that, during the nineteenth century, either (i) there was labor-saving bias in technological change in American industry, whereas the bias in British industry was capital-saving, or (ii) there was labor-saving bias in the industrial sectors of both countries, but the bias was greater in the United States. In fact, Asher's results confirm that there was labor-saving bias in technological change in the cotton and woolen textile industries in both countries. This clear indication that the American industries experienced labor-saving technological change accords at the industry level—although admittedly only for one industry—with Abramovitz and David's findings for the American economy as a whole.[12]

Refinement of the theoretical arguments was initiated by Peter Temin.[13] He attempted to restate Habakkuk's thesis as three conceptually distinct statements that (i) Americans characteristically *employed more capital equipment* than did their British counterparts, (ii) Americans surpassed the British in the *invention* of labor-saving machinery, (iii) Americans surpassed the British in *both the invention and innovation and diffusion of new machinery.*

The first statement, he argued, referred to selection of different input combinations from an array of possibilities within a state of technology common to both countries. In other words, the optimal factor combinations in the two countries reflected their respective factor endowments (and prices). Presumably production was more capital-intensive (and, consequently, less labor-using) in America because of the relatively high price of labor.

Statements (ii) and (iii) together referred to intercountry differences in technologies. According to Temin, Habakkuk had been arguing that technological progress in America was both more rapid and more labor-saving (that is, technological progress led also to the use of more capital-intensive techniques in the United States). Temin summarizes these points in his "Basic Theorem of Labor Scarcity"—either "more" (British-American differences in the choice of technique) or "better" (labor scarcity's effect on the peculiar nature of American invention and innovation) machinery is sufficient to explain the greater productivity of American workers.[14]

Temin derived a two-sector model (agriculture and industry) which appeared to validate the "more" machinery version of Habakkuk's thesis. But, this conclusion was apparently contradicted by the fact that prevailing interest rates in the United States exceeded those in Britain. Temin concluded that the Habakkuk thesis was incompatible with theoretical analysis. In fact, however, Temin had incorrectly specified his production function: with a common technology, the greater abundance of natural resources in America would have raised the productivity of capital and labor at the margin in both agriculture and industry as compared with Britain, which implies both relatively high wage rates *and* high rates of return on capital in the United States. The result does not imply, as Temin believed, a lower capital intensity of American manufacturing. In fact, its implications about relative capital intensity are indeterminate.

Another problem in developing a theoretical explanation of the Habakkuk thesis concerns the theoretical underpinnings of an *ex ante* bias towards labor-saving innovations, that is, the proposition that Americans consciously attempted to invent labor-saving devices. In fact, after the work of W. E. G. Salter[15] and others, the notion of *ex ante* factor bias in technological change has been rendered questionable. With a firm in competitive markets and in least-cost equilibrium, all inputs are equally costly and productive at the margin. Consequently, there was no reason for a high wage to rent ratio in the United States to stimulate Americans to search for methods which saved on labor rather than other inputs. *Ex ante*, entrepreneurs search for cost-saving innovations, and only *ex post* are these innovations observed to be specifically labor-saving or capital-saving.

How does one then deal with the question of a conscious search by Americans for innovations which would economize on labor? One possibility is the "expectations" scheme put forward by Nathan Rosenberg.[16] While accepting Salter's reservations, Rosenberg argues that relative factor prices may influence not only the choice of technique among known techniques but also the direction of technical change if there are firmly held expectations about the likely course of relative price changes in the future. With respect to the nineteenth century United States, it is plausible to argue that businessmen inferred a historical trend for the capital intensity of production to increase and that, extrapolating this trend into the future, they believed that labor costs would continue to rise (because of high wages, persistent pressures of a tight labor market, and the high degree of labor mobility) relative to the cost of capital. Therefore, he concluded, businessmen would be inclined to seek inventions which would economize on labor. Another possibility concerns the socioeconomic climate of the nineteenth century, and does not depend on expectations of changes in relative factor prices. Here, the point is simply that, in general, industrial development in the nineteenth century was oriented about the development of a machine technology, both in the United States and in Great Britain. The search for new, cost-reducing methods of production was consequently directed towards the development of machinery. The concentration of effort in machine development involved external effects among branches of machine development, and resulted in a rapid generation of technological invention.

A promising approach by Paul David tries to make explicit the connection between abundant natural resources and labor-saving technological change.[17] According to David, producers do not normally have a choice among an infinite number of alternative production techniques as neoclassical economic theory presumes. Rather, David believes that producers are confronted by a small number of alternative basic processes. Once a basic process has been selected because of relative factor prices—initially in the United States because of high labor prices and resource abundance—technical change is conceived as a search for cost-reducing innovation within the basic process, what David labels a "myopic exploration" of the basic technique.[18] Technical progress is "localized": that is, it proceeds among a narrow band of alternative technical solutions about the basic process chosen initially. Within the band, there exists a set of potential techniques that have a high probability of technical success. The set changes with changes in the state of knowledge, but any of the techniques can be developed if it becomes commercially profitable to do so.

Thus, the initial choice of technique in America is explained by labor scarcity and resource abundance, with resources and capital being jointly substituted for labor in production. Once America adopted the labor-saving basic process, the search for new inventions was invariably pointed in a labor-saving direction, constrained as it was by the fundamental commitment of existing production to a labor-saving technology. As David concludes,

> Even if the same labor-capital price ratio had faced producers in Britain and America, the comparatively greater availability of natural resources would have suggested to some American producers the design, and to others the selection for use, of more capital-intensive methods. . . . And from such choices immediately would flow the consequences for the global characteristics of the ensuing technological developments in each country.[19]

Although David has left many questions unanswered, he has suggested a promising theoretical connection between natural resource endowment and the rate and pattern of American technological change.[20] This represents a significant improvement over earlier explanations couched in terms of expectations about future relative factor prices and a general "focus" on the development of machine technology.

Changing Profit Expectations. The expected profitability of invention, innovation, and diffusion is generally assigned an important role in explaining technological change. Expected profitability reflects a number of demand and supply forces.

The demand by businessmen for any new invention depends upon several factors. First, demand is influenced by any increase in expected revenue flows to the firm, or reduction in expected cost flows associated with use of the invention. Jacob Schmookler has argued quite forcefully that demand-pull forces are the prime determinant of variations in the allocation of inventive effort to specific industries.[21] Variations in the sale of output induce variations in patenting activity. Another factor influencing the demand for a particular kind of invention lies in the interdependence of component parts of machine technologies. One invention in part of a complex technology may generate pressure for complementary inventions. Inventive activity may thus be led in specific directions seeking to solve particular bottlenecks.

Again, to Schmookler, the composition of consumer demand in the nineteenth and early twentieth centuries was extremely important in explaining the profitability of mechanization. Mechanized industry produced a standardized product rather than a crafted one, and the readiness of the American public to accept homogeneous final products must be acknowledged. In effect, "producer" initiative rather than "consumer" initiative was vital to the mechanization of production, since efficient production of standardized final goods had its roots in machinery which simplified production problems and reduced production costs. This development was embodied in the efficient specialization of the producers' goods sector itself, where quite early a significant degree of standardization in machinery production appeared. This was partly the result of engineering skills being more effectively subordinated to commercial needs and criteria in the United States, whereas in Britain engineers appeared to be preoccupied with purely technical aspects rather than with the production process.[22]

On the supply side, the cost of an invention is dependent upon the supply of factors involved in inventive activity—on the supply of labor and its quality and the state of technical and scientific knowledge.[23] Most important is the realization that technical change results from certain acquired problem-solving skills. The quality of the American labor force has been important here: formal education and literacy were instrumental in raising the productivity of the labor force both as laborers and as prospective inventors and modifiers of technologies developed elsewhere. In the United States, these skills were relatively concentrated in certain sectors of the economy including the machine tool, iron and steel, and steam power industries. From an initial dependence on craft skills, the invention and transmission of new technology came to reply increasingly on organized scientific knowledge and formal engineering and technical training. As Edwin Layton demonstrates, American technology underwent a "scientific revolution" during the nineteenth century, the artisan being replaced by 1900 by the "technologist," possessed of a college degree, a professional organization, and a technical literature.[24] Of course, in the twentieth century, the importance of mechanical skills and aptitudes has been increasingly eroded by the growth of the science-based chemical and electrical industries in which scientific advance underlies technological change.

Expected profitability is also conditioned by the existence of risks or uncertainties which affect the innovation and diffusion process. Risks or uncertainties introduce an element of unpredictability into calculations of an invention's likely profitability. Strassmann[25] has identified four types of risk which the bussinessman must consider: production risks, customer risks, interference risks, and timing risks.

Production risks are associated with the unpredictability of the functioning of new machinery arising from the changing level of production skills and resources of the economy. For example, a new machine may be beset by unanticipated "bugs" which impede its profitable adoption, or its adoption may be delayed or rendered impracticable by the unexpected lack of suitable labor or raw materials. Again, a new technique or production could be liable to an unforeseen rapid rate of obsolescence because of the emergence of other new, competing inventions. Customer risks involve the predictability of individuals' responses—viz., the danger that new machines or their output will not be acceptable for reasons of customer inertia or prejudice. Interference risks involve unanticipated reactions on the part of groups whose socioeconomic status may be affected by the invention. These groups may try to protect the status quo by strategic measures, including the use of strikes by labor unions, patent suits by competitors, tariff changes, and so forth. Timing risks involve the danger of innovating too close to a future business recession.

In fact, Strassman argued, American technological change took place in the nineteenth century in an environment in which there was much less risk associated with innovation than has generally been supposed. For example, production risks were lessened by the complementarity of many inventions; that is, the unexpected dovetailing of inventions in separate industries tended to increase the profitability of many inventions beyond expectations. The rise of engineering and development of scientific knowledge also helped increasingly to lower production risks. Customer risks were low because American consumer demand was quite amenable to consuming standardized products, and the demand for new machinery and equipment reflected the buoyancy of consumer demand.

On the other hand, it is likely that interference risks increased towards 1900 and thereafter. For most of the nineteenth century, America was characterized by a weak union movement, by governments relatively uninterested in policing economic matters, and by an essentially competitive economic framework. By the end of the century, the aura of competition had given way to monopoly and oligopoly elements in industry and the services sector, a stronger union movement, and the threat of government intervention to regulate economic matters. Timing risks, while difficult to predict, did not always lead to innovative failure. In many instances, firms undertook investment in new plant and equipment during mild contractions in order to strengthen their competitive positions.

The existence of risks and uncertainties of many kinds impinged upon the businessman's ability to calculate the expected profitability of new techniques and must have exercised a restraining influence upon the rate of technological advance. But fewer uncertainties appear to have been operative in the nineteenth century United States than historians have generally supposed, and this helps to explain the rapid rate of invention and innovative activity.

Population Size and Distribution. The pace of technological change is positively and strongly related to the rate of invention, and some economic historians have argued that an increasing population may both raise per capita inventive activity and expedite the incorporation of the results of inventive activity into the production process.[26] Consequently, population size and growth, it is argued, has had a positive impact on the growth of per capita output.

The first influence of population size is on effective demand or the size of the market. Market size is a function of average income and the distribution of income as well as population size. Given the level of per capita income in the nineteenth century United States, population growth in itself was important in market creation. The growing market size made possible the exploitation of scale economies in production. These economies of large-scale operation were realized from specialization and division of labor within firms, and from increased specialization among firms.[27] Economies of large-scale production became evident in the iron and steel industry with its growth of plant size and specialized mill activity after 1870. An early example of the growth of specialization among firms is the emergence of a machine tool industry which developed after the realization that machinery could be produced more cheaply by specialized firms than in the users' own machine shops. A case in point is the production of textile machinery. This industry had its origins in machine shops which began as sections within textile firms in New England, became separate firms specializing in textiles machinery, and gradually branched out as tool-making firms catering in addition to a market for producers' goods beyond the textile industries.

Population size also contributes to the rate of invention and innovation. According to Kuznets, there are increasing returns to scale in inventive activity in response to increasing population size, and to increasing population density. In fact, on several occasions, the latter hypothesis has been subjected to empirical testing for the nineteenth century United States in an effort to determine the impact of urbanization on the rate of invention.

These studies have their starting point in a thought-provoking monograph by Alan Pred.[28] Employing data for sixteen cities, Pred argued that inventive activity and the location of inventions tended to be disproportionately urban-oriented in the United States during 1860 to

1910 because urbanization and industrialization provided a social and economic environment appropriate to inventive activity. The quantity of inventions, as measured by patents issued, is assumed to depend upon the demand for new production methods. This demand was concentrated in urban areas where manufacturing was growing rapidly. Coincidentally, on the supply wide, adequate quantities of potential inventors and investment capital were located in cities where manufacturing was found. The search for new techniques by entrepreneurs was facilitated by the enhanced flow of information in urban areas, which increased the probability that potential inventor would learn about an industrial technical problem. Over time, technological convergence tended to reinforce the advantages of urban centers in inventive activity.

This argument has recently been subjected to additional testing by Irwin Feller and Robert Higgs.[29] Feller tried to test some of Pred's hypotheses using data for thirty-five cities, and found a strong relationship between patents issued and urbanization. Inventions tended to be concentrated in the thirty-five largest and most industrialized cities over the period, and differences in the numbers of patents issued in these cities were a function of population and employment patterns. Higg's results are consistent with the hypothesis of a positive linear relationship between inventiveness (inventors per capita) and the proportion of population living in cities.

Why should these results be appealing? Suppose that the quantity of resources directed to inventive activity is assumed to be a function of the expected profitability of invention. Profitability is comprised of a stream of expected revenues generated by the invention and a stream of expected costs of inventing. The expected revenue stream depends upon the market for the invention; if the cost of acquiring information about potential markets is a function of distance, then the costs of obtaining market information are lower in urban communities. And, similarly, with respect to the cost of inventing activity, the basic inputs of inventive capacity and information are likely to be available at lower cost in urban areas because of the greater proximity of information carriers to each other. Consequently, both the stream of expected revenues from and the costs of inventive activity are likely to make inventive activity more profitable in urban compared with rural areas.

Moreover, the effect of urbanization on inventive activity will be conducive to further economic growth and urbanization. Earlier, in chapter 2, it was argued that urbanization reflected changes in the composition of output induced by changing patterns of expenditures towards urban-type products and away from rural-type products as per capita incomes grew. By favorably influencing inventive activity, urbanization also promoted more rapid technological progress which tended to further increase per capita incomes and, consequently, to further increase pressures for unbanization.

Noneconomic Factors.

Were noneconomic factors important in determining the pattern of inventive activity, innovation, and diffusion in American manufacturing during the nineteenth and early twentieth centuries? The American social system has long been regarded as one which emphasized "positive" social values and lacked institutions that might inhibit social and economic mobility. American society was strongly motivated along economic lines. The relatively high levels of literacy and formal education in America were conducive to the high level of productivity of the population, not just as laborers but also as inventors and adapters of technologies developed elsewhere, particularly in Britain. Here the rate and composition of immigration were quite important: acquisition of skills by the American labor force was facilitated by the ease with which her society absorbed immigrants from Great Britain and Europe. Many of the skills associated with nineteenth century machine technology had to be learned on the job, since they included a large proportion of "know-how" or uncodified skills. These were not readily transferable through formal education or print and, thus, their transmission was predicated on a labor force which was well prepared through its educational background to receive and retain technical information and was receptive to the immigration of skilled persons who could impart technical knowledge.

The possible impact of social and cultural factors on the origins and persisting features of the American system of manufacturing has been discussed by many authors. John Sawyer,[30] for example, has argued that a distinctive pattern of manufacturing began to emerge before the Civil War which was influenced by important independent American contributions in tools, techniques, and above all, in ways of approaching and organizing production and distribution. The new patterns of production and the extensive social transformation that they involved met with slight resistance in the United States -- new products, new methods of production, new ways of working, organizing and consuming were facilitated by the prevailing social framework.

Sawyer believes that these basic attributes of the social structure had emerged by the 1850s before the frequently cited explanations for industrial growth—capital accumulation and the large American market—which dominate the interpretation of post-1870 growth. Traditional economic aguments about high wage rates and shortages of skilled labor, improving transportation, and a growing market for manufactures are important but are not sufficient to explain the rapid shift from home and handicraft industry to manufacturing with machine technology. Changes in the social structure were preconditions of the emergence of modern manufacturing.

Sawyer builds his case on information provided by nineteenth century observers of the American scene, and their emphasis on the unique social characteristics of America: higher levels of and more widely diffused general education; absence of rigidities and restraints of class and craft; freedom from hereditary definitions of tasks or set ways of going about them; focus on personal advancement and material success; the mobility, flexibility and adaptability of Americans. These social characteristics are linked directly to economic behavior and, particularly, to the search for and adoption of new and more efficient methods of production involving the use of machinery. In summary, Sawyer argues that a central place in explaining the growth and, more importantly, the machine-technology basis of manufacturing must be accorded the American social structure. While the argument is appealing, there remain problems associated with the reliability of "expert" contemporary opinion and making "exact" causal inferences from characteristics of social structure to individual behavior which must condition reliance on such evidence.

Diffusion of Technological Change

As was suggested earlier, the impression generally conveyed in the literature on American economic growth is that technological change in manufacturing industries was very rapid. The traditional arguments suggest that the rate of invention was high, and that inventions were uniformly innovated with only short time lags behind invention and then rapidly diffused as the profitability of the new techniques became apparent. In fact, the rate at which diffusion occurred varied from invention to invention and from industry to industry as the several factors influencing the rate of diffusion came into play.

Factors Influencing Diffusion

Diffusion is an essentially economic variable. The rate of diffusion is explained by economists principally by considerations of expected profitability and then usually in a demand-oriented framework. That is, economists devote considerable attention to the market's receptivity of new products on the presumption that, once invented, an invention is immediately, technically, ready for use in production. In fact, however, this approach invariably underestimates the technical and economic importance of subsequent improvements in the original invention before its successful innovation precipitates a more rapid rate of diffusion. A number of important considerations that influence the rate of diffusion must be taken into account.

The rate of diffusion of an invention may depend upon improvements to the invention after its introduction because of problems involving the nature of the product produced, input or complementary technical constraints, or because of changes in older technologies which are substitutes for the new. The latter phenomenon is referred to as the persistence of old technologies.

Frequently, the adoption of a new technique of production has been retarded by imperfections—impurities or byproducts—imparted in the production process. One often cited example dating from seventeenth century England was that the use of coal in the brewing industry adversely affected the taste of the product. A more recent example, pertinent in the nineteenth century American economy, concerned the difficulties in the iron and steel industry in controlling the quality of output, which delayed the widespread application of iron products to industrial uses. The introduction of the Bessemer and later the open-hearth process allowed for much greater accuracy in determining the carbon content of iron and steel. These developments indicate a second influence on diffusion, the rate at which subsequent improvements are made in the original invention (in this case, the application of coal to iron and steel production). In fact, diffusion of new technologies can often be delayed by improvements in "old" techniques, and the rate of improvement of technical efficiency in the charcoal-fired sector of the iron industry from 1842 to 1858 is a case in point.[32]

The development of technical skills among users of the new technique is crucial. The length of the learning period for labor depends partly on the extent to which the techniques are really novel or can be managed by the transfer of skills from other industries. For example, railroad shops were, in many cases, adaptations of shops which had originally been developed to work with steam engines in marine use, and were converted with the development of the railroad. In cases where skills are not readily transferable, the time taken to acquire skills—learning-by-doing—helps to determine the rate at which the superiority of new techniques is established vis-à-vis the old. In many cases, the acquisition of skills was rendered difficult and slow because the skills consisted largely in "know-how" and experience, and were not readily transferable through formal education or printed manuals. The supply and geographical mobility of persons possessing such knowledge was a constraint on diffusion. For example, in the puddling process in the manufacture of iron, the iron-master knew by "feel," by experience that is, when the iron was freed from the maximum amount of impurities. Similarly, in the early use of the steam engine, much of the knowledge of optimum pressure levels was a function of experience.

Often, even if the requisite skills were found in the labor force, there would be constraints of a nonlabor kind. The development of skills in the producers' goods industries, and their embodiment in new and better machinery, depended on the development of specialized inputs into machine-making. Examples are the development of precise measuring devices such as the Vernier caliper which allowed for the closer fitting of parts in machines and, consequently, increased efficiency, and the development of high-speed steel which made possible more precise cutting machinery. Again, many new inventions could not be diffused or could not be used to the utmost advantage until complementary inventions were made. In the railroad sector, late nineteenth century innovations like the use of steel rails, the air brake, and the automatic coupler greatly increased productivity.[33]

Finally, the impact of economic, social and political institutions on the rate of diffusion must also be considered. In general, the socioeconomic structure of the United States was conducive to innovation and diffusion. However, to a great extent, the institutional framework affected the way in which the applicability of an invention was conceptualized. Predictions about how a particular invention will fit into the social system and the uses to which it will be put reflect the socioeconomic environment and its perceived needs at the time of development. One of the primary uses to which electric power was expected to be put in the late nineteenth century was street lighting and street railway systems. An afterthought, the application of electric power to industrial machinery had consequences which far outstripped those initially conceived uses.

Case Studies in Diffusion

Let us review the early histories of two industries in order to illustrate the nature of the diffusion process. The first is the machine tool industry which is regarded as a crucial producers' goods industry because of its role in making possible the widespread dissemination of technical knowledge embodied in machinery and equipment after 1840. The second is the cotton textiles industry where attention is focused on the adoption and diffusion of the Draper loom during 1894 to 1914.

Machine Tool Industries. Producers' goods industries such as machine tools are important in the introduction and diffusion of technological change for obvious reasons. First, many inventions are generally innovated into production in the form of a new capital good manufactured by a firm in the producers' goods sector. Firms in this sector have generally been highly specialized, producing a narrow range of outputs in response to the demands of customers in consumers' goods or other producers' goods industries. Second, firms in producers' goods industries are motivated to improve their own efficiency in the production of durable goods. Their success tends to influence the price of their machinery output and, consequently, to influence the rate of investment activity and the rate at which new technology will be diffused. Thus, almost by definition, the machinery-producing industries play a major role in accounting for the rapid production and diffusion of innovations. Machine tools are the most important component of the power-driven metal-working machinery industry.[35]

In the early part of the nineteenth century, there was no separate machinery-producing sector in the United States. Machines were produced in machine shops located on the premises of the machine users -- for example, in the textiles firms of New England. As these shops became successful producers of textile machinery, they emerged as separate firms producing textile machinery and then began to produce and sell a diverse range of other types of machinery, generally the heavier, general purpose machine tools like lathes, planners, and boring machines for the railways. This growth reflected the growth of the market for such machines, and also the accumulation of technical skills and knowledge which, developed in the production of one type of machine, were transmitted to the production of other types. Lighter, high-speed machine tools like milling machines and precision grinders tended to emerge from the initial production requirements of weapons makers, and their development was furthered later in the century by the demands of manufacturers of sewing machines, bicycles, and automobiles.

Thus, the machine tool industry originated out of the manufacturing requirements of a succession of particular industries, and evolved gradually in the second half of the nineteenth century into a separate industry with a large number of firms producing a narrow range of products. The same machines came to be employed in a larger and larger number of industries, and the production of the machines itself became a specialized operation. By 1914 there were more than 400 machine tool manufacturers in the United States, mostly located in the New England, Middle Atlantic and East-Northcentral regions.

The importance of the machine tool industries to nineteenth century technological change is underscored by the fact that industrialization involves the introduction of a relatively small number of similar production processes across industries. These processes involved the growing adoption of a machine technology which employed decentralized sources of power. This similarity was the basis for "technological convergence" in the machinery and metal-using sectors of the economy where, in many industries producing a wide variety of products, component metal parts were converted into a final form before they were assembled as final outputs.[36] The use of machinery in these many industries involved a relatively small number of types of operations (turning, boring, drilling, milling, and planing, among them) and a similar group of technical problems (including power transmission, control devices, feed mechanisms, and friction reduction). Technological convergence occurred precisely because these processes and problems were common to the production of this wide range of different end-products, and was predicated on the technological interrelations of seemingly unrelated industries. In the nineteenth century, for example, there was significant technological convergence among firearms, sewing machines, and bicycles.

Technological convergence was important both for the development of new techniques and their diffusion, and for the growth of specialization among firms. For example, individual firms producing milling machines would not likely have emerged if only firearms manufacturers used milling machines; with technological convergence, milling was an important operation in a large number of metal-using industries, and this permitted considerable specialization. In fact, Rosenberg believes technological convergence to have been as important a factor as the expansion in demand for final products in explaining the high degree of specialization in the machinery-producing sector.

Moreover, the machine tool industry was to play an important role both in the initial solution of technological problems and in the rapid transmission and application of new techniques to other users. Indeed, Rosenberg argues that the industry was a center for the acquisition and diffusion of new skills and techniques in an economy based on machine technology. New skills or techniques were developed or perfected in response to the demands of specific customers, and the machine tool industry then transferred these techniques to other machine-using sectors of the economy.

By economizing on the use of labor and by making possible mass-production through interchangeable parts, the machine tool industry helped to raise output and, consequently, incomes per capita.

Draper Loom in Cotton Textiles. The power loom had become almost ubiquitous in the American cotton textiles industry by 1860. It was subjected to continuous technical development until about 1880 in order to increase the speed at which looms could be operated and the number of looms an individual worker could operate. The number of looms one worker could tend was limited because of the need for manually inserting a new bobbin of yarn in the shuttle every few minutes.

The Draper loom, invented between 1888 and 1894, was an automatic shuttle-changing loom which allowed for automatic replacement of empty bobbins without stopping the loom. It was about three times more expensive to purchase than the dearest nonautomatic loom, but the Draper Company claimed it lowered labor costs by permitting an individual worker to operate more looms and also reduced skill requirements. This led to a reduction in weaving costs per unit of output, although there was some increase in repair costs.

The interest of economic historians in the Draper loom arises from the apparent slow rate of adoption of the loom in the New England textile industry after 1894. The traditional explanation in American historiography of this diffusion lag was the alleged conservative bias of the textile firms' managements, which led to the technological obsolescence of the industry and to the relative decline of New England as a textile-producing area. However, the economic rationality of management in delaying adoption of the loom must not be prejudged: it depends upon the profitability of adopting the new technique compared with continuing production with existing equipment. In considering this question, Irwin Feller looked at two points: (i) the rate of adoption of the Draper loom in New England compared with the South, and (ii) the consistency of the rate of adoption in New England with the rate necessary for long-term survival in competitive markets.

The data on Draper loom sales indicate a slightly higher sales volume in the South compared with New England to 1909, and a sharp relative increase in sales in the northeastern area from 1909 to 1914. Throughout the period, the ratio of Draper looms to total looms was higher in the South, with the result that in 1914 the automatic loom was fifty-two percent of the southern capacity compared with about forty percent in New England.[38] The question, of course, is whether this sequence of events is explained by economic irrationality on the part of northeastern management, or by the possibility that it was profitable to adopt a new technique for expanding output in the South but simultaneously unprofitable to *substitute* it for an older technique still serviceable and in use in the North. In fact, the latter proposition appears the more valid, especially since firms in New England bought the Draper loom after 1909 when they greatly increased capacity and made some transition from the old to the new loom in existing capacity.

Why this difference in regional rates of diffusion? The reason lay in the nature of competition in the textile industry. The South had emerged by 1890 as a threat to New England in the production of coarse textiles, and had begun to encroach on the better-quality textiles markets as well. During the 1890s New England firms shifted their output mix towards better quality textiles, and virtually abdicated the coarse textiles market to southern producers. These more expensive fabrics could not, for technical reasons, be produced with Draper looms. In spite of the Draper Company's attempts to improve the loom to meet the requirements of the New England industry, the fact remains that the output mix in those mills militated against adoption of the loom, whereas the southern mills' coarse textiles could be produced most efficiently on Draper looms. By 1909, however, the loom had been made suitable for a greater variety of fabrics, and was diffused into the New England industry rapidly thereafter.

Thus, there is an economic explanation for the differential regional rates of diffusion. In the 1890s the Draper loom had limited applicability to the output mix produced in New England. Moreover, cost savings generated through use of the loom, even when it had been technically adapted for use in the New England industry, were not great enough to warrant general replacement of all existing capacity. By 1909 the loom was clearly superior to nonautomatic looms, and was purchased to expand capacity in the New England industry. Quite clearly, undue emphasis had been placed on managerial conservatism in New England in the prewar period.

Even with the prewar upsurge in adoptions of the automatic loom and high wartime profits, the New England industry soon fell upon difficult times. Does technological obsolescence explain the long-term decline of this industry which dates from the liquidations and exodus of northern firms to southern locations beginning in the mid-1920s? It appears that the New England industry was, on average, still using a backward technology compared with southern manufacturers: if New England mills had been more up-to-date, would they have had a better chance of withstanding southern competition? Or, even if they had been reequipped with the most efficient technology, would the New England textile industry still have suffered a relative decline?

Feller argues, quite convincingly, that New England mill owners saw their disadvantage, not in terms of the vintage of their plant and equipment, but in high labor and other costs which would have continued to hamper the industry even if best-practice techniques were employed. New England owners acknowledged that southern mills had a significant cost advantage—even with the same technology, cost differentials favored southern mills by about fifteen percent in the mid-1920s, mainly because of lower wages.[39] New England firms had a choice of investment strategies -- either to modernize under unpromising cost conditions vis à vis southern mills, or to continue operating with obsolete equipment until falling profits precipitated closure. In fact, New England owners made a rational decision in the mid-1920s not to continue modernizing at a time when southern firms were doing so. Regional differences in the diffusion of the automatic loom were not the determining factor in the movement of the cotton textile industry from New England to the South, although they may have affected the rate and timing of changes in the regional industries. Ultimately, the inherent cost advantage of southern firms, due mainly to regional wage differences, was the decisive factor in the decline of the New England cotton textile industry.

Conclusion

Most nineteenth-century inventions emanated from the curious minds and mechanical skills of craftsmen and technicians laboring in small workshops. By the end of the century, the source of invention shifted towards the professional scientist and his well-equipped scientific laboratory. Invention depended more and more on the simultaneous development of theoretical work in new branches of science, and their practical application in chemical, electrical, and other industries. Technology's growing science base has continued -- even accelerated -- in the twentieth century.

There remains a tendency, however, for historians to substitute the biographies of noted inventors for more careful analysis of the social processes of invention, innovation, and diffusion. I have tried to remedy this defect in this chapter by examining the various ways in which both economic and noneconomic factors may have influenced technological change. And I have emphasized in particular the theme of America's abundance of natural resources and its relationship to the developing labor-saving bias in American techniques of production. Even so, the study of the inventor/entrepreneur—both as an individual and as a social type—can prove fruitful, and to this subject we now turn.

4

The American Industrial Entrepreneur

Introduction

A dramatic feature—and perhaps the overriding feature—of the American economy during the late nineteenth century was its predominantly private nature; that is, although state and federal governments guided and promoted economic development, the United States was still essentially a market economy characterized by private ownership of the means of production and distribution, and by private initiative in economic matters. In essence, a large range of economic functions was concentrated in the hands of individual decision-makers in the United States in this period. These individuals acted within a social environment which was peculiarly favorable to the pursuit of economic opportunities. In this environment, the process of economic change involved the introduction of new products and new methods of production and the exploitation of new markets and new resources, and all of these changes were introduced by individual merchants and industrialists.

What was the particular nature of the entrepreneurial role in the nineteenth and early twentieth century American economy? One aspect of this role is related to the motivation of entrepreneurial behavior toward commercial success, and to the influence of factors such as social origin on entrepreneurial recruitment. Indeed, it is possible to examine case studies of entrepreneurial success in industry and to try to infer from these examples the influence of social structure on entrepreneurship and to assess other factors which might influence the emergence of entrepreneurial capacity.

The Entrepreneurial Function and Its Determinants

Entrepreneurship is a concept which, in the study of economic history and economic development, has always been regarded as extremely important. But at the same time, it is a concept which has been very difficult to pin down or to define precisely. The usual starting point is the Schumpeterian version of the entrepreneur and his role in economic growth. In discussing economic change, Joseph A. Schumpeter[1] distinguished between adaptive response and creative response on the part of businessmen. Adaptive response involves the firm in major or minor changes that remain within the range of current practice. Creative response, on the other hand, involves going beyond existing practices or techniques, and requires the doing of new things or the doing of things that are already being done, in a new way. In other words, creative response is innovation, and its study is the study of entrepreneurship.

Schumpeter's entrepreneur was a rather heroic figure, who engaged in innovation and who willingly bore uncertainty in order to innovate new processes or new products in the economy. This kind of heroic role for entrepreneurship may be limited to relatively few cases, among them certain American entrepreneurs—titanic figures like Carnegie from the iron and steel industry, Edison in the electrical industry, and Ford in the automobile industry. However, it is important also to emphasize adaptive response. This clearly involves the entrepreneur in a less sensational role whereby he continually adjusts his entrepreneurial responses, choosing among already innovated processes and modifying them to be consistent with his maximizing behavior.

In particular, there appear to be two aspects to entrepreneurship: first, the entrepreneurial function itself, and second, investment strategy and responses to uncertainty.[2] The entrepreneurial function is relatively straightforward. The entrepreneur can be regarded as a person (or firm) who invests time, energy and capital in economically significant pursuits. In the Schumpeterian world, the emphasis is placed on the actual decision-making process rather than the factors motivating the entrepreneur to behave the way he does. On the other hand, many historians believe that it is extremely important to analyze the psychological and social underpinnings and determinants of entrepreneurial behavior.

Since the entrepreneur invests time, energy, and capital in economically significant pursuits, it is necessary to look at the investment process. What is particularly compelling about the investment process is that it proceeds in the face of uncertainty. An aspect of this considered in the previous chapter was the dependence of the expected profitability of technological innovation partly upon uncertainty and the predictability of revenues and costs. One way of approaching the classification of investment is to argue that it embodies either creative or adaptive response in the decision-making process. Investment carried out as an adaptive response involves routine decision making; that is, the effects of the decision-making process are considered predictable. For example, the technical processes are known and are being adapted to the production of a slightly different product, or a slight alteration in technique within that known process is being introduced. The process of "technological convergence" cited by Nathan Rosenberg in the diffusion of machine tools in the nineteenth century is a good example. Machine tools which were originally developed in the textile industry were subsequently adapted for use in similar processes in other industries, such as the railroad machine shop industry. Machine tools originally developed in the firearms industry were later adapted for use in the sewing machine industry and, still later, in the bicycle and automobile industries. Machine tools performed tasks that were common to production processes of very different industries. Thus, in Rosenberg's terms, they were "technologically convergent." Another example of adaptive response is the subsequent refinement of Edison's invention of the phonograph in the 1870s. Although Edison invented the phonograph, he did not foresee its most likely uses. In fact, he thought of the phonograph as a device mainly for business use (like the contemporary dictaphone), for recording speeches, teaching languages, and providing literature for the blind, but he did not foresee the role which his invention was to play in entertainment. The modern phonograph industry was developed by his competitors.

The other kind of investment activity that can be fitted into the Schumpeterian framework takes the form of creative response which embodies innovative decision making. As a creative response, investment strategy occurs in a developmental situation and appears as a shaping action. Here, the constraints of the institutional framework are not binding on entrepreneurial response. Edison's invention and early innovation of the phonograph represents a creative response, whereas, as noted above, the later improvements in the phonograph represent adaptive responses.

How does the entrepreneur decide to respond creatively rather than adaptively, and to innovate changes in technology or new products, especially when called upon to undertake investment in the face of uncertainty? And what factors influence the entrepreneur's expectations about the profitability of innovation, and how exactly are these expectations formed in the context of uncertainty?

If the entrepreneur is considering undertaking an investment, then he also must consider the extent to which there are uncertainties impinging upon the prospective profitability of this investment. One possibility is that he may try to develop techniques that tend to minimize uncertainty by building what Easterbrook calls "security zones" for investment. That is, he can undertake some kind of action to modify or to expand the market for a new process or new product. This, in many cases, is not an economic function at all, but one which involves noneconomic actions, including the use of social and political influence in order to gain acceptability for (to reduce uncertainties confronting) the investment project.

Edison, for example, was able to rely on his friendship with Henry Ford and on financial connections with J. Pierpont Morgan in order to obtain capital to finance his innovative activity at crucial points in the 1880s and 1890s. Eli Whitney was able to finance the development of his firearms industry in the early part of the nineteenth century on the basis of political connections with the federal government, which enabled him to secure advance payments and to avoid penalties on his government musket contracts. These are two cases in which businessmen employed noneconomic connections to reduce uncertainty by building some kind of security zone for investment.

There are two sorts of variables which need to be considered in regard to entrepreneurial response. One is obviously the social and political environment, and the way in which it represents uncertainties to the entrepreneur. The other is the determinants of entrepreneurial capacity. For example, consider two entrepreneurs of identical quality. It stands to reason that the entrepreneur who faces greater uncertainty is likely to be less innovative in his investment activities solely because of the burden of greater uncertainty; it is more incumbent on him to try to build a security zone through political or social connections in order to reduce uncertainty. Again, if there exist two social environments that are approximately equal in their degree of uncertainty to entrepreneurs, then the entrepreneur possessing the greater ability is likely to more successfully combat that uncertain environment.

In nineteenth century America, entrepreneurship flourished in a social environment whose institutions and goals were extremely favorable to the individual entrepreneur as the archetype of private capitalist development.[3] There were certain features of that social environment which were especially important. Hardened patterns of social stratification and well-defined functions for individuals did not exist: the society was not rigidly structured in the pattern of European society in the nineteenth century. In part, this reflected the absence of hereditary privilege and prestige such as those enjoyed by the aristocracies of continental Europe and Great Britain. Thus, traditional ways of looking at property, occupations, business activity, and roles were absent.

On the positive side, certain inheritances from the European environment were conducive to entrepreneurial development. The legacy of Puritanism and its encouragement of pursuit of rational self-interest manifested in hard work and material success. The legacy of eighteenth century Lockeian individualism and its emphasis on the natural rights of liberty and property provided the philosophical basis of laissez-faire. American faith in human progress towards the end of the nineteenth century became associated with the doctrines of Social Darwinism.[4]

Generally, Americans held an optimistic belief in increasing material welfare and in the glorification of economic advancement. These were characteristics of American society in the nineteenth century upon which contemporary European and British visitors to North America and Americans themselves frequently commented. The American was depicted as individualistic, optimistic, and enterprising. This image was conveyed by the emphasis on "industry, sobriety, and frugality" and on achievement in business and making money in various publications, ranging from the homely encouragement of self-reliance and success by Benjamin Franklin in *Poor Richard's Almanack* during the mid-eighteenth century to the crass braggadocio of nineteenth century tycoons like Andrew Carnegie in *The Gospel of Wealth* and his *Autobiography*. The cult of the "self-made man" was firmly implanted in American society. Success was up to the individual, since American institutions by creating an egalitarian society made the individual's pursuit of economic gain a matter of his own character and determination.

These tenets—individualism, competition and mobility (both social and economic), achieved rather than ascribed or hereditary status, emphasis on material success and ownership of material possessions—all tended to stimulate the emergence of creative and aggressive entrepreneurship.

Owing to the general character of this environment, entrepreneurs invested under nearly ideal conditions in nineteenth century America. A philosophy which condemned government regulation of economic affairs at the same time approved strong government support for private investment. Effective government regulation of the transportation and banking sectors and of monopoly power was slow to develop in the nineteenth century, and government powers were employed to stem the rise of labor organizations. On the other hand, for example, Eli Whitney's firearms manufacturing firm was an early recipient of government financial assistance. More significantly, strong government financial support enabled private firms to initiate the development of transportation improvements, both canals and railways, under mixed enterprise conditions.

The lack of negative government interference was complemented by the weakness of opposition by organized labor and agriculture for most of the nineteenth century. Thus, American entrepreneurs operated for the most part within an environment in which neither government nor economic power groups were able to restrict the rapid exploitation of economic opportunities. And indeed, in many areas, government actually encouraged investment in new lines.[5] In sum, the result was that technological change and innovation became primary ingredients in the transformation of the American economy away from its earlier staple orientation and scattered markets to the truly national economy of the late nineteenth century, predicated on production for the domestic market and rapid industrialization.

Only toward 1900 did some elements of the favorable social framework appear to recede. Uncertainties were inherent in the kind of chaotic competition that emerged in the latter part of the nineteenth century, and these uncertainties led businessmen to control their markets by pooling arrangements, trusts, mergers, and consolidations. In turn, agricultural and labor groups were induced to promote countervailing action. The result was the growth of labor unions and farmers' groups, and the emergence of organized pressure groups generally. On the regulatory front, political and social uncertainties engendered in the growing competition among groups resulted in government intervention in and regulation of the private sector of the economy.

The determinants of entrepreneurial capacity involve the ability of a society to produce entrepreneurs and innovators, not just the conditions under which the entrepreneur makes decisions. What factors influence the quality of entrepreneurship or the innovational capacity of businessmen, and what factors determine the quantity of potential entrepreneurial types?

One approach to assessing the determinants of entrepreneurship is that of David McClelland[6] a social psychologist who has argued that changes in the supply of entrepreneurial capacity are a function of shifts in personality traits. He argues that human action is motivated toward the pursuit of satisfaction. Humans wish to satisfy a wide range of psychological needs, amond them the need for knowledge, the need for affection or affiliation, the need for power, and the need for achievement. The latter represents the desire to do well, not so much for social recognition or for prestige, but, according to McClelland, for a sense of personal accomplishment. The need for achievement is inner-motivated and "*n*-achievement" is the factor which McClelland puts forward as the major explanatory determinant of entrepreneurial capacity.

The important thing is to try to explain the relationship between *n*-achievement and the intensity and drive with which a chosen path of activity is pursued. Here, the chosen path of activity is entrepreneurial activity. How then does high *n*-achievement lead to more rapid economic growth? The relationship can be broken down into two parts: do individuals with high *n*-achievement behave like entrepreneurs, and do entrepreneurs have high *n*-achievement?

According to McClelland, psychological tests administered to sample populations from the United States and other countries indicate that high *n*-achievement is highly correlated with the principal entrepreneurial personality characteristics. These personality characteristics include positive attitudes towards risk-taking, willingness to expend energy, willingness to innovate, willingness to make decisions and to accept responsibility for them.

The next step involves the determination of what it is that produces high *n*-achievement in populations. He argues that *n*-achievement is an acquired characteristic, a result of childhood influences which operate during the period four-to-ten years of age. This finding, of course, raises the question of parental upbringing.[7] It is parental upbringing and differences in patterns of child-raising which determine whether children will have high levels of n-achivement that persist into adulthood. High levels of motivation toward achievement are associated with certain kinds of parents—with parents who set high levels of aspiration for their children and who tend to be affectionate. Further, in such families, the mothers tend to be domineering and the fathers usually do not interfere directly with the child. According to McClelland, parental upbringing of this kind produces children who are "trained" for initiative and self-reliance. The single most powerful additional influence appears to be religious background: high *n*-achievement is highly correlated with Protestantism, because Protestantism is an individualistic creed rather than one based in authoritarian relationship or ritualistic contact with God.

This explanatory framework certainly fits in with what is known of American social structure and economic success, and represents a plausible explanation for the large supply of American entrepreneurship of high innovative capacity. On the other hand, it is possible to turn McClelland's argument around. Perhaps the expression of high *n*-achievement in business appears in children of societies which have experienced economic growth. In other words, only in societies where high levels of economic performance have already occurred do parents induce in their children the predisposition to manifest high levels of *n*-achievement in entrepreneurial or business-type roles in society. The American experience is consistent with both interpretations.

The Industrial Entrepreneur: A Closer Look

The theoretical underpinnings of the study of entrepreneurship are poorly developed, and there are many difficulties in assessing the personality traits of entrepreneurs. Nevertheless, it is useful to examine more closely the American enterpreneur because the growth of the American economy was the outcome of myriad individual actions. Some of the most dramatic in their economic consequences were innovative actions of industrial entrepreneurs. But first it must be recognized that there are certain basic methodological problems in analyzing entrepreneurial history.[8] One is the choice of an appropriate frame of reference. Whom do you decide to study, for example? The tendency is to study only successes, entrepreneurs who have "made it" and seldom to look at entrepreneurs who have failed. It may be, of course, that there are interesting lessons to be inferred from failure as well as from success, but unfortunately not enough work has been done in this area to report here. Another problem involves the heterogeneous kinds of information with which the entrepreneurial historian must deal: data pertaining to markets, technology, and other economic variables; social variables including the environment and the structure of the society in which the entrepreneur works; the even more complex data concerning entrepeneurial personalities; and the way in which personality characteristics lead entrepreneurs to operate within the environment. Are they profit maximizers? Are they always profit maximizers?[9]

Characteristics of the business elite

According to the age-old stereotype in American history of the "rags-to-riches" (or Horatio Alger) success story, the saga of the "typical" American industrial or financial giant begins with a poverty-stricken boyhood. Often he was an immigrant. He probably had no father or at best was the son of a laborer. Because of his very poor beginnings and/or the early death of his father, he was forced into employment when he was 12 or 13 years of age, and received little or no formal education. But America was the land of unlimited opportunity, and so frequently—and incredibly—this poor boy would by early middle age achieve immense wealth and power. Andrew Carnegie and Henry Ford were giants who epitomized the "American dream" come true.[10] Can this stereotype be confirmed by looking at data on American business leadership?

In a series of collective biographies," the origins and careers of more than three hundred business leaders of the late nineteenth and early twentieth centuries were studied by Miller and by Gregory and Neu.[11] Gregory and Neu selected business leaders from the textile industries which were the oldest of the great industries, the steel industry which was the newest, and the railroad industry which was the largest in terms of capital accumulation. Data was compiled for the offices of treasurer (really the chief executive) and agent (who acted as superintendent or general manager of operations) for thirty large textile firms. These firms included the largest cotton-producing firms with over one million dollars capitalization and seventy thousand spindles, the largest woolen manufacturing firms with over six hundred thousand dollars capitalization and forty-nine sets of cards, and the one silk firm with capitalization of a million dollars. As far as steel executives were concerned, data were taken from thirty large steel firms for the offices of president, vice-president, general manager, superintendent, and partners. And finally, in railroads, the sample included executives from the largest seventeen companies with minimum capitalization of twenty-four million dollars in 1880. Many of these firms were still family concerns or partnerships, especially in the steel industry, although the corporate form was already common in textiles and railroads.

What were the characteristics of these business leaders? Their average age was about forty-five years. They were overwhelmingly Protestant (ninety percent) in religion. Very few were immigrants: ninety percent were born in the United States and only ten percent were foreign-born. In fact, few were the sons of immigrants: of the native-born, only three percent were the sons of foreign-born fathers. Some sixty-five percent of the native-born had been born in New England, an indication of the tendency for American industrial leadership to come disproportionately from the old northeastern seaboard states. About nine-tenths of the leaders were of British ancestry. Thus top-level leadership in American industry, at least in the sample for the 1870s, was overwhelmingly native-born of native American families, and not immigrants on the way to success.

One variation of the stereotype presented above is that many business leaders were likely to have been refugees from the farm, since over seventy percent of American population in the 1870s was still rural. But, in fact, half of the business leaders of the 1870s were born in places which had more than 2,500 population at the time. (There is some question whether the remaining half can be considered of farm origin, because many communities of below 2,500 population were commercial towns serving rural hinterlands.)

The occupations of their fathers are interesting. More than half (fifty-one percent) had fathers who were businessmen: of these one-third were merchants and one-third were manufacturers. Many textile leaders in the 1870s were themselves sons of textile men, and many steelmen were the sons of steelmen. There seems to have been some tendency for the business leaders to come from business-oriented family backgrounds and for many of them to follow similar industrial occupations to their fathers. As far as education is concerned, about one-third had attended primary school, about one-third had gone to secondary school, and about one-third had some years at college. As a result, about forty-five percent were nineteen or over before they started to work. Thus, the social origins of this sample of business leaders lay primarily with business families of fairly high social standing. Their careers most certainly did not conform to the "American dream."

The Horatio Alger stereotype was implicitly examined in Miller's study, which employed data on business leaders of the period 1901 to 1910—a sample of 190 men who were chief executives of American business firms, either presidents, chairmen of boards, or partners in unincorporated investment banking houses. The largest number, sixty-four, were from mining or manufacturing firms, fifty-eight were from railroads, over thirty from public utilities, and the rest were scattered among commercial banks, investment banks, and insurance companies.

The career composition of this group differed from the sample of leaders of the 1870s. Bureaucratic hierarchies in business management had become common by the 1900s with the emergence of "big business," and the elite of business leaders in 1901-10 reflects this process of bureaucratization.[12] Independent enterprise, more common in the 1870s, had not been entirely superseded, but about half of the men in the sample had been salaried officeholders virtually throughout their entire business careers; that is, they had been and continued to be members of the business bureaucracy.

Now, what of their characteristics? Their average age in 1900 was about fifty years. Insofar as origin is concerned, again there were very few immigrants in the sample, about ninety percent having been born in the United States. More than four-fifths were the sons of American-born fathers, although a decreasing relative importance of New England as a source of business leadership is noticeable. This, of course, was to be expected with the westward migration of American population, commerce, and industry after 1870. More than eighty percent were still of British ancestry, but the decreasing relative importance of English compared with Irish and Scottish origin is clear. About twelve percent were of German descent compared with only nominal German representation in the 1870s. Again though, the predominance of Anglo-Saxon and nonimmigrant backgrounds is apparent. As far as religion is concerned, 90 percent were Protestants. Some three-fifths had been born in urban places, an increase from the 1870s' sample.

The occupations of fathers were even more business-oriented in this sample: fifty-five percent were the sons of businessmen, and only fourteen percent were sons of farmers. Their educational background had changed somewhat from the 1870s in favor of higher education; the proportions completing primary school were twenty-two percent, secondary school thirty-seven, and attending or completing college thirty-one percent. Once again, forty-five percent were nineteen or over before going to work.

Overall, the business leaders comprising the sample for the early 1900s were quite similar in their social characteristics to those of the 1870s' sample. Business leaders continued to have their origins mainly in business families of fairly high social standing. The stereotypical success story of American folklore was becoming increasingly rare.

Several additional collective biographies, prompted by the Miller-Gregory-Neu findings, have generally confirmed their results for selected cities and industries. Gabriel Kolko's "Brahmins and Business" concludes that long-established socio-economic elites continued to dominate Boston's economic development from 1870 to 1914, because status and access to existing economic and political power conferred a significant competitive advantage on members of "old" families, particularly in raising financial capital.[13] Ghent and Jaher in their study of 1186 Chicago business leaders, whose careers covered the period from 1830 to 1930, concluded that few went from "rags-to-riches," even in this relatively new midwestern urban environment.[14] However, most members of Chicago's business elite were self-made men, especially in manufacturing, meat-packing, and railroading. And John Ingham has completed a similar analysis of 696 iron and steel manufacturers in six cities (Philadelphia, Pittsburgh, Cleveland, Youngstown, Bethlehem, and Wheeling).[15] In the older, established cities like Philadelphia, the leading iron and steel manufacturers had their roots in antebellum, pre-industrial upper social classes. This was less true in the newer cities like Wheeling, where "humble" origins for business leaders were more common. Typically, however, Ingham's iron and steel manufacturers "came from the 'first families' of their communities" and further, he concludes, "the industrial revolution, whatever the changes it brought in the economic and technological spheres, did little to disturb the hegemony of the antebellum social upper classes over economic affairs."[16]

The most unique, and perhaps the most interesting of these studies is Bernard Sarachek's attempt to appraise some of the psychodeterminants of business success.[17] Sarachek identifies a set of business leaders who meet his criteria as entrepreneurs, and then examines such formative behavioral influences as childhood deprivation, father-son relationships (whether the subject was orphaned, rejected or poorly fathered, or had a supportive father) and birth-order as well as the more standard variables like social origin, father's occupation, and so forth.[18] Interestingly, he finds that a high proportion of his 187 entrepreneurs experienced a disadvantaged childhood, mostly in terms of relationships with their fathers and often in terms of economic hardship. Frequently, those with deceased or inadequate fathers began working at an early age and fit many of the "rags-to-riches" characteristics. But those with supportive fathers were in most cases similar to the members of the Miller-Gregory-Neu business elite.

As we have seen, there are several, acceptable approaches to identifying and classifying members of the American business elite, whether one focuses on a handful of men who rose from humble beginnings to immense wealth and power as did the Beards, or on compiling a list of several hundred business leaders whose membership in the elite is a function of executive status or occupation or industry group. Whatever the approach, it is important to reflect on the significance of these studies—to examine what they do tell us of successful entrepreneurship and business leadership, and what they do not tell us.

Clearly, it is useful to know who the members of the business elite were, what attributes they shared, and their links to economic, social and political power. These are interesting and valid historical concerns. But a note of caution is essential. These studies provide only a list of the characteristics of a given population of successful businessmen, and nothing more.[19] The population of the Miller-Gregory-Neu studies, for example, is a sample of successful businessmen selected according to arbitrary criteria. It is not a random sample, and hence its representativeness is suspect. Nor are the characteristics of the sample subjected to any tests of statistical significance. Consequently, we cannot draw inferences from these studies about what attributes constitute necessary or sufficient conditions of business success. We know precisely what characteristics are possessed by businessmen appearing in Miller-Gregory-Neu's lists, but we do not know whether having these characteristics increases the probability of succeeding.[20]

Four Case Studies

The entrepreneurial dimensions of American business leadership can also be appraised by an examination of the business careers of a "vital few" entrepreneurs.[21] If the set is confined to those particularly associated with industry, the three most obvious ones are Thomas Alva Edison, the great inventor and innovator in the electrical industry, Andrew Carnegie, the doyen of the iron and steel industry, and Henry Ford who pioneered and later revolutionized the automobile industry. It is also worthwhile to examine the innovative achievements of J. Pierpont Morgan, who was not an industrialist per se but played an important role in the development of new organizational forms in American business. As a leading financier, he is included because of his contributions, and those of others like him, to the increasing scale of American enterprise in the late nineteenth and early twentieth centuries. However, the same caveats apply here as in the case of "collective biographies." The appeal of "selective biographies" of a few, carefully chosen business princes is the richness of the individual's personality, his achievements, and his interrelationships with other business, social, and political figures. But, these studies too have limited prescriptive value because the subject may be unrepresentative of businessmen in general.[22]

Edison.[23] Consider first the case of Thomas Alva Edison. During his lifetime, Edison registered 1,328 patents in his name, and a host of new industries were created as a consequence of his experiments with electrical energy and the innovations they engendered. Edison came from an old American family of middle-class standing. His father was a self-employed merchant and, during Edison's early childhood, the family was prosperous. Even so, Edison had little formal education and, with a decline in the family's fortunes, he was forced into employment at about twelve years of age. He began by working at menial tasks, but his activities were characterized by his inquisitive nature and guided by his anxiety to learn beyond the skill levels required by his immediate employment. In addition to his curiosity, he possessed tremendous energy, and these two characteristics together with an inventive knack which was unparallelled among American industrial inventors and researchers, were to shape his career.

Edison was a self-taught man. His experimentation proceeded less by theoretical work and more by trial and error, in which success seemed to be a product both of his great energies and his exceptional intuition. Indeed, this seems to have been the style of industrial inventors and innovators in both Great Britain and in the United States. Edison was an example par excellence. Most of the inventions for which he is most noted were developed between 1869 and 1881 when he acted primarily as an industrial researcher rather than as the innovator he was to become. These inventions were financed by and related to the growing private sector of the economy, especially the telegraph industry. He began in 1869 with Western Union, a leading firm in the telegraph industry which was to become a major growth industry in the 1870s. Edison's early inventions during 1869 to 1874 were associated with the telegraph. Subsequently, he did inventive work with the telephone and concurrently invented the telephone with Bell and Gray in early 1876. In 1877 at the request of Western Union, he "reinvented" the telephone and is credited with having brought the telephone to the state of a commercially successful innovation even though later, after protracted negotiations, Bell's patent for telephone equipment was recognized by Western Union.

The telephone was followed by the invention of the phonograph in 1877. Here, as was mentioned earlier, Edison failed to understand some of the potential applications of this invention, believing that the phonograph was not destined for entertainment or amusement, but rather for use in business much as the dictaphone is used now. His best-known invention is the incandescent lightbulb, which was created in 1879 and like the telephone and phonograph proved to be an invention of enormous economic potential.

Edison's innovations made possible the growth of electrical companies. In 1881 he formed the Edison Electric Illuminating Company to develop lighting for office blocks in New York City. The firm became solidly established during the 1880s. By the end of the decade, Edison's achievements had laid the foundations for the future success of Consolidated Edison and General Electric, and other giant electrical generating and equipment firms of the twentieth century. The Edison enterprises were consolidated into Edison General Electric, a New Jersey Corporation, in 1889. With mergers and with his patents receiving final court approval in Pennsylvania in 1889 and New York in 1891, the Edison empire had stabilized.

In 1892 Morgan stepped into the electrical industry and organized General Electric Limited, comprised of Edison General Electric and Thomson-Houston Electric (a major alternating current equipment manufacturing firm) as principal partners. This left only Westinghouse as the major independent firm standing between Edison-related enterprises and monopoly of the industry.[24] In the short period of some fifteen years, Edison's enterprises had moved from the invention stage through the innovation stage to major financial reorganization which established the resulting firm as the largest supplier of electrical equipment as well as a continuing source of invention and innovation.

Edison had some curious failings, two of which were a profound distrust of financiers—a suspicion inculcated when he was fleeced by Jay Gould in the early 1870s—and a stubborn refusal to accept the applicability of alternating current systems in the electrical industry. The latter was to prove his major technical failing, just as his distrust of financiers was to prove his main innovative failing.

Carnegie[25]. Andrew Carnegie's entreprenueurial career personified the "American dream." Carnegie came to the United States around 1850 as an immigrant, lived in abject poverty, and had little formal education. He was forced to begin work at the age of thirteen. True to the stereotype, his early employment involved menial occupations, beginning as a bobbin boy in a textile mill and culminating in a position as a messenger in 1855 with the Pennsylvania Railroad. Through his tremendous energy and capacity for work, in 1859, when he was twenty-three he became superintendent of the Pittsburgh division of the railroad. As superintendent of the railroad, Carnegie found time to undertake personal investments as a sideline, and was quick to capitalize on the wartime demand for iron by the Union Army. As early as 1862, he became a partner in the Keystone Bridge Company, and in 1864 he organized a company to build blast furnaces in the Pittsburgh area. In 1866, he formed the Pittsburgh Locomotive Works. Here is an early version of the process of vertical integration at work: by 1866, Carnegie had investments in all stages of the iron production process from the basic blast furnace at the one end to bridges and locomotives as final products at the other.

Despite, or perhaps because of, his lack of formal technical training, Carnegie is best known for his talents as a competitive innovator. He was by all accounts the greatest innovator in the history of the American steel industry. It is strange, then, that he should be remembered for the remark "pioneering don't pay." Carnegie was not a foolhardy innovator, but took risks only when the techniques had been proven elsewhere and there was little doubt they would pay under his management. His emphasis on commercial success is certainly consistent with the innovative process as discussed thus far.

There are two kinds of innovations that Carnegie is noted for, the first technical, and the second organizational. Carnegie introduced both the Bessemer and the open-hearth processes on a widespread basis in the American industry. In 1873 the Bessemer process was an innovation which was quite close to the technological frontier. It had been "proven" in the British industry and, after extensive discussion with Bessemer in 1872, Carnegie became so committed to Bessemer's process that he began construction of a new plant embodying it in 1873. At this time, his general superintendent was William Jones. Jones is generally credited with adapting the Bessemer process for efficient production by introducing several inventions to enable a continuous movement of steel from the blast furnaces through the converters to ingot-casting and the rolling mills without reheating.

In 1893 Carnegie introduced the Siemens open-hearth process to his Pittsburgh works. This process had been experimented with since 1888 at Homestead. Then, at the beginning of the depression of 1893, Carnegie undertook a massive rebuilding and expansion program in which he replaced all blast furnaces and Bessemer converters with open-hearth furnaces. This made him the most efficient competitor in the American steel industry.

His other major innovations were organizational. In fact, Carnegie is often credited with taking the first steps toward "scientific management" in the steel industry. He introduced strict cost accounting for each process in the steel industry as early as 1870, and brought the science of chemistry into the blast furnace area, by complementing the "practical" or "intuitive" steel maker with a more scientific approach to steelmaking. This also spilled over into assessing such incidental aspects of steel as the quality of ore deposits and the selection of ore lands for lease or purchase. In order to obtain a secure supply of inputs, Carnegie leased ore properties in the Mesabi range from Rockefeller, secured his coke sources through a partnership with Frick, acquired railway connections to Lake Erie, and built more steamships to carry ore on the Great Lakes.

At the other end of the spectrum, he introduced active marketing of iron and steel products into the steel industry; instead of waiting in Pittsburgh for orders, he went out after business and left technical management of the steel industry to skilled personnel.

Above all, Carnegie adapted private ownership and the partnership form in a skilful way. Like Edison, he distrusted financiers. He was not interested in incorporating, but relied on the use of partnerships so that he could fund expansion by internal financing, ploughing back profits into new plant and equipment instead of dividends. The cash reserves accumulated in this way allowed him to purchase and rebuild in depressions (for example, he acquired the Homestead works in 1885 and the Duquesne works in 1890) and allowed his to become the most efficient and competitive of the steel firms.

His use of partnership was interesting for a second reason. Young men had opportunities to become partners of Carnegie on a merit basis; that is, he would select—and he was well known for his ability to evaluate manpower—especially talented young men from his plant to become partners. He also gave bonuses for good work to factory hands and supervisors. Some of his selections for promotion from his labor force are legendary. Charles Schwab and William Corey, who eventually became presidents of the United States Steel Corporation, were both picked by Carnegie from the mills for advancement.

By 1900 more than one-quarter of American steel output was produced by Carnegie and his firm was by far the most efficient. Meanwhile, the second and third largest companies, Federal Steel and National Steel, had both developed operations resembling Carnegie's and, in addition, had made alliances with several producers of finished steel products, among them National Tube, American Bridge, American Tin Plate, and American Sheet and Wire. Because Carnegie was already strongly based in steel inputs, he threatened to move fully ahead into production of finished steel products. This threat of open competition from Carnegie's efficient firm prompted J. P. Morgan to initiate a major reorganization of the steel industry at a time when Carnegie was beginning to lose enthusiasm for industrial conflict. After protracted negotiations, Carnegie sold out to Morgan, who reorganized the Carnegie holdings together with Federal Steel and National Steel and several end-product companies to form the giant United States Steel Corporation in 1901.

After 1901 and his retirement from business, Carnegie became more concerned with social reform, and indulged his interests in universal education, in great virtues like heroism, and in the spiritual evolution and perfectibility of man, a curious avocation in later life for a man who had long been regarded as the most ruthless competitor in American industry.

Ford.[26] From his youth Henry Ford was interested in mechanical things. Thus, it was natural that he eventually became a master mechanic after leaving the farm and going to Detroit as a young man to find employment as an apprentice.

As an innovator, Ford is noted for his extension of mass-production techniques in the substitution of machinery for skilled labor. Standardization in production was his watchword; the moving assembly line was his most important contribution. His innovative work in the development of the automobile began with a successful five-year effort to construct a homemade prototype and was followed after 1896 by attempts to place the production of automobiles on a commercial basis. In 1903 Ford founded the Ford Motor Company. In 1908 Ford build the Model-T and in the following year decided to make the T his only model, to paint it black, and to make it inexpensively for the wide middle-class market. A simple practical machine, the "Tin Lizzie" was instrumental in breaking down the barriers between rural and urban American and bringing America's regions even closer together.[27]

Contrary to popular opinion, Henry Ford was not the father of mass production. Oliver Evans' "automatic" flour mill, built in 1785, was an early successful example of continuous processing, and interchangeable parts were a result of innovations in firearms production at the turn of the nineteenth century. But, Ford was its twentieth century proselytizer, even going so far as to author an article entitled, "Mass-Production" for the *Encyclopedia Britannica* in 1926. Wrote Ford, "Mass-Production is the focussing upon a manufacturing project of the principles of power, accuracy, economy, system, *continuity* and speed . . . And the normal result is a productive organization that delivers in quantities a useful commodity of standard material, workmanship and design at minimum cost."[28]

"Continuity" is the key word in the foregoing statement. Ford conducted mass production at a speed and on a scale that was unique. In his concern to increase output while lowering unit costs, he relied on unskilled labor and moved the skill back in the production process to the technology and design of equipment. This made possible the crucial element in his innovation—the introduction and perfection of the moving assembly line in which the work was carried from worker to worker each of whom was stationed at different points of assembly. The assembly process employed earlier in the nineteenth century had normally been discontinuous: that is, inputs were brought as needed to stationary assembly points at which one or a few workers would assemble the final product. The continuous assembly process was introduced in the meat-packing industry during the 1870s and 1880s and introduced to the automobile industry by Ford.

The experimentation with the moving assembly line was conducted by Charles Sorensen, Ford's production manager, during the period from 1908 to 1913, and Ford introduced the process into the Highland Park Plant and later into the Rouge River Plant once the moving assembly line principle had been perfected.

Ford's keynote was productive efficiency. So linked was he in the popular mind with productive efficiency and the assembly line that he became known as the "father of mass-production" as his techniques spread into other industries and became part of standard American manufacturing practice. Unfortunately, the legacy of the assembly line has been a bitter one. More far-reaching has been the moving assembly line's insistence on machinelike repetition of tasks which has dehumanized labor and turned the day's work into a crushing burden of tedium. If Ford is remembered economically for productive efficiency, he is remembered socially for his own poor record in labor relations and his legacy of monotony to the manufacturing worker.

Morgan. J. Pierpont Morgan was a powerful financier. But it was as an organizer of industry that he left an indelible mark on American economic history.[29] He was after all a financier and not an industrialist, but his career epitomized the great organizational change in American industry at the turn of the twentieth century whereby investment bankers made significant contributions to the increasing size of enterprise and management techniques.

Morgan was certainly different in his origins from the archetypal business tycoon of American folklore. He was not from humble beginnings, but rather was the son of a successful investment banker and, as a result, had significantly more formal education. After university studies, he began work in a New York banking house in 1857, and early proved to be a prodigy of the banking system. His first successes lay within the usual merchant banking line, but by 1869, while yet in his early 30s, he gave an indication of his abilities as an innovative organizer of capital. It was in 1869 that he participated in the "Susquehanna Railway War" and plotted the strategy that led to the defeat of Jay Gould and Jim Fisk. In 1871 he began a partnership with the Drexels of Philadelphia and by then had links in Philadelphia, New York, London, and Paris. It was this framework which allowed Morgan eventually to become the most powerful international investment banker in the world and facilitated his placement of American railway, government, and industrial securities in the European market. His major successes in the 1870s were refunding the Federal debt and the profitable sale of Vanderbilt's New York Central stocks in the European market.

His early organizational achievements lay in the amalgamation and reorganization of railroads in the 1880s and 1890s, during a period when the great wave of speculative construction was past and more attention was being directed to the profitability of traffic earnings. Railroad reorganization offered great potential profits for men of finance like Morgan. Profitable reorganizations were based on the simplification of corporate structure, the linking of small lines into systems with control by Morgan-appointed management, and the addition of "water" to the capital stock.[30] Among the railroad reorganizations which he engineered were the "Southshore Settlement" between the New York Central and Pennsylvania railroads in 1885, the "gentlemen's agreements" in 1886 among eastern railroads and investment bankers (a cartel meant to regulate business in an "orderly" way), followed in 1888 and 1889 by the organization of cartel agreements among the midwestern and southern railways. In 1890 this series of agreements facilitated the formation of a Railway Advisory Board to handle rate-making policy in accord with the Interstate Commerce Act. Morgan's abilities as an organizer of capital culminated in the early 1900s with the reorganization of United States Steel—the first multibillion dollar corporation in American history with a capitalization of nearly $1½ billion.

Morgan's hallmarks were tight organization and central control over his holdings and the development of "community of interest" among potential competitors in output and pricing policies. So successful was he that government began to move against Morgan's concept of cartelized growth and develop a set of regulatory policies intended to maintain the competitive characteristics of the American economic system.

It is interesting, at this juncture, to reflect on the growing influence of finance capitalists such as Morgan on industrial operations. In the late nineteenth century, many American transportation and industrial corporations had growth ambitions which seemed to far outstrip their abilities to generate investment capital by ploughing back earnings. Their owners, many of them individual entrepreneurs or partners, sought access to holders of savings in the economy who desired to acquire earning assets. In order to do so, it was expedient for these firms to borrow or sell stock in capital markets and these transactions were arranged by investment bankers.

The important role played by men like Morgan in the development of large scale enterprise was to facilitate the union of finance and industry. In general, economies of large scale production and marketing plus the desire to win control over markets made expansion a highly prized goal, an end for which access to capital markets was essential. The union of technological change and the capital market provided an opening for growth where reliance upon corporate savings alone would have constrained management unnecessarily, and the mobilization of private savings for industrial management for expansion was the outcome. In this process Morgan was the giant among investment bankers. According to the "Morgan Plan," the decisions of industry came to be powerfully influenced by the demands of financiers. Financiers set terms for repayment of debt and, in many cases, the borrowers were forced to regulate their activities in order to meet repayment schedules and even to accept financiers as members of their boards of directors or as members of their executive management. In many cases the management of industrial enterprises fell less and less to industrialists and came more and more under the influence of financiers. Men like Carnegie and Ford who were able to expand operations on the basis of retained earnings had much greater freedom of action than other industrialists who did seek access to the capital market and, consequently, had the encumbrances of finance capitalism forced upon them. While the financiers did raise capital for the expansion of industry, and the strings which they attached in many cases led to more effective management of enterprises, some financiers used their power to manipulate financial markets, water stock, and reduce competition in various product markets, and these abuses brought an outcry for corrective government action.[31]

The Four: A Summing Up

Do these examples of "great" entrepreneurs tie in with the collective biographic data for business leaders in the 1870s and the 1900s, and McClelland's criteria of successful entrepreneurship? Do they share any common characteristics with respect to national ancestry or origin, religion, farm or nonfarm origin, fathers' occupations, and educational characteristics?

Attacking this second set of questions first, only Morgan seems to have had well-to-do origins. Carnegie's father was originally a craftsman, but the development of the power loom in the weaving industry in Scotland had reduced him to penury and forced his emigration to America where he was no more successful. Ford came from a modest family farm. Edison was originally of middle-class origins, but of declining status as his family fell upon hard times in his youth. Only Carnegie was an immigrant. All were of British origin, and all were Protestants. There is certainly a mix in their rural-urban origins; Ford was raised on a farm, but Carnegie was originally from a small Scottish village and would be classified as rural in origin according to the Miller-Gregory-Neu sample. Morgan was brought up in luxury in the heart of New York's fashionable area. Edison was from a small market town in Ohio. Their experiences with formal education varied from Morgan's university education, to Ford's primary school and apprenticeship, and to the distinct lack of formal education of Carnegie and Edison. Indeed, both Ford and Edison—undoubtedly extrapolating from their own experiences— demonstrated a disdain for formal education which extended to the role of scientists and other highly educated people in industry.

McClelland's characteristics of entrepreneurs are compatible with the profiles of the four giants whose careers we have just reviewed. All of them were what might be called risk-takers rather than risk-averters, although Carnegie, as was noted earlier, had a cautious approach to innovative activity in unproven technical processes. They all possessed boundless energy: all worked long days and frequently worked around the clock without sleep, and expected their closest collaborators to do likewise. Only Edison was an inventor, but Edison, Carnegie, and Ford were all innovators of the highest order. Morgan was an innovator of a different sort, but he was responsible for the development of Morgan-style management in the great corporations around the turn of the century.

Of course, all were willing to make decisions. Edison closely supervised all experimental work conducted in his laboratories and took credit for it. Ford and Carnegie were characterized by ruthlessness in the plant and close supervision of all operations. And finally, all were willing to accept responsibility. In fact, no one individual entrepreneur ever accepted more responsibility than Pierpont Morgan did in his handling of the 1907 financial panic when, according to many contemporaries, his leadership prevented the collapse of the American economy.

With respect to parental upbringing and religious influence which McClelland emphasizes, it is difficult to be precise. It does appear, for example, that Carnegie's father was quite ineffectual and that his mother provided him with any guidance and leadership qualities that might have existed in the home. In the case of Ford, there is more evidence, which indicates that his mother was domineering and a staunch Calvinist and that she probably imbued Ford with his work ethic. About Edison and Morgan, it is difficult to say. However, it clearly would be foolhardy to generalize from this scanty evidence on the upbringing of these four tycoons to McClelland's emphasis on child-rearing and family life in the development of entrepreneurial capacity.

Conclusion

The concept of entrepreneurship remains intriguing yet elusive. The determinants of entrepreneurial ability are now almost exclusively the concern of sociologists and social psychologists. The concept has virtually disappeared from the literature of theoretical economics; the firm of neoclassical economics is entrepreneurless.[32] But to historians, the American industrial entrepreneur authored the growth of manufacturing and the changing scale and organization of enterprise in the late nineteenth and early twentieth centuries. While the determinants of entrepreneurial capacity may not be wholly understood, entrepreneurship appears to be influenced by a host of sociocultural factors -- child-rearing practices, family life, education, the structure of society, and so forth. Indeed, most American business leaders in this period were the products of business-oriented, economically successful family environments. And the nineteenth century United States provided a fertile social environment within which entrepreneurship flourished. Whether the culmination of enterpreneurial skills in great personal wealth and power resulted from a "fair share" of the benefits of creative achievement or from predatory exploitation of the "oppressed majority" is the subject of a later chapter.

5

Organizational Change in Manufacturing

Introduction

In pre-Civil War America the manufacturing sector was characterized by small family firms, usually employing handicraft technology, which produced primarily for the local market. By 1900 the manufacturing sector was dominated by large enterprises in both the major producers' goods and consumers' goods industries producing for essentially national markets. In many cases, these enterprises resulted from both vertical and horizontal integration among firms. Horizontal integration consists of the combination of two or more firms or plants producing essentially the same product into one new larger firm, and vertical integration involves the location of a sequence of processes in the production of a good within one firm, from the acquisition of raw materials through the production processes to the marketing and distribution of the final product. In some cases, integrated firms emerged in response to the businessman's quest for production and marketing efficiency, and in other cases, the quest for market control and the dissolution of competitive forces provided the impetus. And, of course, profit-maximizing strategy often called for vertical and/or horizontal integration through mergers and consolidations because of both efficiency and market-power effects.

By 1900 the owner-managed, small-scale manufacturing firm had been relegated to a minor position in most industry groups.[1] Its place was taken by the large firm whose affairs were conducted by a single function, departmentalized management in which ownership and control were increasingly separated. But problems emerged with this kind of administration, in large part because management became more complex as many functions were combined in one firm with vertical integration, expansion, and product diversification. By 1920, a new, innovative, administrative procedure had been introduced, based on a decentralized, multidivisional structure. Thus, a division and specialization of managerial functions analogous to the earlier division and specialization of labor appeared in the late nineteenth and early twentieth centuries, and contributed to greater efficiency in manufacturing. "Big business," characterized by large-scale operation and professional, bureaucratic management, had arrived.

Changes in the Concept of the Firm

Increasing reliance on the corporate form of enterprise was a distinctive feature of manufacturing growth after 1870. As businessmen pursued efficiency and power to the logical outcome of increased size, the corporate form was amended to facilitate consolidations and mergers. By 1900 American industry was dominated by big business through the corporation.

The Corporation and Its Growth

The corporate form has many distinctive characteristics that commended it to businessmen in the nineteenth century. In the first place, it endows the firm with a "personality," because it represents the creation of a separate legal entity. Having a legal personality simplified the acquisition of capital because it allowed for investment by many small shareholders. The corporate form also facilitated the management of large accumulations of capital because, through the separation of ownership and management, it permitted the rise of a professional managerial class. Second, the corporation confers limited liability upon shareholders, who are only liable to the extent of the capital which they have invested in the corporation. Third, within the terms of its charter, the corporation retains the advantage of proprietorship and partnerships in that it is free from interference by government. If the government wishes to interfere with the corporate sector, it can do so only by changing the legislation under which the corporations have been chartered, or await changes in interpretation of corporate charters by the courts.

Study of the corporation in American economic history is hampered by the fact that there is no complete time series dealing with incorporations by all states taken together. There exist only *some* state series and, consequently, this places serious limitations on reconstructing and generalizing about the pace and pattern of incorporating activity.

The legal form of corporate charters was greatly liberalized in the nineteenth century. The corporate charter lays out the conditions under which the corporation can perform its several functions — for example, obtain capital, undertake different lines of business, or hold stock in other corporations. The early history of the corporation in the late eighteenth and early nineteenth centuries in the United States revolves around the issue of special charters by state legislatures.[2] Special charters provided very strict provisions for guaranteeing the public interest, which included a carefully defined function for the enterprise and limited scope for its activities. In many cases the requirements were that all capital be paid up in the firm before operations began, and that the firm adopt a rigid capital structure that could be changed only by appeal to the legislature. These, among many other features of the special charter, made it extremely difficult for corporations to adapt production to changing circumstances or to develop new lines of activity.

In part this policy reflected the contemporary belief that the corporate form should not be resorted to unless the public interest was involved. In fact many of the early corporations under special charter were conceived as agencies of the state to meet community needs. Here, for example, can be included turnpikes, banks, the early railroads and canals, many of which in essence took the form of public utilities.

Although there were relatively few general incorporation laws passed before the latter part of the nineteenth century, the few that were enacted are alleged to have stimulated some manufacturing incorporations, especially the significant number of textile firms in Massachusetts which were incorporated in the early part of the century. As time passed it became less necessary to demonstrate a public interest in order to receive a corporate charter, and the corporate form was adjusted to meet the increasing demand for industrial incorporations, especially after 1870. The restrictions of the special charter gave way to the more liberal provisions of general incorporation laws which removed control from the legislatures to the corporations themselves. Corporate management was strengthened by such changes as the introduction of proxy voting, the simple majority vote of shareholders, the authorization to exchange shares for property, and the waiver of rigid capital structure requirements. All of these features of general laws of incorporation made it possible for further development of the corporate form and its expansion and refinement in the development of consolidations and mergers in the late nineteenth century.

General incorporation laws had become fairly widespread by 1875; among the more important were those of New York in 1846, Ohio in

1851, and Pennsylvania in 1873. Those of New Jersey in 1875 (amended in 1889) and Delaware in 1897 proved to be especially important. New Jersey was the legal home of most of the very large corporations in the late 1890s and early 1900s, and Delaware was to play this role after 1915.

Corporations gravitated to particular states because of the comparative liberality of their general incorporation laws, and both New Jersey and later Delaware had very liberal laws. Both states wanted to attract incorporations because of the income generated by chartering fees and annual franchise levies. From table 5.1 it is possible to see the trend

Table 5.1 Number of Corporations with Authorized Capital Stock of $20 Million or more, Chartered Under General Laws, in New Jersey and Delaware

New Jersey		Delaware	
Year	**Number**	**Year**	**Number**
1890	3	1916	11
1	3	7	27
2	1	8	10
3	2	9	96
4	0	1920	110
5	0	1	51
6	1	2	77
7	3	3	67
8	7	4	55
9	50	5	103
1900	11	6	104
1	12	7	166
2	11	8	343
3	5	9	619
4	5	1930	253
5	8	1	121
6	2	2	41
7	1	3	12
8	4	4	8
9	5	5	12
1910	0	6	12
1	3	7	11
2	4	8	5
3	2	9	4
	0	1940	2
1915	0		

NOTE: The firms comprising the large corporations incorporated in New Jersey from 1881 to 1902 are identified by name and date of incorporation in Evans, work cited below, p. 48.

SOURCE: Evans, *Business Incorporations in the United States, 1800-1943,* Tables nos. 17 and 18, p. 49.

of large incorporations (with capitalization of 20 million dollars or more) in both New Jersey and Delaware. In 1889 New Jersey amended its general act of incorporation in order to permit holding companies; that is, the amendment permitted corporations chartered in New Jersey to hold stock in other corporations whether chartered in New Jersey or elsewhere. This appears to have induced many firms to incorporate locally in New Jersey. Note that about ninety corporations were chartered by New Jersey in the period from 1898 to 1902, fifty in 1899 alone, the peak year of New Jersey's incorporation series. Delaware's general incorporation act of 1897, plus subsequent liberalizing amendments, attracted large numbers of incorporations after 1915, especially in the peak periods of incorporation of 1919 and 1920 and 1928 through 1930.

Overall, there were three periods of intensive chartering of very large corporations in New Jersey and Delaware, centered on the years 1899, 1920, and 1929. About one-half of these firms were manufacturing corporations, and the remainder were public utilities and services.

The Emergence of Noncompetitive Elements

The increasing use of the corporate form and the trend toward very large firms were facilitated by general laws of incorporation. The growth of the unit size in the firm and its individual plants resulted from the pursuit of production and marketing efficiency or from the attempt to secure some form of market control. After 1889 the laws were conducive to the development of the holding company and of consolidations and mergers.

What do we know about the historical antecedents of the growth of noncompetitive elements in the manufacturing sector? In the 1870s there were strong competitive pressures confronting the manufacturer, which became even more serious with the onset of the depression of 1873. This protracted depression brought about attempts to develop cooperation among manufacturers in order to avoid the costs of competition. Several forms of cooperation emerged. First were pools or "gentlemen's agreements" in which individual firms made a cartel agreement to share traffic or markets rather than to compete by prices. These pools tended to be quite unstable because there were incentives to chisel and the agreements were not enforceable in the courts. In fact, by 1887 railroad pools had been declared illegal by the passage of the Interstate Commerce Act.

The second form of cooperation was the trust, which was a much tighter form of organization than the pool. In the trust stockholders in member firms would delegate their voting rights to a board of trustees by depositing their shares in a special trust and receiving trust certificates in return. The trustees would then operate the firms as a unit in order to achieve their goals which generally involved a reduction of competition. The Standard Oil (1882), cotton oil (1884), linseed oil (1885), whiskey (1887), sugar (1887), and lead smelting (1887) trusts were extremely powerful in their respective industries until they were finally declared illegal under the Sherman Act of 1890.

The third form of cooperative enterprise was the holding company, which emerged under provisions in general acts of incorporation and permitted corporations to hold shares in other corporations. This pattern of stockholding continued to be illegal in many other states after New Jersey introduced the holding company amendment to its general incorporation act in 1889. Nevertheless, it was the holding company form which first promoted the link between manufacturing enterprise and the investment bankers, and made possible the financiers' role in the direct management of large manufacturing corporations.

The ultimate form of cooperation was to bind firms together by common ownership ties through consolidation or merger.[3] Consolidations and mergers were linked to the growing emphasis on horizontal and vertical integration in manufacturing industry, but the Supreme Court's initial interpretation of the Sherman Antitrust Act of 1890 may also have given a strong boost to the merger movement. The act declared illegal "every contract, combination in the form of trust, or otherwise, or conspiracy in restraint of trade." In the E. C. Knight case of 1895, the Court ruled that a merger of several companies into the American Sugar Refining Company was not a violation of the law, in spite of the fact that the new company had increased its share of national production from sixty-five to ninety-eight percent. In other cases, culminating in the Addyston Pipe case of 1899, the Court ruled that attempts by competitors to control markets by cartels or agreements were illegal. In effect, the Court had decided that agreements in restraint of competition were illegal but mergers were not. It was not until the Northern Securities case of 1904 that the Court declared the illegality of a merger destructive of competition. The evidence suggests that the Supreme Court's interpretation of the Sherman Act was a factor in the wave of mergers during the period 1895 to 1904.

The 1880s and the 1890s mark the emergence of the first great integrated enterprises in the American economy.[4] Firms began to consolidate their manufacturing activities in a few but growing number of large and efficient plants. In these enterprises, however, the act of production became no longer the sole function performed by the firm. Integrated firms moved into other functions, into marketing activities and the distribution of products, into the procurement of raw materials, and frequently into the distribution network itself in the form of ownership of transportation systems, both to collect raw materials and to distribute final products.

Multifunction enterprise, according to Chandler, resulted from two different types of growth strategies. In the first, a single company began to expand and to integrate through creating its own marketing organizations. This pattern of expansion was characteristic of many firms producing new consumers' goods for whom existing marketing arrangements were unsatisfactory. In particular, agricultural processing firms integrated forward in this fashion. There are quite a few examples of this — meat, tobacco, flour, and bananas, among others. Perhaps the best-known example is that of Gustavus Swift's meat-packing firm. Swift saw new opportunities for the marketing of meat products with the development of the refrigerated railroad car, which after 1878 permitted the marketing in eastern cities of refrigerated meat that had been slaughtered and dressed in the Midwest. Developing this technique in spite of the opposition of livestock butchers in northeastern cities and the need to "educate" the public to eat refrigerated beef, Swift created a national distribution and marketing organization around a network of midwestern branch plants where the livestock slaughtering and packing was done. By 1892 there were Swift meat-packing plants in Chicago, Omaha, and St. Louis, and in the 1900s more were constructed in several other midwestern centers. Swift's approach made economic sense: it was cheaper to ship dressed meat than livestock, so he located his packing plants near the livestock markets. Swift also moved "backward" into the systemization of livestock buying and "forward" into the development of by-product uses, and further development of his marketing organization.

By 1900 the great, vertically integrated Swift organization was ensconced in central offices in Chicago. Other meat-packers like Armour, Cudahy, and Morris followed suit. Also, some firms producing consumers' durables goods integrated forward by creating their own marketing organizations. One example was the Singer Sewing Machine Company, which replaced the agency system by establishing sales offices throughout the United States, staffed with salaried employees who knew the product from inside out. Other examples from producers' durables industries can be cited, especially in the new electrical industries. Here, as with the sewing machine, marketing was a technologically complicated process, and, consequently, highly trained salesmen were required who understood both the workings of the machinery and the special requirements of their customers. The sales process, manufacturing, and engineering design were so closely interrelated that integration forward into marketing was a natural concomitant of the production of heavy electrical equipment. Both General Electric and Westinghouse followed this pattern.

The second growth strategy which Chandler describes is the horizontal combination of firms that often preceded vertical integration. Here, he points to instances of trade associations, pools, trusts, and holding companies that were legally joined in the great wave of mergers and consolidations at the end of the century. These firms first consolidated their manufacturing activities, and then integrated forward into marketing and distribution or backward into procurement of raw materials. Many of these firms produced "older" staple products. With their industries unorganized, the production and marketing activities of many of these firms had been characterized by sharp competition (viewed by them as industry overcapacity), and these dangers had prompted their cooperation, first informally and subsequently along formal lines.

Noted examples are the members of the petroleum-refining and the iron and steel industries. In the petroleum industry, the emergence of Standard Oil of Ohio as the dominant firm is particularly interesting because it pioneered the use of the trust form in 1879. During the 1870s, Rockefeller had brought Standard of Ohio to a position of dominance in the refining industry in the United States through the acquisition of refineries in Ohio, Pennsylvania, and New York (these were the principal producing and marketing areas at the time). By 1878 Standard had control of ninety percent of American refining capacity and this position was reinforced in the first trust agreement of 1879 and the amended one of 1882. Rockefeller had decided earlier not to try to gain control of crude oil production because the existence of many producers guaranteed a competitive price of crude and thus low acquisition costs. By the late 1880s, however, he began to integrate backward into the production of crude in order to assure himself of a steady crude supply. The firm's expansion in the 1890s culminated in Standard Oil of New Jersey, a holding company, which absorbed the whole group of Standard Oil companies in 1899. In 1911 the Supreme Court ordered the dissolution of Standard Oil of New Jersey. This action, combined with the general westward movement of crude oil production and increased demand for refined petroleum products with the growth of the automobile industry, led to the relative decline of Standard Oil. The market outgrew Standard Oil's dominant position, leaving the effect of its antitrust conviction somewhat uncertain.

Another interesting example is provided by the iron and steel industry. As described earlier, Carnegie Steel had integrated its manufacturing properties and adopted the open-hearth furnace to become the largest and most efficient producer of basic iron and steel in the American industry by the mid-1890s. Carnegie had also integrated backward in the 1890s by securing coking-coal reserves, acquiring control over Mesabi ore lands, purchasing ore ships, and developing a railroad connection from Pittsburgh to Lake Erie.

Other steel companies had followed the same strategy by building efficient production facilities in the vicinity of Pittsburgh. The Federal Steel Company, for example, formed in 1898 under the leadership of Judge Elbert Gary with financial supervision from the Morgan firm, closely resembled Carnegie's operation. One major difference was Federal Steel's alliance with several producers of finished steel products, among them National Tube and American Bridge, which effectively meant that it was integrated forward into the production of finished producers' goods. National Steel, the third largest producer of basic steel in the United States, was also integrated forward to producers of finished iron products, including the American Tin Plate Company, the American Steel Hoop Company, and the American Sheet Metal Company.

With the emerging rivalry of Federal Steel and National Steel with their forward integration into finished producers' goods, Carnegie announced his intention to follow suit by initiating the production of finished producers' goods as well. In 1901, this threat prompted Morgan to organize the merger of Carnegie interests with Federal and National plus a sizeable number of finished goods' companies to form the giant United States Steel Corporation. At the time, United States Steel controlled about sixty percent of national unfinished steel output and enjoyed strong backward and forward integration into raw materials and producers' goods.

Mergers and Consolidations

In our study period, there were two periods of concentrated merger activity, the first from 1887 to 1904 and the second from 1916 to 1930.[5]

The first merger wave was the culmination of a process by which many industries populated by many small-or medium-sized firms were transformed into concentrations of a few large corporations. The peak activity from 1898 to 1902 was preceded by a smaller number of mergers in the 1880s and early 1890s and was succeeded by a period of very low merger activity. The first merger wave produced such giant firms as United States Steel, American Tobacco, International Harvester, Anaconda Copper, and American Smelting and Refining. Even in the period of low merger activity after 1904, some very important firms were created, including General Motors (1908) and the precursor of International Business Machines (1911).

The second merger wave resulted in part from the appearance of new leading industries. It can also be considered as an attempt to restore the levels of concentration achieved earlier, but reduced by government and Supreme Court activity in the intervening years. In fact, the period from 1926 to 1930 represents a peak of merger and consolidation activity in a long uptrend which began about 1916 or 1917 and increased through the 1920s, peaking only at the end of the decade. Among the major consolidations achieved in this period were Union Carbide and Carbon (1917), Transcontinental Oil (1919), Allied Chemical and Dye (1920), Bethlehem Steel (1916, 1922-1923), and Continental Can (1927-1930).

An indication of the chronology and magnitude of merger activity for the period is presented in table 5.2. The net number of firms disappearing because of consolidation or merger is one index of the extent of activity, and the second is the dollar amount of merger capitalizations, that is, the sum of the sizes of the merged or consolidated firms. Both measures substantiate the argument that there were two subperiods of intensive combination activity.

The composition of consolidations and mergers in this period is quite interesting. First, the majority of the mergers occurred in the food, chemical and petroleum products, and the primary metals industries, with less but significant activity in metal products, nonelectrical machinery, and transport equipment. The first four of these industrial groups accounted for about two-fifths of firm disappearances and three-fifths of merger capitalizations during the period 1895 to 1920 — primary metals alone accounted for 13.1 percent of firm disappearances and 30.2 percent of merger capitalizations.[6]

Shifts in the composition of merger activity reflected differential rates of growth, different sizes of industrial firms, and previous merger activity in the different industries. For example, merger activity in the petroleum industry only tended to increase after 1915. Even though the petroleum industry was increasing rapidly in relative size, combination activity was slow from 1895 to 1915 because of previous merger activity and had to await industry growth and the 1911 dissolution of Standard Oil of New Jersey before further merger activity occurred. Another illustration is provided by the chemical products industry in which the average size of industrial firm was increasing quickly, as an index of wage earners per establishment shows. Chemical products ranked high in merger capitalizations during 1915 to 1920. Primary metals and food products, the leaders in merger activity from 1895 to 1904, were outstripped by petroleum products and chemical products in the later period.

The second change in the composition of merger activity concerns whether firms grew by consolidation or acquisition. In the period from 1895 to 1904, there appears to have been much greater reliance on consolidation, compared with the post-1915 period when there was much greater reliance on acquisition. The choice whether to merge by consolidation or acquisition depended upon many things, including the size of the firms, their capital resources, and legal considerations. If, for ex-

Table 5.2 Recorded Mergers in Manufacturing and Mining and Merger Capitalizations, 1895-1930

Recorded Mergers			Merger Capitalizations
Year	Nelson	Thorp	$ millions
1895	43	—	40.8
1896	26	—	24.7
1897	69	—	119.7
1898	303	—	650.6
1899	1,208	—	2,262.7
1900	340	—	442.4
1901	423	—	2,052.9
1902	379	—	910.8
1903	142	—	297.6
1904	79	—	110.5
1905	226	—	243.0
1906	128	—	377.8
1907	87	—	184.8
1908	50	—	187.6
1909	49	—	89.1
1910	142	—	257.0
1911	103	—	210.5
1912	82	—	322.4
1913	85	—	175.6
1914	39	—	159.6
1915	71	—	158.4
1916	117	—	470.0
1917	195	—	678.7
1918	71	—	254.2
1919	171	438	981.7
1920	206	760	1,088.6
1921	—	487	n.a.
1922	—	309	n.a.
1923	—	311	n.a.
1924	—	368	n.a.
1925	—	554	n.a.
1926	—	856	n.a.
1927	—	870	n.a.
1928	—	1,058	n.a.
1929	—	1,245	n.a.
1930	—	799	n.a.

NOTES: 1. n. a. means not available. Merger capitalizations are available only for the Nelson series, and are measured by authorized equity capitalization or gross assets of the consolidation.

2. The Thorp and Nelson series are not comparable. The larger number of disappearances in the Thorp series is likely due to a more complete reporting of small and large mergers; Nelson's series likely includes only mergers from the larger merger population. See Nelson, work cited below, pp. 25-29, for a discussion of these issues.

SOURCES: Nelson, *Merger Movements in American Industry, 1895-1956,* p. 37; *Historical Statistics of the United States,* ser. V30-31, p. 572.

ample, several large firms were combining, then it was likely that they would opt for consolidation and establishment of a new legal entity, whereas if a large firm were combining with a small firm, the large firm usually acquired the smaller firm. Since it normally involved the formation of a new corporation, consolidation frequently required access to new and large sources of capital.[7] Consequently, the availability of capital resources likely affected the decision to undertake consolidation rather than acquisition.

Another variable was the state of incorporation. As has been seen, many state corporation laws began to give greater choice to firms as to the lines of business and financial structures which they might choose. New Jersey, New York, and Delaware led as states of incorporation for consolidations and mergers in the period from 1895 to 1920 because their liberal corporate statutes not only encouraged incorporation but also provided great leeway in incorporations that involved amalgamation.

Finally, merger activity appears to have been periodic, that is, to have occurred in clusters or in waves. Apart from the concern to acquire dependable raw material supplies or the need to contact the ultimate buyer directly, arguments based on the businessman's desire to exploit economies of scale in production and marketing are difficult to substantiate because of data limitations. The great bulk of combinations were comprised of horizontal integrations, especially consolidations, at least in the period up to 1902, which are only vaguely related to scale economies. Vertical mergers were smaller in number than is usually believed, except in the case of the primary metals industry where concern to acquire both secure sources of supply of raw materials and assured markets for basic iron and steel appear to have been extremely important. The later stages of the period featured both more merger activity and vertical integration. There was great diversity among the industries in which mergers and consolidations occurred, and it is highly unlikely that there should have been a simultaneous onset of economies of scale in these many diverse industries.

A rather more convincing rationale is the argument that businessmen wished to control a large part of an industry in order to decrease competition and to increase market control.[8] This goal is consistent with the preponderance of horizontal integration or consolidation up to 1902. In fact, George Stigler has styled the first merger wave as "merger for monopoly." In his discussion of horizontal combinations, Stigler pointed out that the leading firm usually merged more than fifty percent of national production. By leading to market control—in many cases, to near-monopoly—such mergers permitted prospective monopoly profits to be capitalized and distributed among the owners of the merged firms and the promoters of the new corporation. As indicated above, J. Pierpont Morgan pioneered the tactics for profitable production of monopolies.[9]

Some evidence of the extent of market control achieved by firms participating in this early merger wave is indicated in table 5.3.[10] Much of the merger activity in this period led to dominant shares in the market for the firms which underwent merger. The table divides firms into categories: those achieving between 42.5 and 62.5 percent of market dominance, between 62.5 and 82.5 percent of market dominance, and 82.5 percent and over. Some firms are designated only as "large." In the category of greatest dominance, near-monopoly was achieved by firms producing many different kinds of products—from American Brake Shoe and Foundry on the one hand, to American Caramel and American Chicle, and United States Bobbin and Shuttle. Many firms appear to have achieved dominance of between two-thirds and four-fifths of the national market, including American Can, American Locomotive, International Harvester, National Biscuit, and United States Steel Corporation. Certainly, these data are consistent with the argument that firms underwent merger and consolidation in an attempt to secure market control.

In the 1920s merger movement, there was a higher incidence of vertical integration and diversification than in the earlier one, partly because consolidation into a single dominant firm was discouraged by antitrust laws. When they did occur, consolidations were concentrated among companies smaller than the largest one, the merged firms occasionally becoming the second largest firm in the industry. In steel, for example, merger activity was carried out by the Bethlehem and Republic Steel Companies. Bethlehem increased its share of national production from less than one percent in 1908 to almost fifteen percent in 1948, and Republic from two percent to a little more than nine percent during that period. Meanwhile, the share of the dominant firm, United States Steel, fell from fifty percent in 1908 to thirty-three percent in 1948. Similar mergers were concluded in other industries—among producers of cans, cement, petroleum, agricultural implements, glass, and automobiles.[11]

Finally, one should not ignore the role which the emerging American capital market was playing by the late 1890s in permitting investment bankers to marshall funds for the financing of mergers and consolidations.[12] The growth of the capital market—and, in particular, the emergence of the New York Stock Exchange—can be looked on as an enabling condition that facilitated the emergence of large-scale enterprise.

Table 5.3 Mergers Achieving Market Dominance, 1895-1904

Company	Net Firm Disappearances	Capitalization (millions of dollars)	Percentage of Market Controlled
42.5%-62.5%:			
Allis Chalmers	3	50.0	50
American Felt	4	5.0	60
American Shipbuilding	7	30.0	60
American Stove	8	5.0	60
American Writing Paper	27	25.0	55
Asphalt Co. of America	12	30.0	35-50
Computing Scale	2	3.5	50
Distilling Co. of America	73	125.0	60
International Paper	24	45.0	60
International Salt	27	30.0	30-60
National Candy	13	9.0	55
National Enameling & Stamping	9	30.0	55
National Glass	18	3.0	50-70
Royal Baking Powder	4	20.0	58-65
Rubber Goods Manufacturing	6	50.0	40-60
Standard Table Oil Cloth	6	10.0	50
United Button	2	3.0	45
U. S. Cotton Duck	12	50.0	45-65
U. S. Envelope	9	5.0	50-60
U. S. Shipbuilding	8	45.0	40-60
Virginia-Carolina Chemical	15	10.0	60
62.5%-82.5%:			
American Can	64	88.0	65-75
American Car & Foundry	12	60.0	65
American Fork & Hoe	12	4.0	80
American Hide & Leather	21	35.0	75
American Locomotive	8	50.0	70
American Radiator	3	10.0	80
American School Furniture	24	10.0	80
American Sugar Refining	6	145.0	70-90
California Fruit Canners	9	3.5	65
Casein Co. of America	4	6.5	70
Central Foundry	30	14.0	80
Chicago Pneumatic Tool	4	7.5	80
Federal Publishing	3	6.0	75
General Chemical	15	25.0	70
Harbison-Walker Refractories	10	27.6	70
International Harvester	4	120.0	70
International Steam Pump	4	27.5	80
National Biscuit	27	55.0	70
National Fireproofing	22	15.5	65

National Novelty	19	10.0	70
Otis Elevator	6	11.0	65
Standard Sanitary	8	5.0	80
Union Bag & Paper	5	27.5	80
U. S. Gypsum	29	7.5	80
U. S. Steel	170	1,370.0	65
82.5% and over:			
American Brake Shoe & Foundry	4	4.5	90
American Caramel	1	1.5	90
American Chicle	5	9.0	85
American Grass Twine	3	15.0	90
American Linseed	6	33.5	85
American Pneumatic Service	2	15.0	87
American Seeding Machine	7	15.0	90
American Smelting & Refining	12	65.0	85
American Tobacco	162	502.0	90
Diamond Match	38	19.5	85
Du Pont (E.I.) de Nemours	65	50.0	85
General Electric & Westinghouse	8	162.0	90
National Carbon	10	10.0	87
Pullman	1	74.0	85
Railway Steel Spring	7	20.0	95
U. S. Bobbin & Shuttle	4	2.0	90
"Large":			
American Agricultural Chemical	32	40.0	
American Sewer Pipe	6	10.0	
Borden	6	20.0	
Brewery Consolidations (12)	97	67.1	
Corn Products Refining	3	80.0	
Ice Consolidations (4)	61	74.4	
International Nickel	3	24.0	
International Silver	16	20.0	
National Lead	18	25.0	
United Shoe Machinery	3	20.0	

SOURCE: Nelson, *Merger Movements in American Industry, 1895-1956,* pp. 161-162.

Changes in the Administration of the Firm[13]

As the scale of enterprise increased in the late nineteenth and early twentieth centuries, geographical expansion, vertical integration into new functions, and product diversification (the move into new products) rendered the old styles of business administration inefficient. These factors induced the innovation of new techniques of business administration in large industrial firms and their subsequent diffusion throughout the manufacturing sector. These innovations occurred in three stages: first, during the manufacturing sector's early emphasis on small-scale industrial enterprise; second, during the development of integrated, multidepartment enterprise beginning in the 1880s; and third, in the post-1920 phase, featuring decentralized, multidivisional enterprise.

The small-scale industrial firm of circa 1870 could be managed by one or a few men who handled all basic managerial activities including fiscal administration, operational supervision, and entrepreneurial activity. Even in the largest firms of the day which were already using the corporate form, chiefly in railroads and textiles, there were usually only very few senior executive personnel, generally the president or treasurer, and a general superintendent. It was the expansion of railroads that first pointed out the need for a new administrative structure, and was to provide precedents for industrialists when the scale of industrial firms skyrocketed.[14]

In the 1870s and the 1880s the modern factory emerged as one of the obvious imperatives of the new machine techology. As the structure of enterprise began to increase in scale to meet the opportunities inherent in mass production, industrialists began to feel the need to improve the administration of their plants. A major step was the development of "systematic management."[15] The interest in systematic management arose as a result of the impact of increasing plant size and complexity on the efficiency with which internal operations could be managed, that is, in response to growing pains that showed up as waste and confusion. Litterer argues that the growth of operating inefficiency resulted from two basic forces: first, a breakdown of coordination and central office control of the component activities from the receipt of an order, to its processing through the engineering, foundry, machining, and assembling departments, and ultimate shipping by the shipping department; second, a disintegration of effective interplay between higher and lower levels of management, based partly on the inadequacy of information flows in the large firm.

Management had been concerned with refining the performance of isolated activities within the firm at the expense of the integration or linking of activities. By the 1880s this neglect had become apparent, and had precipitated a search for solutions. Several different lines were followed. First, there was increased attention paid to the scheduling of activities in the firm, which resulted in better production and inventory control methods. The use of shop order sheets was begun in the early 1880s, and was refined to provide a more detailed information flow between the shop and the central office in specifying what work was done, when it was begun, and when it was finished. Second, higher management began to supervise organizational matters more directly. To do this, management required new, reliable information and the development of cost accounting techniques to provide more detail more quickly.[16] Third, the higher level of management could reserve for itself the more significant decisions and permit lower management to execute the decisions. The increasing reliance on decision rules in such areas as personnel matters facilitated the tasks of both top management and lower management.

Growing interest in improving the internal management of the industrial plant culminated in the "scientific management" movement of the 1890s and early twentieth century, which was to reach its zenith in the writings of Frederic W. Taylor.[17] His early papers, "A Piece Rate System" and "Shop Management," presented in 1895 and 1903 respectively, outlined his basic ideas. Taylor believed that the secret to improving worker efficiency lay, first, in obtaining more information about the job (analyzing the worker's movements, experimenting to find optimum size and weight of tools, and the like) and, second, in offering incentive payments for good performance. He developed principles for designing the most efficient physical layout of the factory, and emphasized the official routing of work and careful scheduling of production of orders. In essence, careful analysis and measurement were the underpinnings of scientific management. Taylor's work prepared the way for the widespread adoption of the principles and practices of scientific management by 1920.

As has been shown, the horizontally and/or vertically integrated enterprise emerged in the late nineteenth century as one element in the businessman's response to the growing national and urban market. Accordingly, industrialists had to build departmental structures to administer a number of units or plants and to set up central offices for management of the company as a whole. New administrative needs were emerging not just from increasing size of the firm per se but, more importantly, because the firms were assuming new functions.

By 1900 in many cases the horizontally integrated firm had already embarked on vertical integration as well. It not only manufactured goods but also itself purchased or produced raw materials, and sold directly to retailers; that is, it had become a multifunction enterprise. Thus, administrative changes were required. As far as production was concerned, standardization of processes and concentration of production in efficient plants could be achieved only if there were a transformation from a loose combination or federation of firms to a consolidated firm. Upon combination, the constituent firms were disbanded. Factories formerly managed by the heads of member firms were placed under salaried managers. Even then, the economic benefits of consolidation were not conferred automatically upon the firms but required careful attention to the administration of manufacturing, marketing, procurement of raw materials, and coordination of all these activities. The result was the development of the centralized, departmental structure between 1900 and 1920, in which the sales, manufacturing, purchasing, and finance activities of each firm were placed in a large single-function department (see Figure 1). An integrated, multidepartment enterprise naturally involved the development of a central headquarters to supervise the activities and plans of the departmental units.

Examples of the early development of multidepartment enterprise are Standard Oil in the 1890s, Du Pont and the National Biscuit Company in the early 1900s, and the iron and steel industries.

The weakness of this system was that there were still a few men — the president and the vice-presidents or department heads — who formed the top executive group and who were obliged to make a great number of complex decisions. There was also a problem of coordination. Usually, both the president and the vice-presidents had spent their early careers in single functions of the enterprise (for example, in manufacturing or in marketing). The result was that they often encountered difficulties in taking a corporation-wide view as compared with a more limited marketing-view or production-view. In Chandler's opinion, this led to major entrepreneurial weakness on the part of such firms.

Beginning in 1920 an organizational structure was devised which permitted an effective administration of a number of vertically integrated subsidiaries or divisions. Chandler calls this administrative form the decentralized, multidivisional enterprise. It arose because of increasingly complex administrative problems both in some new industries (for example, the electrical, automobile, and chemical products industries) and in some technologically complex older industries (for example, petroleum products, rubber products, and agricultural implements). These complex administrative problems resulted from the growth strategy that had been adopted in these industries.

Vertical integration, diversification into new lines of products, and expansion into foreign markets all increased the number and complexity of entrepreneurial and operational activities in the firm, and rendered increasingly formidable the tasks to be performed at headquarters by top-level management. Two kinds of responses were undertaken by the organizational leaders among industrial firms. The first was an adaptive response which brought about further refinements in the structure and administration of the functional department. The second was a creative response leading to the development of the new multidivisional, de-

Diagram 1: The Integrated, Multidepartment Enterprise

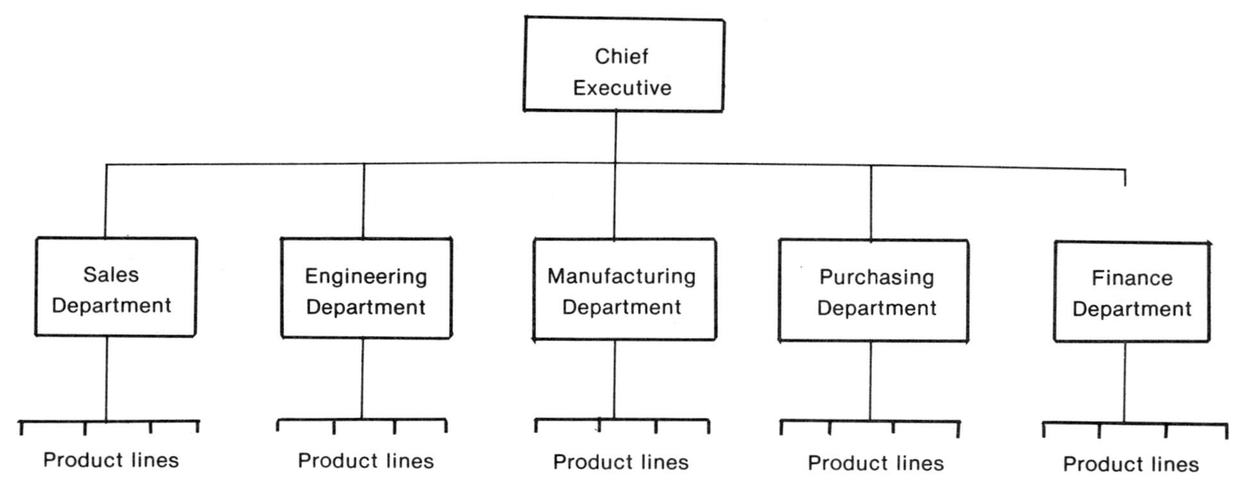

centralized structure which made use of the autonomous, multidepartment division based on a region or a product line (see Figure 2). This managerial system was innovated in General Motors, Du Pont, and Standard of New Jersey in the 1920s, and was rapidly diffused throughout the remainder of the American industrial sector only after World War II.

This creative response was made necessary because of the inherent weakness of centralized, functionally departmentalized, operating companies, and loosely held, decentralized holding companies. The key organizational weakness of such firms was an increase of the administrative load on senior executives so great that they could no longer handle their entrepreneurial responsibilities. The operations of vertically integrated enterprise, whether through expansion or diversification of products, became increasingly complex. Short-term, operational activities became more and more time-consuming. The multidivisional structure was necessary to enable general or head-office executives to concentrate on entrepreneurial activities, while lower-level executives focused on operational activities in autonomous, self-contained, operating divisions.

Finally, the personalities and training of the organizational innovators probably help to explain the development of new administrative techniques. Indeed, an engineering training together with an interest in systematizing and defining organizational relationships seems to have been characteristic of the leading organizational innovators at General Motors, Du Pont, and Standard of New Jersey.

According to Chandler, the significance of these innovations was great. By relieving top-level management from responsibility for operating duties, the new administrative forms freed them for more strategic, decision-making activity. Moreover, general executives were less likely to reflect the position of just one part of the firm — one division, or one department. The emergence of well-trained, general office advisory staffs enabled senior management to make decisions in the corporation's interest independently of pressures and information provided directly by operating divisions and functional departments.

Today, only two basic forms of management structure continue to be used by large industrial firms—the centralized, functionally departmentalized form perfected by General Electric and Du Pont prior to the First World War and used by companies manufacturing a single line of goods for one product or regional market, and the decentralized, multidivisional type developed in the early 1920s at General Motors and Du Pont and subsequently diffused among companies producing several lines of goods for a number of product or regional markets.[18]

Diagram 2: The Multidivisional Structure

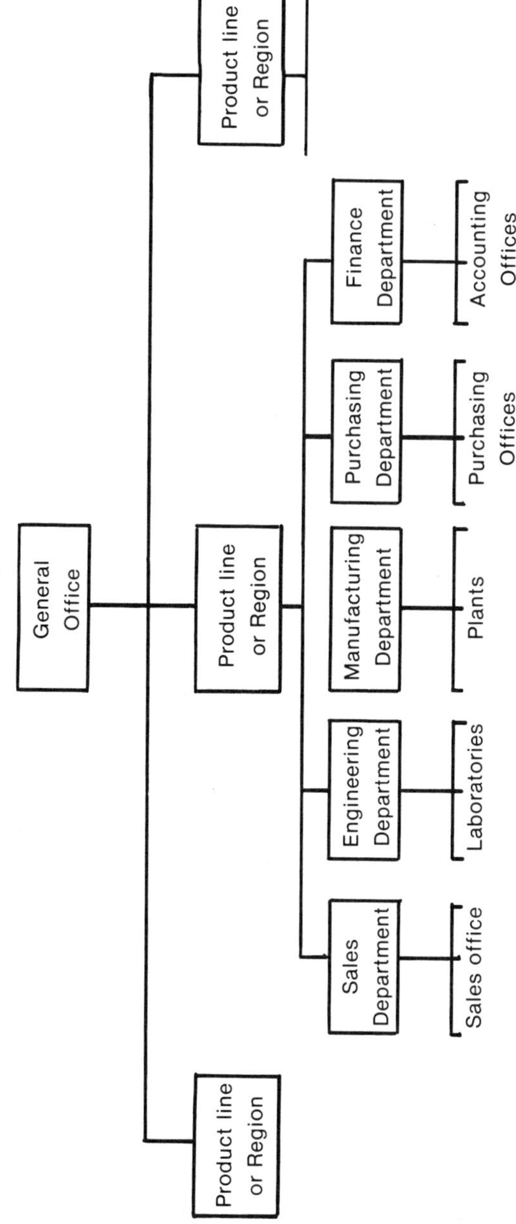

SOURCE: This chart is adapted from Chandler, *Strategy and Structure*, p. 10.

A Case Study: Du Pont

The history of the Du Pont firm illustrates the evolution of management innovation in the large, integrated, industrial firm.[19] Du Pont, as a family firm, had been the leading member of the Gunpowder Trade Association since its formation in 1882. The Du Ponts had carefully invested in other large explosives firms as well in order to guarantee the "community" of interest of the industry. But little attention had been paid to the administration of the business itself.

In 1902 on the death of Henry Du Pont, the firm was reorganized to include many of the other firms in the explosives industry as the E. I. Du Pont de Nemours Powder Company, which controlled about two-thirds of industry output. Manufacturing operations of the enlarged firm were concentrated in a few of the larger plants close to the principal markets, and three administrative departments were established to coordinate the work of the plants, one for each of the major product groups—black powder, smokeless powder, and high explosives. A national marketing organization was grafted onto the sales department of one of the constituent firms in the consolidation, and engineering, traffic, and purchasing units were retained. A new development department, designed to improve products and manufacturing processes, was added. Each major department was to have a vice-president whose primary responsibility was long-term planning and appraisal of operations in his area, and a director who supervised daily operations. The head office was comprised of the president and vice-presidents serving as an executive committee concerned with long-term planning and appraisal for the firm as a whole, and an administrative committee comprised of the directors. A finance committee represented the shareholders' interests but was largely submerged within the executive committee. Shortly after its formation, the new Du Pont firm had concluded the development of a centralized, functionally departmentalized structure, with its central office located in Wilmington. A heuristic depiction of this structure is presented in Figure 3.

Through the years to 1921, this administrative structure was further refined, but no substantive alterations were introduced. During the period 1911 to 1914 the firm was transformed from a family enterprise to a professionally managed one in the interests of more effective administration. The auxiliary staff units in the general office were expanded, and some of the responsibilities of the executive committee and finance committee were redefined. Much attention was given to improving the collection and use of data in the efficient administration of the firm. A subcommittee of the executive committee considered company organization in 1919 and recommended that the company's operations be divided

Diagram 3: The DuPont Organization, 1911

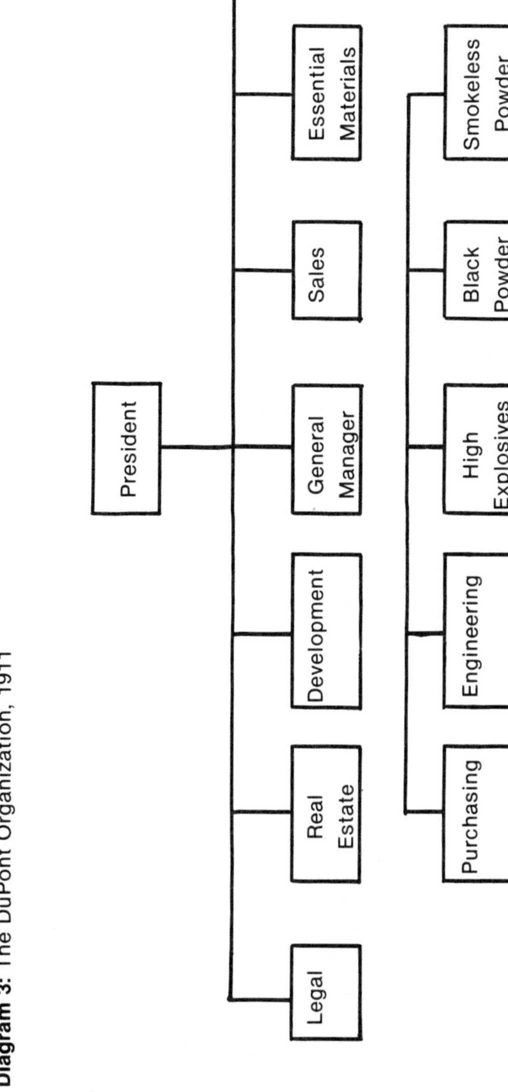

SOURCE: This chart is adapted from Chandler, *Strategy and Structure*, p. 62.

into four functional divisions—production, sales, development, and finance—with the general office auxiliary staff being absorbed into the departmental headquarters. Other than this, the central office organization was to be little changed. The final revisions adopted by the company's senior management retained separate purchasing, chemical, and engineering departments. The revised organizational framework represented the ultimate refinement in "traditional" administration of the giant, vertically integrated, industrial enterprise. The departmental directors administered operations in each major function, and the vice-presidents in charge of the functional departments, together with the president and senior vice-president as "general" officers, comprised the executive committee and undertook entrepreneurial decisions.

But the refinement of the centralized, functionally departmentalized structure at Du Pont was accompanied by the beginnings of serious organizational problems that, within two years, caused the firm to redesign the administrative structure completely.

Du Pont's early experiments with diversification after 1908 and, then, more substantial diversification into the chemical-based industries after World War I were responses to the threat of excess capacity. By early 1919 the company was firmly established in chemical, paint and varnish, celluloid, and artificial leather production, as well as in the manufacture of explosives. Also the production of dyestuffs was in an experimental stage, and the decision had already been made to begin producing rayon.

Diversification greatly increased the demands on Du Pont's administrative officers. The basic problem was that executives with experience primarily in explosives were now being called on to make decisions involving the manufacture and sale of paints and varnishes, dyes, chemicals, plastics, and so forth. The differences among these product lines adversely affected the efficient working of both the functional departments and the general office by making more complex the assessment of departmental operations, the conclusion of policies affecting several functions in many industries, and interdepartmental cooperation. The emerging problem was escalated to crisis proportions by the deterioration of Du Pont's profits position during the postwar recession.

In short, Du Pont's postwar organizational problems arose out of the strategy of product-diversification. Diversification simply put too much strain on an organization designed to manage a single line of products (powder and explosives) and unable to adapt to administering several different product lines. Du Pont responded by appointing a second subcommittee on administrative structure in 1920 which concluded that the profits problem was really an organizational one, in large part reflecting the especially difficult problems in the sales area. As the committee saw it, Du Pont's traditional product lines were finished or semifinished goods distributed on a tonnage basis, and the newer lines required a different approach geared to the merchandising of small, packaged goods. It was in this latter area that profit margins were low. During 1920 the paint and varnish operation was operated as a "pilot" case along the lines of a product division combining all functional aspects. This was followed in 1921 by the expedient of "divisional councils" on product lines.

The decline of profits in the first half of 1921 brought on full-scale reorganization in September of that year. Five product divisions (or industrial departments) and eight staff divisions (or auxiliary departments) were established. The treasurer's department was retained. The reorganized structure along autonomous division lines is depicted in Figure 4. Responsibilities were divided on the principles of decentralized, multidivisional structure. The executive committee had no direct reponsibilities for operations, but were concerned with planning, appraisal, and coordination—essentially just the entrepreneurial functions. This had, of course, been the intention in the earlier period, but failures of administrative structure had constantly involved the senior executives in operational matters. In addition, each member of the committee was to oversee, in an advisory capacity *only*, one functional activity (sales, purchasing, manufacturing, and chemical and engineering activities) in all five industrial divisions. The information gathered here was to assist the executive committee to fulfill its primary duties. The heads of product divisions, general managers, were to take full responsibility for all aspects of divisional operations, and report to the executive committee. The eight functional departments were retained to provide advisory services to both the product divisions and to the executive committee. The treasurer's department continued to be responsible for overall accounting practices and the presentation of data.[20]

Thus, by late 1921, Du Pont had created a new structure of autonomous, multidepartment divisions and a general office of senior executives assisted by staff specialists. The divisions each had central offices which supervised all aspects of the divisional product line, and the general office concentrated on overseeing the administration of the multi-industry enterprise and planning its future growth strategy.

An Aside: The "New Imperialism" of the Multinational Corporation[21]

Early in their foreign investment experience, Americans demonstrated a marked preference for direct investment which confers ownership and legal control over foreign assests, to portfolio investment where the form

Diagram 4: The DuPont Organization, 1921

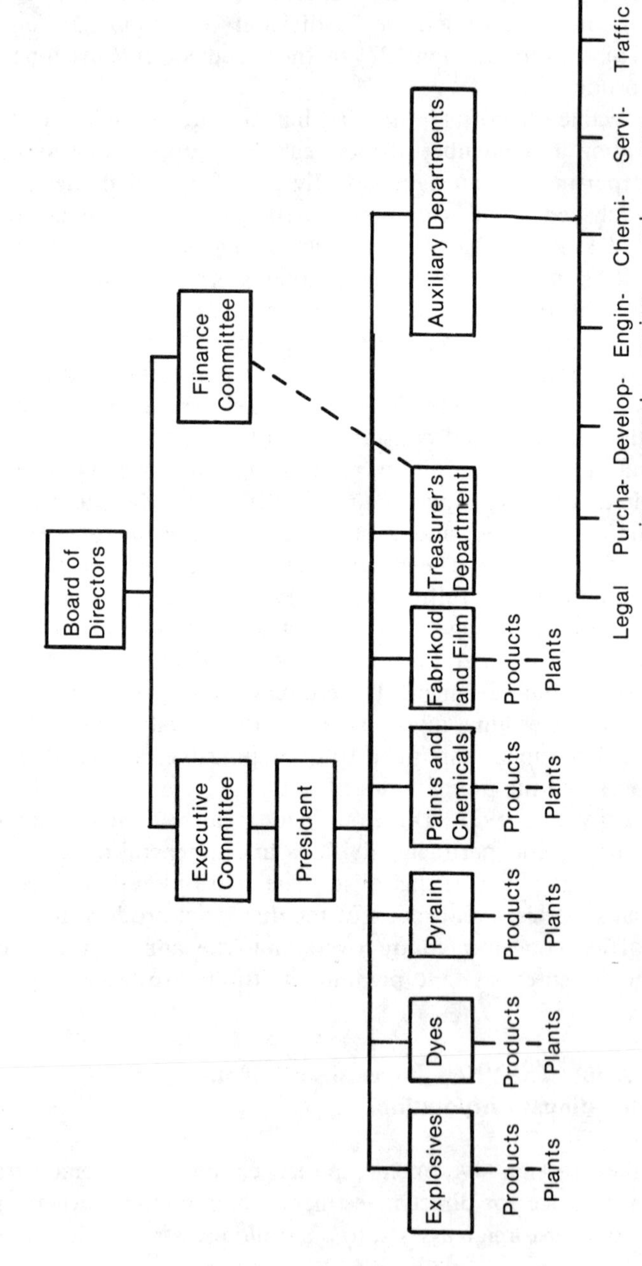

SOURCE: This chart is adapted from Chandler, *Strategy and Structure*, p. 109.

or amount of the investment do not involve legal control. Commonly, control has been exercised through capital investment in a branch plant or subsidiary where the American investor retained voting control. Ownership rights have facilitated not only consumption abroad of American products but also extension of American technology and management techniques.

The book value of United States direct investments abroad have increased from about $600 million in 1900 to approximately $70 billion in 1970. Table 5.4 shows the industrial distribution of American foreign direct investment from 1897 to 1966, and Table 5.5 shows American

Table 5.4 Industrial Distribution of U. S. Foreign Direct Investment, 1897-1970 (book value in billions of dollars)

	1897	1914	1929	1940	1950	1960	1970
Manufacturing	.09	.48	1.81	1.93	3.83	11.05	32.26
Petroleum	.09	.34	1.12	1.28	3.39	10.81	21.71
Mining	.13	.72	1.19	.78	1.13	2.95	6.17
Public Utilities	.17	.39	1.61	1.51	1.42	2.55	2.87
Trade	.06	.17	.37	.52	.76	2.40	6.55
	.64	2.65	7.53	7.00	11.79	31.82	78.18

NOTE: Totals include miscellaneous investments.
SOURCE: Wilkins, *The Emergence of Multinational Enterprise,* p. 110, and *The Maturing of Multinational Enterprise,* pp. 182, 330.

Table 5.5 U. S. Foreign Direct Investment in Manufacturing Subsidiaries, by Areas, 1897-1970 (book value in billions of dollars)

Year	All Areas	Canada	Latin America	Europe and UK	All other Areas
1897	.09	.06	.003	.04	.001
1914	.48	.22	.04	.20	.02
1929	1.81	.82	.23	.64	.13
1940	1.93	.94	.21	.64	.13
1950	3.83	1.90	.78	.93	.13
1960	11.05	4.83	1.52	3.80	.90
1970	32.26	10.06	4.62	13.71	3.87

NOTE: Totals include miscellaneous investments.
SOURCE: Wilkins, *The Emergence of Multinational Enterprise,* p. 110, and *The Maturing of Multinational Enterprise,* pp. 182, 330.

direct investment in manufacturing subsidiaries by geographic region. Although most of this increase has occurred since the mid-1950s, the export of capital from the United States as direct investment began in the nineteenth century, as an outgrowth of industrialization and the rise of "big business." The United States exported capital in the form of direct investment even though it was a large net borrower of portfolio capital. By the 1920s the United States had ceased to be a net borrower: Americans held large foreign portfolio investments, and direct investments continued to expand. During the 1930s many nations adopted defensive measures to protect national economies by increasing tariffs and creating other barriers to trade. Direct investment provided a means of crossing tariff barriers: by building a manufacturing or assembling plant in the host economy, the American parent firm became "localized" and benefited from tariff protection to produce for the local market. Since World War II the level of direct investment has increased substantially, reflecting the growth of new investment opportunities for Americans abroad, especially in Europe.

American direct investment initially followed expansion of the domestic market into nearby areas like Canada and Mexico. As Mira Wilkins has pointed out, there were two prerequisites of international business—improvements in transport and communications to lower costs and risks of foreign business, and the prior development of large-scale enterprise producing for the national market.[22] Both of these conditions were met in the United States by the 1880s.

At first American businessmen undertook foreign investments in order to expand sales. For some firms, it was a response to the depression of 1893–1897. For others, it was a natural extension of mass production for the national market. To export surplus commodities in similar market areas abroad required the establishment of a foreign sales and distribution network at relatively low cost, and represented a special case of vertical integration forwards into mass distribution. By the mid-1880s sewing machines, petroleum products, electrical equipment, chemicals —all were being marketed abroad by American companies.[23]

Moreover, by 1900 there were already many American industries which were beginning to manufacture or assemble their products abroad, or to invest in extracting raw materials from foreign resource bases. In many cases, American firms were pressured or encouraged by foreign governments to undertake direct investment of this more substantial type. For example, the protectionist National Policy tariff adopted in Canada in 1879 represented a deliberate attempt to attract direct foreign investment, and the Canadian patent acts of 1872 and 1903 required foreign patent-holders to begin local manufacture within two years in order to retain Canadian patent rights. Not only did Canadian policy lure American investors northwards, but Canada had other advantages. It was, after all, an adjacent country, rich in natural resources, with a similar language and culture, a stable government, and generally friendly relations with the United States. By 1914 Canada had more American-controlled manufacturing plants than any other country—the great names in Canadian manufacturing were Ford, General Motors, Goodyear, United States Rubber, DuPont, International Harvester, and so forth.[24]

Whereas market orientation may have been the most important factor in the expansion abroad of marketing and manufacturing operations, proximity appears to have been most important in raw materials investment. Canada was an early recipient of American direct investment in this sector: copper and nickel, asbestos, timber and newsprint pulp, and hydroelectric power attracted American investment before 1914.

During the 1920s the American government became even more favorably disposed to foreign trade and investment, and American direct investment increased across a broad range of manufacturing industries. Moreover, as domestic supply shortages began to develop in various natural resources, American investment in securing foreign sources of raw materials became an even more important part of direct investments, particularly in the energy sector. Continued expansion of American enterprise abroad has been a feature of the international economy since World War II. As Raymond Vernon's work indicates, the American-controlled multinational corporations are very large, profitable, and are widely diversified: indeed, they are dominant firms in the United States economy and in United States foreign transactions, and are dominant firms in host countries as well.[25]

But what are the impications for the host country?[26] First, extraterritoriality—the extension of foreign laws and regulations to the host country—can be a problem. The United States Trading with the Enemy Act prohibits trade by American parent firms and by subsidiaries with certain countries whereas Canadian law, for example, has no such general prohibition. American balance of payments guidelines to parent firms during the 1960s and 1970s were also applied to foreign subsidiaries, worsening the operating performance of the subsidiaries and, in some cases, limiting the effectiveness of host country economic policy. Second, the extent of the host country's economic gains from foreign enterprise depends partly on the government's success in taxing profits accruing to foreign owners. Corporate transfer pricing—the setting of prices for transactions between parent firm and subsidiary to minimize tax burdens—provides one way of escaping host country taxes. Third, host countries often complain that research and development expenditures are concentrated in the parent firm rather than the subsidiary, at a substantial cost to the development of scientific research in the host country. Finally, the sheer size of many multinationals is worrisome to many governments: the annual sales of General Motors exceeds the Gross National Product of well over one hundred countries. The global strategy of giant international corporations means that the subsidiary operates as an instrument of the parent firm with little regard for national economic goals. What is to be produced? Where will the output be sold? Where will supplies be purchased? What funds will be remitted to the parent firm? These decisions are dictated by the multinational's desired internal transfers between parent and subsidiaries rather than by market forces. Host governments have little input into the decision-making process, and almost no political recourse against unwelcome decisions.

Today, American-based firms account for some two-thirds of all foreign direct investment in the world economy. Distinctly American in ownership and management, American multinationals are perceived by many national governments to pose a real threat to their security. Moreover, the multinational corporation has been regarded in host countries as the agent of American imperialism, a tool to penetrate and control their economies. Now, however, the multinationals' great economic power and size even renders dubious the proposition that they are ultimately responsible to the American government!

Conclusion

The ascendancy of "big business" in the late nineteenth and early twentieth centuries was embodied in profound organizational changes in the manufacturing sector. The rise of the corporate form, and the growing incidence of mergers and consolidations which changed the structure of enterprise were accompanied by new developments in the administration of the firm and the rise of professional management. After 1900 functionally departmentalized administration came into wide use. But business administration became increasingly complex because of vertical integration, expansion, and diversification into new products, with the result that by 1920 some firms began experimenting with a new, decentralized, multidivisional structure which facilitated the concentration of top-level management on entrepreneurial decision making and left responsibility for operations in the hands of executives in autonomous, self-contained, operating divisions. This new administrative structure became widely diffused in American industry after the Second World War. Modern industrial firms still employ one or the other of these two basic administrative structures developed in American business between

1880 and 1930. Thus, according to Chandler, "In many sectors of the economy the visible hand of management replaced what Adam Smith referred to as the invisible hand of market forces . . . Modern business enterprise . . . became the most powerful institution in the American economy and its managers the most influential group of economic decision makers."[27] The rise of modern business enterprise and the ascendancy of managerial capitalism are indeed among the major economic achievements of the early twentieth century. But as glorious as it yet appears, the triumph of "big business" has been tainted because the effective replacement of the "invisible hand" of market prices by the "visible hand" of corporate management in large sectors of the American economy has imposed substantial external costs on the American public. We shall return to this issue in chapters 7 and 8.

6

Technological and Organizational Change in Agriculture

Introduction

The role played by agriculture in post-Civil War American economic development had many dimensions. First, the agricultural sector continued to provide foods and fibres to the growing American population. Agriculture's growth was distinguished by significant changes in the composition of output and by the increased productivity of inputs. Second, agriculture released factors of production to nonfarm employment. In particular, technological change, contributing to increased output per unit of labor, was vital in releasing farm labor to the rapidly growing manufacturing and services industries. Third, the increase in farm population and income generated increasing demand from rural areas for the products of village and urban industries.

Two dramatic features of American agricultural change in this period were geographical expansion and the growth of regional specialization. Expansion was based primarily on additions to the supply of agricultural land with westward-moving settlement until 1900. After that date farmers resorted to more intensive farming and the development of "scientific" agriculture. The mechanization of farm equipment has generally been regarded as the single most important factor in raising agricultural labor productivity. Horsepower was initially the primary motive force, but after the First World War the internal-combustion engine and its application to the farm tractor and truck changed the mode of power on the farm.

The American domestic market, reflecting increases in population and incomes per capita, grew relative to the export market for agricultural products from 1870 to 1930. Within the domestic market, urban-rural population shifts meant that the domestic market became more and more an urban one.

These developments together with transportation improvements combined to increase regional specialization in agriculture. One result of the growing domestic demand was a shift towards products with higher income elasticity of demand—that is, toward beef, dairy products, fruits and vegetables. The production of market garden products was increasingly adopted in the northeastern states near the growing urban centers and subsequently on the west coast. Dairying, instead of continuing to be widely dispersed and noncommercialized, became concentrated in sectors of the Mid-Atlantic states and the Midwest. Grain and livestock were more and more the special products of the prairie and plains states.

Sources of Output Growth

The sources of output growth in the agricultural sector are increases in the quantity of inputs and changes in factor productivity. Several sources of output growth can be mentioned briefly. First, the availability of new lands, in particular, the westward movement of the agricultural frontier, implied changes in the regional shares of output in the United States, especially for corn, small grains, and livestock products. The Midwest and the plains states emerged as major producers of these products by 1900. The derivative effects of the growth of markets and transportation improvements in promoting regional specialization and the concomitant changes in yields per acre associated with regional specialization are often considered together with westward expansion. Second, the improvement of farming techniques, the development of mechanical equipment, and the growing use of chemicals and fertilizers helped to promote the growth of output. In particular, the mechanization of agriculture helped to reduce labor inputs per acre and to promote labor productivity.[1]

Westward Expansion and Regional Specialization

The dramatic post-Civil War expansion of agriculture and settlement of the western frontier brought about the rapid growth of several agricultural products. Wheat, oats, and corn production grew rapidly up to World War I, and leveled off thereafter. Wheat output rose from 254 million bushels in 1870 to 897 million bushels in 1914 and remained over 800 million bushels in 1929. Corn output increased from 1.1 billion bushels in 1890 to 2.5 billion bushels in 1914, and fell to 2.1 bushels in 1929. The output of cotton, which was still the nation's major export crop, rose from 4.4 million bales in 1870 to 16.1 million bales on the eve of the First World War, falling back to 14.8 million bales by 1929.[2] Output increases in livestock were also considerable: the numbers of cattle increased from about 31 million in 1870 to just under 60 million in 1914 and 1929, whereas hogs increased somewhat less, from 33.8 million in 1870 to 52.9 million in 1914 and 59 million in 1929.[3]

Substantial changes in the regional composition of agricultural output reflected patterns of regional specialization and concentration of production which emerged after the Civil War and were solidified by 1900.[4] Cotton production continued to dominate in the South, and advanced westward into Texas and Oklahoma. Stimulated by decreases in the real cost of transportation connected with railroad expansion, winter wheat production was concentrated in central Kansas and Nebraska and spring wheat production in Minnesota and the Dakotas. The Corn Belt of Illinois, Iowa, Kansas and Nebraska was established.

Table 6.1 shows that the westward movement of wheat and corn production into the prairie and plains states was largely completed by 1900. Complementary to corn growing, hog-raising was concentrated in a band from Illinois down into Texas.

In the northeastern states, the composition of agricultural outputs changed substantially as farmers shifted out of cereals and livestock into vegetable and fruit production, dairying, and poultry products. These outputs were dependent upon ready access to urban markets, and changes in the output mix reflected the changing urban-rural composition of population in the United States.

Did the growing regional specialization of American agriculture contribute to making American agriculture more productive? The westward movement of the frontier and the emergence of specialized corn and small-grain farming in the prairie and plains states have been singled out as responsible for increased productivity in grain farming. In particular, western lands were alleged to be more fertile for grain raising. This question is closely examined in the first case study later in this chapter. Moreover, changes in transport costs to urban markets help to explain regional expansion and specialization.

Mechanization

A major contributor to the growth of farm output was mechanization. There have been two mechanical revolutions in agriculture. The first,

Table 6.1 The Leading Wheat and Corn States and Percentages of United States Crop, 1869-1899

	1869	1879	1889	1899
Wheat	55.7%	53.4%	50.2%	49.0%
	Illinois	Illinois	Minnesota	Minnesota
	Iowa	Indiana	California	North Dakota
	Ohio	Ohio	Illinois	Ohio
	Indiana	Michigan	Indiana	South Dakota
	Wisconsin	Minnesota	Ohio	Kansas
	Pennsylvania	Iowa	Kansas	California
Corn	72.0%	78.9%	80.7%	75.5%
	Illinois	Illinois	Iowa	Illinois
	Iowa	Iowa	Illinois	Iowa
	Ohio	Missouri	Kansas	Kansas
	Missouri	Indiana	Nebraska	Nebraska
	Indiana	Ohio	Missouri	Missouri
	Kentucky	Kansas	Ohio	Indiana
	Tennessee	Kentucky	Indiana	Ohio
	Pennsylvania	Nebraska	Kentucky	Texas
	Texas	Tennessee	Texas	Kentucky
	Alabama	Pennsylvania	Tennessee	Oklahoma

SOURCE: Fred A. Shannon, *The Farmer's Last Frontier: Agriculture 1860-1897* (New York: Holt, Rinehart and Winston, 1945), p. 163.

from manpower to animal power, dates from the 1840s to the early part of the twentieth century. The second, from animal to mechanical sources of power, occurred in the period during and after World War I. In this later period, the introduction of the internal-combustion engine, and its application to the tractor and the truck, and rural electrification were of primary significance. The development of new types of machinery which were used as agricultural inputs tended to be labor-saving—that is, tended to increase the output of farm products per unit of labor input. One important indirect effect of mechanization in the nineteenth century was the release of labor to other rapidly expanding sectors of the economy.

The basic competitive structure of agriculture helps to explain why mechanical techniques of production were rapidly adopted in agriculture and readily diffused. There was a demand for improved techniques of production which promised cost reduction to the farmer who adopted them. This is an extremely important point but one which is quite difficult to substantiate. Generally speaking, historians have often described the farmer as being inherently conservative and reluctant to take risks in adopting new techniques. On the other hand, more recently some historians have begun to take a different stance. For example, Richard Hofstadter has argued that the United States agricultural economy was much different from European traditional agriculture:

> If a rural culture means an emotional and craftsmanlike dedication to the soil, a traditional and pre-capitalist outlook, a tradition-directed rather than career-directed type of character, and a village community devoted to ancestral ways and habitually given to communal action, then the prairies and plains never had one. What differentiated the agricultural life of these regions from the practices widespread in European agriculture—or, for that matter, from the stereotype of the agrarian myth—was not simply that it produced for a market but that it was so speculative, so mobile, so mechanized, so "progressive", so thoroughly imbued with the commercial spirit. . . . The characteristic product of American rural society was not a yeoman or a villager, but a harassed little country businessman who worked very hard, moved all too often, gambled with his land, and made his way alone.[5]

The impression that the farmer was above all a businessman underlies the competitive framework within which mechanical devices were adopted and rapidly diffused. The farmer was anxious to adopt machinery for use in the grain harvest because it reduced labor costs and also lowered uncertainties about the availibility of labor and payment of harvest wages, associated with the peak-load labor requirements of harvest time.

As was indicated in Chapter 3, many writers have ascribed an important role to economic conditions in explaining the direction of inventive activity and the rate at which new techniques were innovated and diffused in the nineteenth century American economy. Irwin Feller has provided an index of inventive activity in agriculture based on data on patents granted from 1837 to 1890.[6] The patent data cover total "pure" agriculture and three component series (earth preparation and planting; harvesting; and bee culture, livestock, and miscellaneous). Feller found that there was a sharp rise in inventive activity in agriculture after 1851. The soil preparation, planting, and harvesting series tend to move together, which suggests that there was some common determining influence at work on both series. This finding undermines the proposition that inventive activity is provoked by bottlenecks, since this hypothesis would imply uneven development in preharvest and harvest inventive activity, with important inventions in the one series leading (or lagging) those in the other series. The apparent simultaneity in the appearance of preharvest and harvest patents caused Feller to look for explanatory factors other than bottlenecks.

Accordingly, Feller attempted to determine whether the series for patents granted was closely related to changes in the general state of agriculture. Since the farmer was becoming increasingly caught up in market forces, one plausible hypothesis was an application to the agricultural sector of Schmookler's proposition that inventive activity was a function of market pressure. Feller used data on value added in agriculture as a proxy for investment, prices, costs and output on the assumption that variations in value added were market-determined. He discovered a high correlation between value-added and inventive activity. Similarly, he found a high correlation between data on gross investment in agriculture and patents issued. These findings provide some basis for concluding that inventive activity in agriculture was determined by market forces, although the question of a more specific relationship remains open.

It is one thing to emphasize the role of market forces in the allocation of inventive activity and the composition of patents issued and another to emphasize the direct influence of market pressure on the innovation or commercial adoption of new techniques of production. In fact, as in the case of manufacturing development, the emphasis in discussions of agricultural development has tended to be on the growth of output and productivity change. This stress implies that innovation, not invention, is the more important concept, if only because not every invention is commercially successful. Therefore, more significant than the pace of inventive activity is the fact that the adoption and diffusion of mechanical inventions in the agricultural sector increased rapidly during the last half of the nineteenth century.[7]

Many of the most significant mechanical inventions of this period were developed for grain farming, and the following discussion is oriented largely around new equipment applied in raising wheat, oats, and corn. The mechanical inventions can be classified by function as (i) soil preparation and planting, (ii) harvesting, and (iii) postharvesting. The sequence of operations in the agricultural year imposed differential demands for labor, with peak-period demands in harvesting for small grains and cultivation for corn. Improvements in all three stages of this sequence led ultimately to an increase in the acreage which one man could farm. By the 1870s all stages of grain production took place with the aid of horse-drawn machinery.

To expedite soil preparation and planting, plows, seed-drills, harrows and cultivators were developed. In prairie agriculture the development of a strong, light plow was imperative. Western lands were characterized by a thick sod which was tough to break and by heavy soils which stuck to the plow moldboard when wet and became too hard to plow when dry. The first steel plow—steel plate combined with wood—is generally credited to John Deere in 1837, and it was followed by the sulky plow, which permitted the farmer to ride behind his horses. The chilled-iron plow was invented in 1867 by James Oliver and was followed by the chilled-steel plow. This was a distinct improvement over the older iron or steel moldboard and wooden plow. In addition seed drills, available as early as the 1840s, were in fairly common use by the 1870s. Horse-drawn cultivators had replaced the hoe and human labor in both corn and cotton by 1860. Straight-toothed harrows were used in preparing plowed fields for seeding. The spring-tooth harrow was invented in 1869 and was soon followed by the disc-harrow, and these found some use in the 1870s.

Harvesting of wheat and oats involved reaping, raking, binding, and shocking activities. For corn, picking and husking were involved. Mowing machines, reapers, binders and corn-harvesters were all experimented with and innovated during this period. The mechanical reaper had been invented in crude form as a wheeled platform with a cutting edge independently in the 1830s by Cyrus McCormick and Obed Hussey, and by the 1850s, the mechanical reaper was in widespread use for small-grain farming in the Midwest.[8] The early reapers delivered cut grain to a platform from which the grain was raked to the ground at first by hand and by the 1850s by the machine itself. Subsequently, in the 1860s binding was done from the platform by hand labor. The major further advance was the development of the automatic binder, culminating in the twine-binder in 1878; self-binding had become fairly widespread by 1880. The combine followed soon afterwards.

Postharvesting activities included threshing and winnowing or fanning of small grains, and corn shelling. Threshing was less urgent than reaping since grain was fairly safe once placed in the stack or mow, and could be completed during the farmer's off-season. Threshing and fanning mills were developed between 1840 and 1880, and refinements included the application of the steam engine in the 1870s. To sum up, Allan Bogue writes:

> The economic and social implications of mechanization were great. Most obvious and most stressed, of course, was the saving of human labor or increase in productive potential that came from shifting work previously done by human muscle to iron hands and straining animals. The man who could sickle less than an acre of grain in a day could cradle at least two; place him on the seat of a Virginia reaper, and he could cut ten to fifteen acres per day, with the aid of one man to rake the grain clear from the table. By the 1860s, the self-rake reaper had eliminated even these men. With the flail, one man labored all day to separate some seven bushels of wheat from its straw. Using horses to tread the grain, he could raise his product to fifteen bushels. The horse-powered, custom threshing machine of the late 1860s more than doubled this output, and the figure rose still more during the succeeding decade.[9]

The application of machinery to the corn crop was somewhat different from the experience in small-grain farming. Implements had been developed by the 1830s which greatly increased the productivity of labor in planting and cultivating corn, but corn-harvesting machinery presented a dilemma. The major reason was that corn picking involved operations which were inherently difficult to mechanize, although the fact that there were no peak-period labor requirements for corn harvesting may have had some impact.

Certain features are common to nineteenth century mechanization. First, much of the machinery was especially suited for the flat geographic terrain of the Midwest. Small-grain agriculture dominated this area by 1890, and this pattern of regional specialization was apparently a function of the innovation and widespread diffusion of agricultural machinery peculiarly suited for use in the area. In particular, the fall in labor costs associated with mechanization made possible concentration on small-grains production.

Second, from the technological point of view, mechanization in grain harvesting was made easier because it was a straightforward matter to machine-duplicate the sweeping actions involved in reaping. On the other hand, problems delayed the development of mechanical devices when they were required to duplicate the picking or grasping motion of the human hand—for example, in cotton picking, corn picking, and in the milking of dairy cattle. These activities were slow to be mechanized.

Third, the application of mechanical sources of power to agricultural acitivity was largely unsuccessful in the nineteenth century. To a limited degree, steam engines were employed in plowing and harvesting, but the steam engine's applicability was limited by its poor power-to-weight ratio and because it was so cumbersome. It was used, in its stationary form, in threshing and winnowing the harvested crop, but as a source of mobile power it could not compete with the horse. Horse-drawn farm equipment remained ascendant until World War I. In fact, the adjustment of mechanical power sources to agricultural machinery had to await the twentieth century application of the internal-combustion engine to the tractor and the truck which were adapted to the family-size farm, and the development of rural electrification.

Finally, there is the question of the role played by factor endowments in the development of mechanized agriculture. The Habbakuk thesis that factor endowments in the United States explained the propensity of Americans to invent and innovate labor-saving devices in manufacturing is pertinent to agriculture as well. The same factor endowments held for agriculture, and Habbakuk's thesis could be extended to provide an economic "explanation" of a labor-saving bias in American agricultural inventions and innovations as an adjustment to factor proportions—in particular, the relatively high price of labor. In this case, after Habbakuk, American agricultural inventions would have been labor-saving by design. The case of mechanization of peak-period activities like small-grain harvesting which was very demanding of labor time comes to mind.

The objections raised earlier to the Habbakuk thesis with respect to technological change in manufacturing can be made to its extension to agriculture. As we saw, inventive and innovative activity is factor-saving *ex ante*, and only *ex post* can it be classified as either labor-saving or capital-saving.

However, there may have been external effects from technological progress in the manufacturing sector on agricultural technology. The gains in agricultural technology may simply have represented agriculture's share in the general advance of machine technology. Of course, one great advantage of advances in machine technology was that new machines were patentable, and could be embodied in specific marketable forms which found ready use in all farming areas. Consequently, a disproportionate share of inventive activity may have been devoted to the development of agricultural machinery for this reason. In any case, mechanical techniques developed rapidly compared with the belated development of improved seeds, fertilizers, and farm practices. These inputs tended to be more specific in their applicability because of the effect of local variations in soil and climate and the need to await the prerequisite scientific advances in biochemistry and genetics.

Agricultural Organization and Practices

With the exception of cotton in the South, the American agricultural sector has always featured the owner-operator in which farm acreage and equipment were under the direction of a single-farm family sometimes working with one or a few hired hands. Thus, the family farm continued to be the primary organizational form in the Northeast and Midwest in the nineteenth and early twentieth centuries.

The family farm is identified with independence and self-sufficiency. Independence and self-sufficiency may still have characterized the family farm in the immediate post-Civil War period, but increasingly the farmer was brought inexorably into the market economy. Not only was a larger portion of farm output produced for commercial markets, but also increasing product specialization implied the destruction of self-sufficiency. Many former farm functions were absorbed by the manufacturing and services sectors. For example, many domestic "industrial" activities such as the production of home-spun yarn and clothing and canned preserves were substituted by purchased goods. A larger portion of the farm family's consumer needs were being met in the market place. More importantly, the semimanufacture of many farm products was eroded by commercial enterprise. For example, farm slaughtering of livestock, customary in the pre-Civil War period, was rapidly displaced in the 1860s by local, commercialized, slaughtering activity and then by centralized slaughtering with consolidation of meatpacking in giant firms like Swift. Finally, in this period, the farmer became increasingly concerned with the purchase of specialized inputs, both services and equipment. In prairie agriculture, professional sod-busting crews who would break the tough prairie sod for the initial plowing and professional threshing crews of migratory workers in the harvesting season were common place as early as the 1850s. With the development of the internal-combustion engine and growing dependence on the tractor and truck, the farmer was forced into the market on a continuing basis for the purchase of fuel and repair services. These pressures were subsequently reinforced by rural electrification, the growing use of chemical fertilizers, and greater recourse to purchased capital goods.

Some changes in the nature of farm holdings did occur. Increased tenancy rates in agriculture from 1880 to 1920 are often cited by writers who argue that the family farm was not an ubiquitous form of ownership in the American Midwest.[10] However, tenant farmers in this area did work their farms along family-farm lines. Some early examples of corporate farming occurred first with the development of large "bonanza" farms in the Dakotas in the 1880s and then again beginning in the 1920s.[11]

The discovery and application of better farming practices is an important aspect of agricultural organization. Three sources of improved practice stand out. The first was the familiar "demonstration effect": individual farmers, generally prosperous ones, were the customary source of improved practices. Experimentation was the route whereby the "proper" season for breaking prairie sod, the "best" depth of the breaking furrow, the "prime" sowing time, and the "highest yield" seed grain were found. Improved practices were disseminated primarily through the forum of neighborhood discussion and observation. In any case, improved farming practices were not easy to conceal or monopolize.

In addition, local newspapers and periodicals contained guidelines for farmers in advice columns by agricultural experts and journalists, factual reports of grain and market activities, and advertisements. Agricultural periodicals carried reports on a wide selection of agricultural matters. State agricultural societies and state and county fairs exhibited crops and livestock, displayed machinery, and presented speeches by agricultural experts, including successful farmers and representatives of agricultural colleges and farm organizations.[12]

Finally, farmers' organizations and government-supported agricultural institutions emphasized the importance of better farm practices. The Patrons of Husbandry (or the Grange) were extremely concerned with the education of farmers in better agricultural practices. The agricultural colleges established under the Morrill Act (1862) and the agricultural experiment stations established under the Hatch Act (1887) were instrumental in the dissemination of careful farm practices. By 1900 these agencies had thoroughly investigated the principles of scientific rotation of crops and had actively publicized the need for conservation of moisture and top soil in plains agriculture through dry farming techniques.

Careful practices appear to have spread slowly. Some techniques were peculiar to local climate and soil conditions and to different types of crops, and this hindered diffusion. Moreover, in the early years of agriculture, improved practices did not appear to be important, largely because of the original fertility of the soil. In particular, little attention was paid to good crop rotation and plowing techniques in early midwestern commercial agriculture. Later, careful practices spread as the soil was deprived of its original fertility.

If the typical American agriculturist was so market-oriented, why did careful practices spread so slowly? The slow development of soil management probably reflected the farmers' initial focus on the efficient use of fertile lands before problems of soil conservation became apparent with repeated cropping. For example, many farmers appear to have believed that the recently broken western soils did not need manuring, and this belief was corroborated by the results of experiments at the Illinois Experiment Station in the late 1880s which showed that manure and commercial fertilizers did not influence yields sufficiently to justify their application. Moreover, specific locational factors—including variations in soil conditions, climate, and other growing conditions—retarded dissemination. It was late in the nineteenth century before the pejorative use of "book farming" had largely disappeared from common usage.

Agricultural Research

The development of "scientific" agriculture and agricultural research has been mostly a twentieth century phenomenon. Advances in soil chemistry and the development of new seeds and animal strains have made possible more intensive utilization of farm acreage and increased outputs per acre.

Why did developments in scientific agriculture lag behind advances in mechanization? Clearly, the reason is that the "life" processes are inherently more complicated than mechanical processes. As a result, a prerequisite of the development of scientific agriculture was increased investment in human capital and the progress of scientific knowledge in genetics and biochemistry. These sciences were in a crude state in the nineteenth century, and were not sufficiently advanced to permit scientific agricultural research until the twentieth century.

In the nineteenth century agricultural research proceeded largely on the basis of trial and error methods. Such methods were characterized by high risk. Although individual farmers experimented with improved practices, the federal and state governments played an important role by establishing institutions which sponsored agricultural research and disseminated the results. The first State Department of Agriculture was established by Georgia in 1874, and North Dakota in 1889 founded the first "Northern" department. State governments were primarily concerned with agricultural education. On the federal level the United States Department of Agriculture was established in 1862 and elevated to Cabinet status in 1889. Many divisions or bureaus were established to undertake specialized research and testing. The divisions of Chemistry in 1862, Statistics in 1863, Entomology in 1863, Botany in 1868, and Plant Pathology in 1888 were the most important creations in the nineteenth century. After 1900 the bureaus of Weather, Animal Industry (which investigated tick fever, bovine tuberculosis and hog cholera), and Plant Industry (which inquired after the eradication of plant disease and the suitability of new foreign plants and introduced short-kernel rice, drought-resistant durum wheat, alfalfa, and seedless grapes) were established.

Government attempts to sponsor research and disseminate results had a practical orientation from the beginning. The Morrill Act (1862) saw the federal government endow state governments with parts of the national domain for the establishment of agricultural colleges. it was followed by the second Morrill Act (1890) and the Nelson Amendment (1907) which increased the colleges' financial support. In the land-grant colleges, agricultural teaching and research was emphasized. The agricultural experiment stations were introduced under the Hatch Act (1887) and extended by the Adams Act (1906). The type of research done in the stations was practical and reflected differences in local conditions. For example, the experiment station in Illinois published results of tests on several varieties of seed corn in the late 1890s and recommended varieties particularly suited to the various regions of the state to farmers. Another interesting example is the active role played by stations in Minnesota and Wisconsin in the development of hybrid corns in the 1930s.

The sponsoring of research was only one of the responsibilities of these institutions. The communication of results to the farmers was another extremely important activity. Dissemination of research results was achieved through official publications and local demonstrations sponsored by government agencies. After 1902 many of these activities were directed by the Office of Farm Management under the Federal Department of Agriculture. Subsequently the Smith-Lever Act (1914) promoted cooperative extension work through county agents, in order to get research results directly to the farmer and to facilitate adaptation to local conditions. These efforts culminated in the establishment of the Agricultural Extension Service in 1923.

Finally, governmental activity included regulatory functions over grades and standards in agricultural production and distribution. Branches of the Federal Department of Agriculture gradually developed responsibility for regulatory activities. The Bureau of Animal Industry, for example, was authorized in 1884 to regulate the shipment of livestock, but the authorization proved to be inadequate until the passage of the Meat Inspection Act (1906) and extension to dairy exports in 1908. The Pure Food and Drug Act (1906), the Grain Standards Act (1916), the Cotton Futures Act (1914, revised 1916), and the Warehouse Act (1916) all extended government regulatory functions.

Case Studies of Productivity Growth and Diffusion

This section examines three case studies of productivity advance in American agriculture in the nineteenth and twentieth centuries. The first is a study of labor productivity growth in small-grain and corn production between 1840 and 1910, the second deals with changes in labor productivity in dairy farming between 1850 and 1910, and the third concerns influences on the rate of adoption and diffusion of hybrid corn beginning in the 1930s.

Grain farming, 1840-1910[3]

In their classic study, Parker and Klein began with the premise that productivity growth in grain production derived largely from westward expansion and technological change in the nineteenth century. Fortunately, sufficient data existed to permit an estimate of the growth of labor productivity and the relative importance of other factors contributing to increased productivity in grain farming.

The three major grain crops — wheat, oats, and corn — accounted for about 55 percent of the land harvested in the United States in 1910, and between 1840 and 1910 their outputs increased by 653 percent, 690 percent, and 695 percent, respectively. For these terminal dates, data on labor inputs by activity and by region were compiled. Next, they were combined with estimates of the growth in output per man-hour for each crop, for the regions and for the United States as a whole. The study estimated changes in labor productivity only, since difficulties with data on capital inputs precluded the specification of an aggregate production function for grain farming and the concomitant estimation of total factor productivity increase.

Two basic sets of factors are considered to have been responsible for productivity growth: the growth in the supply of productive factors and improvements in knowledge about the most efficacious ways of combining them in production. The increase in factor supplies in the nineteenth century was dominated by the "westward movement" of the agricultural frontier which brought new areas under cultivation. The movement of small-grain farming into western lands is thought to have increased output per unit of labor, assuming that the movement was into lands of relatively higher average fertility than lands already being cultivated in grains and that increased regional specialization occurred. Technological developments, especially mechanization and improvements in agricultural implements, are thought to have increased labor productivity as well.

The data for 1840 reflect farming conditions before the major westward movement and most important mechanical changes took place, whereas by 1910 most of the significant mechanical inventions in grain farming were widely disseminated and the western frontier had largely disappeared.

The Parker-Klein analysis involved the use of *ceteris paribus* assumptions in which each element was allowed to vary and to influence output growth in turn, the others remaining unchanged by assumption. Parker and Klein then asked, how would productivity have changed from the level of the 1840s if westward movement alone had taken place without technological change, and how would productivity have changed from the 1840s if technological change alone had occurred in the absence of westward expansion?[14]

Labor-using agricultural operations were divided into three groups: soil preparation and cultivation, operations on the standing crop, and those on the harvested crop. Preharvest operations on wheat and oats were defined to include plowing, sowing, and harrowing, and for corn to include field preparation, planting, and hoeing or cultivating. Per acre labor inputs in these activities were assumed to be fixed, given the state of technology. Harvest activities, which were also assumed to be fixed per acre, were defined for wheat and oats as reaping, raking, binding and shocking, and for corn as picking or husking. Finally, postharvest activities, fixed in terms of labor requirements per bushel under given technological conditions, included threshing and winnowing of wheat and oats and shelling of corn.

Table 6.2 shows significant increases in the indexes of labor productivity from 1840 to 1910 for all three grains. The labor productivity index in wheat reached 417 in 1910 compared with the base value in 1840. For oats the corresponding index reached 363 and for corn, 365. What was the relative importance of the various contributing factors to productivity growth? The index for each grain was constructed of three parts: (1) average labor requirements per acre in each region; (2) average crop yield per acre in each region; (3) the importance of each region in national output. These components of the overall index provided the required information.

In essence, the partitioning proceeded as follows. Consider the case of westward movement alone. Labor inputs per acre and grain output per acre were assumed to be constant at their 1840 levels in each region, and each region was weighted by its share of national output in 1910. This was equivalent to assuming that westward movement occurred in the absence of technological change in small-grain farming. Derived in this way, the index of labor productivity depicted in Table 6.2 shows that only a small portion of the total increase in labor productivity was due to westward expansion: for wheat, the index was 109, for oats 123, and for corn 130. In other words, little productivity increase would have occurred because of the movement to western lands alone.

Again, the effect on labor productivity of more capital per worker and improved methods were considered separately, where improved methods were defined to include better farming practices, seed and livestock breeds, and equipment. Productivity increase not accounted for by westward movement was allocated between changes in yields in each region and reductions in labor inputs per acre due to mechanization. Yields per acre changed little: with labor inputs per acre and the regional distribution of acreage held at the 1840 level, the application of 1910 yield levels produced indexes showing only a slight increase in labor productivity in wheat to 118, in oats to 106, and in corn to 119. The effect of westward movement and improvement in crop yields combined raised the indexes to 118, 118, and 143 for wheat, oats, and corn respectively. This left the remaining large increase in labor productivity to be explained by mechanization and by any further interaction effects among the sources of productivity change.

The effect of mechanization alone was very substantial, producing an index for wheat of 246, for oats of 186, and for corn of 227. Moreover, to the extent that much of the machine technology developed for grain farming was particularly suited to the terrain of the Midwest, mechanization and westward movement should be considered together. The indexes showing the combined effects of westward movement and mechanization are 377 for wheat, 372 for oats, and 330 for corn.

Thus the mechanization of grain farming was found to be the single

Table 6.2 Productivity Growth in Grain Farming, 1840-1910

	Indexes Showing Separate Effects of:					
Crop	**Total labour productivity**	**Regional shift**	**Yield Increases**	**Mechanization**	**Regional shift and yield increases combined**	**Mechanization and regional shift combined**
Wheat	417	109	118	246	118	377
Oats	363	123	106	186	118	372
Corn	365	130	119	227	143	330

SOURCE: William N. Parker, "Productivity Growth in American Grain Farming: An Analysis of its Nineteenth Century Sources," in Fogel and Engerman, eds., *The Reinterpretation of American Economic History,* pp. 177, 181.

most important factor in explaining the growth of labor productivity. For wheat and oats, the greater importance of the mechanization of harvesting and threshing operations stands out compared with advances in plowing and planting. For corn, the greatest gains were in preharvest operations, especially in the mechanization of planting and cultivation of young plants, which allowed the abandonment of hoe cultivation.

Dairy farming, 1850-1910[15]

In 1850 almost all American dairying was noncommercial, and was conducted essentially as an adjunct of rural and town self-sufficiency, providing milk, butter and cheese for the family. Local markets were small, and perishability coupled with poor transport conditions restricted the size of any given market to a few miles. Specialized dairy cattle had not yet been introduced.

By 1910, however, dairying had become a significant branch of commercial agriculture, with production of fluid milk, butter and cheese for urban markets, with some regional specialization and some specialization within regions as well. Fluid milk was typically produced by farms located close to markets and butter and cheese on more distant farms. An interesting contrast emerges with the Parker-Klein study in that there were virtually no mechanical improvements in dairying before 1900. Most of the influence on dairy output came from improved feeding, care, and breeding practices—all of which were very labor-intensive—and these advances are reflected in improved animal yields rather than in increased labor productivity.

Bateman first estimated the growth in the average milk yield per animal to be about fifty percent between 1850 and 1910. The changes in national average milk yield per cow are summarized in table 6.3. The

Table 6.3 Average Milk Yields per Cow in the United States, 1850-1910

Year	Average Yield per Cow (pounds per year)
1850	2371
1860	2559
1870	2670
1880	2797
1890	3050
1900	3352
1910	3570

SOURCE: Fred Bateman, "Improvement in American Dairy Farming, 1850-1910: A Quantitative Analysis," p. 257.

potential sources of growth in milk output were the lengthening of the annual milking season resulting from the commercialization of dairying, advances in the care and feeding of dairy cattle and in breeding and breeds, the diffusion of better techniques to regions where poor practices had prevailed in 1850, and the interstate relocation of dairying activity (that is, the dairying equivalent of the "westward" movement of small-grain farming).

In attempting to determine the relative importance of these sources of increased yield per cow, Bateman employed the partitioning technique used in the Parker-Klein study. First, he examined the effect of the westward movement of dairying; that is, he asked how the national average milk yield per animal would have changed between 1850 and 1910 if there had been no advance in technique and no spread of techniques in a westward-moving dairy agriculture. A constant level of techniques was simulated by holding state average yields constant at their 1850 levels. The effects of westward expansion were then quantified by examining the percentage change in the national dairy herd located in each state: there was a relative increase over the period in the proportion of all dairy cattle in medium-yield and no-yield states as of 1850, and a decrease in the proportion in high-yield states. In other words, the effect of westward expansion alone was to reduce average yields per animal, Westward expansion was significant only as it interacted with and induced improvements in dairying techniques.

The advance and diffusion of techniques was regarded as a product of increased commercialization of dairy farming. Commercialization presented farmers with an incentive to introduce new techniques and to imitate practices which raised annual yields per animal. Bateman pointed out that there were really no major advances in breeding methods or breeds, nor any noticeable change in the rate of diffusion of superior dairy breeds during the period. Some improvements occurred slowly until the mid-1880s, with a slight quickening thereafter. However, there were decided improvements in the care and feeding of dairy animals throughout the period, with the most notable changes being a lessened reliance on natural pasturage and more emphasis on commerical feeds and balanced feeding programs. These changes were widely diffused during the period. Bateman's calculations indicate that, in comparison with the 1850 milking season, the increased daily yield per animal associated with improved care and feeding amounted to nineteen percentage points of the increase in the national average yield per animal from 1850 to 1910.

Bateman also assessed the impact on average yields of the lengthening of the annual milking season. In 1850 cows were milked an average of

237 days per year, and were allowed to "go dry" over the winter months. With the growth of the market for fluid milk and milk products and with improvements in transportation, the average milking season averaged about 300 days in 1910. The increase in the milking season was found to be the single most important source of increasing animal yield, accounting for twenty-seven percentage points of the fifty percent increase in average milk yield.

Finally, the interaction or combined effects of the increase in the milking season and improved daily yields resulting from improved care and feeding accounted for the balance of yield increases. In sum, of the average increase in yield of 1199 pounds of milk per animal from 1850 to 1910, the extended milking season represented 629 pounds, increased daily yields represented 449 pounds, and their combined effects accounted for the remaining 121 pounds.

Bateman then proceeded to employ his output series together with estimates of average annual labor input per animal to assess the changes in average labor productivity in dairy farming for the period. In fact the sources of higher yields were associated with larger daily and annual inputs of labor time. The increase in the amount of labor input required per animal reflected the slow progress made towards labor-saving mechanization in dairying. According to Bateman, this was based partly on technical difficulties with, for example, machine-milking. It was also related partly to the possibility that the opportunity cost of labor in dairying may have been low—farmers may have performed dairying tasks only when other farm chores permitted, and women and children could be used in milking and other aspects of dairying owing to the lightness of the work.

Bateman made estimates of labor input for milking, and care and feeding. Milking time per animal appears to have been invariant between high-yielding and low-yielding animals, but increased in proportion to the increase in the average milking season from 237 days in 1850 to 300 days in 1910. This accounted for an increase in average annual milking time from some 50 hours per animal in 1850 to about 75 hours in 1910.

Changes in care and feeding accounted for an even larger increase in labor time. Average care and feeding time per animal was estimated by Bateman to have increased from approximately eighteen hours annually in 1850 to about sixty-six hours in 1910. Daily feeding and care varied among farms and regions according to the degree of emphasis placed on dairying, climate, herd size, and sanitation regulations. Between 1850 and 1910 no important changes were introduced to reduce time spent on animal care; rather, there were some developments which tended to increase labor time, among them, more restrictive sanitation regulations and the development of specialized winter dairying especially in the Northeast and the Midwest (winter being a season when labor requirements were relatively high and milk yields relatively low).

Thus, the total labor time per cow increased from some 77 hours annually in 1850 to almost 141 hours in 1910. There was some regional variation in labor inputs per animal, the figures being relatively high in the Northeast and Midwest, regions of more severe climatic conditions and greater economic significance of dairy farming.

Bateman's estimates of labor productivity for 1850 and 1910, presented in table 6.4, were "startling" in that direct labor productivity was found to have declined between 1850 and 1910, because the methods by which average annual yields were increased involved greater use of labor through the lengthening of the milking season and improvements in sanitation, care and feeding. The primary impact resulted from the increase in nonmilking labor requirements rather than milking operations.

Why would farmers continue to expand output under conditions of declining labor productivity? Bateman explains that the farmer's attention was focused primarily on the annual milk yield per animal, and this emphasis was encouraged by the apparently low opportunity cost of labor in dairying. The increase in national milk production per animal possibly reflected a reduction in farm underemployment of women and children. Nevertheless, Bateman's conclusion that labor productivity in dairy farming was decreasing over the period and his neglect of the productivities of nonlabor inputs and total factor productivity indicate the need for further research in this area.[16]

Hybrid corn, 1930s and 1940s[17]

Identifying the determinants of the invention, innovation and diffusion of new agricultural products is indispensable for understanding the process of agricultural development. The discovery and subsequent supremacy of hybrid corn provides a particularly dramatic example.

Hybrid corn was first introduced on a substantial commercial scale in the early 1930s, and was rapidly diffused through the Corn Belt and to other areas, although its rate of diffusion varied regionally. For all states the diffusion of hybrid corn tended to follow an S-shaped growth curve: that is, the rate of growth of adoption was slow but accelerating at first, reached a peak, and slowed down once again as adoptions approached the equilibrium level.[1]

After the data for different states had been summarized in this way, the geographical differences in the parameters of the S-curves were analyzed. First, the date of availability of hybrid corn was not homogeneous throughout the United States. In fact, with all agricultural

Table 6.4 Labor Productivity in Dairy Farming, 1850 and 1910

		Milking Labor Productivity			Total Labor Productivity		
Year	**Annual average yield per cow (pounds)**	**Annual average Milking labor time (man-hours)**	**Milking labor per 100 pounds of milk (man-hours)**	**Milk output per milking man-hour (pounds)**	**Annual average total labor time (man-hours)**	**Total labor per 100 pounds of milk (man-hours)**	**Milk output per labor hour (pounds)**
1850	2371	59.25	2.50	40.20	77.04	3.25	30.78
1910	3570	75.00	2.10	47.60	140.60	3.94	25.39

SOURCE: Fred Bateman, "Labor Inputs and Productivity in American Dairy Agriculture, 1850-1910," pp. 221-222.

hybrids development must be carried out separately in each region because of the importance of climatic and soil variations. For a given area, the date at which commercial quantities of superior hybrid seed were first produced was one major determinant of adoption. Griliches regarded a ten-percent planting of corn acreage in hybrid corn as the date at which superior hybrids became available commercially to farmers. Thus, superior breeds became available in Iowa, Illinois, and other parts of the Corn Belt in the mid-1930s compared with the late 1940s in the South.

What explains differences in the date of availability (the origins of the S-curves) in the various states? Griliches argued that hybrid corn seed became widely available at different dates because of economic factors. Innovators among seed producers began production where the expected profits from hybrid corn were greatest. Thus, "good" corn-raising areas were developed ahead of "poor" corn areas; expected profits from the commercial production of hybrid seed were greatest in the Corn Belt of Iowa, Illinois, and Nebraska because the potential market among farmers was largest there.

Along with market size, availability was represented as a function of cost of access to the regional market. The market for corn seed was measured by the density of corn acreage in 1949 and by the density of corn pickers in use on farms. There was a high correlation between early availability of hybrid seed and market density; the lower the market density, the later the date of entry of hybrid corn into an area, and vice versa. Deviations in the correlation between the diffusion of hybrid corn and market density were explained by the cost of entry, which depended on how different an area was from those already entered, and on whether agricultural experiment stations had already developed hybrids adaptable to the area. Cost factors were likely to be similar in contiguous geographical areas. The spread of hybrid corn was more rapid latitudinally than longitudinally, because the length of the growing season was an important determinant of a particular hybrid's adaptability. Moreover, movement northwards tended to be faster than movement southwards because of the existence of larger markets for hybrid seed in the North and the special role that the Minnesota and Wisconsin Experiment Stations had played in the development of hybrid seeds.

Even when hybrid corn became widely available, rates of acceptance (the slope coefficients of the S-curves) by farmers in the several areas varied from high values in the Corn Belt to low values in some regions of the South. These variations, Griliches argued, were explained by demand phenomena — the amount of profit expected to be realized by the farmer in changing from open-pollinated to hybrid corn. Profitability was assumed to depend upon the absolute superiority of hybrids in corn yield in bushels per acre, and on the average number of acres per farm planted in corn. Hybrids tended to outyield open-pollinated corns by fifteen to twenty percent. Rates of acceptance were correlated with yields per acre (the higher the yield per acre with open-pollinated corn, *ceteris paribus*, the higher the increment in total output with hybrids and the more rapid the rate of adoption of hybrid corn) and with acres in corn per farm.

Finally, equilibrium levels of the percentage of total corn acreage planted in hybrid seed (the ceiling levels of the S-curves) were explained. Regional differences in the proportion of acreage planted in hybrids in the late 1950s varied from almost one hundred percent in the Corn Belt to levels of from thirty to eighty percent elsewhere. These differences were explained by differences in the average profit realized by farmers from the shift to hybrids. Areas of high average profit were also areas of low risk of loss from such a shift, whereas marginal areas were associated with greater variability in yields and a higher risk of loss. Variations in the ceilings by region, then, were explained in large part by the absolute superiority in yield of hybrids and the average number of acres in corn per farm.

Griliches has also investigated the social rate of return on public and private funds invested in research leading to the development of hybrid corn.[19] After compiling data on private and public research expenditures on hybrid corn from 1910 to 1955, Griliches estimated the annual social returns to hybrid corn as the value to society of the increase in corn output resulting from its adoption. Subtraction from these annual gross returns of the additional annual cost of producing hybrid seed compared with open-pollinated seed resulted in estimates of the annual flow of net social returns. The rate of return was calculated as that which equalized the present value of the flow of net returns with the calculated value of research expenditures. His results indicated that a social rate of return of at least seven hundred per cent per year was being earned on the average dollar invested in hybrid corn research. As Griliches concluded, his results confirmed that hybrid corn research was undoubtedly one of the most socially profitable uses of funds ever.

An Aside: Agriculture in the Postbellum South[20]

The southern regional economy lagged behind economic progress in the rest of the country from the Civil War to 1930. Easterlin's estimates of personal income per capita presented earlier in chapter 2, table 6, show that southern incomes fell from seventy-two percent of the national average in 1860 to a bare fifty-one percent in 1900, recovering only slightly to fifty-five percent by 1930. Indexes of manufacturing activity show relatively low levels of value added and capital invested per worker in the South. But it is to agriculture, historically by far the largest sector in the southern economy, that the source of poor economic performance is usually traced—and in particular to the "overproduction" of cotton and failure to diversify agricultural production before the First World War. These problems were most serious in the Cotton Belt of the deep South. For example, the growth of agricultural output in five cotton states is depicted in table 6.5 which shows clearly the devastating impact of the Civil War, the partial recovery by 1880, and the slow growth of output through the rest of the century. In fact, southern crop output grew much less rapidly than agricultural output elsewhere in America, and much less rapidly than United States Gross National Product.

Why did southern agricultural performance lag during this period behind the rest of the country? The traditional argument is that, with the collapse of the plantation system and the financial and marketing system based upon it, there emerged in the postbellum South new economic institutions — tenancy, share-cropping, and the crop-lien — which reinforced the South's dependence on cotton and kept the southern farmer in poverty. The most interesting analysis of these developments is Ransom and Sutch's *One Kind of Freedom.*[21]

According to Ransom and Sutch, the nature of emancipation proved to have sinister implications for the future economic development of the South. While blacks made immediate welfare gains in the form of increased income, leisure, and independence after emancipation, they were provided with little opportunity to make further gains. The legacy of slavery was lack of land, capital, and education, and together with the continuing climate of racism, these factors limited nonagricultural employment opportunities and sorely constrained their range of

Table 6.5 Per Capita Crop Output by Decades for Five Cotton States, 1859-1900

Years	Index of Physical crop output per capita 1859 = 100	Annual growth rate (%)
1859	100.0	
		-6.3
1868-70	52.0	
		2.0
1878-80	63.5	
		1.4
1888-90	73.3	
		0.3
1898-1900	75.3	

SOURCE: Roger L. Ransom and Richard Sutch, *One Find of Freedom: The Economic Consequences of Emancipation* (New York: Cambridge University Press, 1977), p. 10.

agricultural choices to wage labor or various forms of tenancy. Indeed, the most common outcome was tenancy on either a fixed rent or sharecropping basis, usually the latter.[22] Tenancy implies a commitment to make cash payments (as does indebtedness), and it is clear that southern farmers became more specialized in cotton during the postbellum period when the world demand for cotton was growing slowly.[23]

One implication of tenancy arrangements was an emphasis on maximizing current yields since all tenancy arrangements were based on a one-year term. As a result, throughout the South, there was a lack of investment in improving the land (drainage, fencing, fallowing, and so forth) and farm capital formation. Expected returns from investment by either the landlord or tenant would have to be shared with the other party, and the tenant in particular had no security of tenure beyond his annual term in which to reap the benefits. Consequently, southern farmers used liberal amounts of fertilizer to increase yields but gave little thought to the long-term consequences of poor farming practices.

Tenancy was but one of the economic institutions established in the postwar decade which were to hamper both black and white farmers in their pursuit of prosperity and independence, although ultimately they bore more heavily on blacks. A second development was the replacement of the prewar financial and marketing structure based on the cotton factor by the rise of small, rural merchants who were able to exert local monopoly power over credit supply and to influence crop choices through the crop-lien system.

This new financial and marketing organization was based on local market requirements. In addition to selling food and general merchandise, the local merchant supplied short-term credit to tenant farmers who lacked capital. In fact, the merchant advanced goods on credit to the farmer to finance his consumption and precrop outlays before harvest. The farmer's collateral took the form of a lien on his future crop. This gave the merchant two forms of leverage and potential sources of profit. First, he sold goods under a two-price system — cash prices and credit prices. The tenant farmer had little choice but to buy on credit, and found himself paying high implicit interest rates. Second, the merchant invariably insisted that this lien be held against a cash crop, normally cotton, which limited the farmer's ability to grow his own foodstuffs and escape the need to buy food from the merchant. The local merchant possessed a "territorial monopoly" which he was able to enforce by acting as sole supplier of credit. The result was an "overproduction" of cotton at the expense of self-sufficiency and diversification, a "trap of debt peonage" which became endemic to southern agriculture.[24] It is one of the great ironies of American history that the grip of cotton, if anything, was strengthened after the Civil War by the new institutions arising from the ashes of the plantation system and slavery.

The root cause of southern rural poverty was institutional according to Ransom and Sutch. The nature of economic institutions explains why both black and white tenants had limited opportunity and incentive for breaking away from the debt-cash crop cycle, and investment in land improvement and rural capital formation suffered accordingly. However, some writers have taken issue with this emphasis on the determining role of economic institutions, notably Robert Higgs. In *Competition and Coercion*[25], Higgs emphasizes the real progress made by blacks under the stimulus of the competitive market economy. Higgs believes that tenancy, share-cropping, and the crop-lien system were all rational tools of the market rather than interfering with it, and consequently these institutional arrangements cannot be regarded as the source of southern economic problems. Rather, largely because of labor scarcity, relative black incomes rose from 1865 to 1914. But the gap between black and white incomes did not close much, and Higgs acknowledges that blacks operated under more constraints in the labor market than whites because of racial discrimination. In fact, Higgs concludes that blacks had to "tread lightly," to behave carefully and with caution, "the very antithesis of that aggressive, pushing behavior for which economically successful Americans have been justly famous."[26] Perhaps no more telling indictment of the economic consequences of discrimination can be made!

Many issues have yet to be resolved. Whether southern farmers voluntarily abandoned self-sufficiency in the hope of clearing their debts and achieving independence, or whether they were "forced" by their creditors into dependence on the cotton market when they preferred self-sufficiency, remains a point of contention. Whether black poverty resulted from the triumph of an iniquitous social institution—racism—over benign, competitive market forces, or whether southern rural poverty was the product of the new postwar institutions is also unresolved. But in a sense these are secondary issues. The fact remains that, whatever the reason, the southern agricultural economy lay moribund until the eve of the First World War. Only then did a set of exogenous forces—the bollweevil pest which induced diversification away from cotton, and improved transportation and wartime demand for labor which spurred northward and rural-urban migration—present southern agriculture with a new lease on progress.

Conclusion

Important technological and organizational changes took place in American agriculture between 1870 and 1930. Westward expansion greatly increased the supply of agricultural land. Patterns of regional specialization developed in response to the increased size and complexity of markets, and growth was increasingly dependent on the domestic market and, in particular, urbanization. Productivity increase was generated by improved farming techniques, especially mechanization which reduced labor requirements per acre and released labor for employment in the manufacturing and services sectors. The spread of better farming practices depended largely upon trial and error experimentation and informal neighborly contacts, with assistance from a growing agricultural press and professional government bodies. But the onset of a more scientific agriculture awaited twentieth century developments in genetics and biochemistry.

Agricultural production continued to be oriented around the family farm. But the most far-reaching in its consequences was the erosion of rural independence and self-sufficiency which resulted from the integration of the farm family into the market economy. Production for the market brought with it not only opportunities for the material benefits of higher incomes and increased consumption, but also greater vulnerability to the vagaries of impersonal market forces, often personified by "greedy" merchants and middlemen. Although agricultural output increased greatly from 1870 to 1930, the farmer did not seem to reap his share of the benefits. If anything, he became more disenchanted about the inequalities produced by the economic system, and thus he played a vital part in the growing public debate on the distribution of wealth and power at the turn of the century.

7

Industrialism, Unrest, and Reform: The Coming of Government Regulation

Introduction

Many authors have characterized the discontent of the late nineteenth and early twentieth centuries as a reaction to the forces of industrialism. First associated with falling prices and widespread unemployment during the severe depressions of the 1870s and 1890s, more important in the long term were changes in the organization of production and distribution accompanying the rise of "big business" and the resulting aura of monopoly. The way in which Americans responded to industrial change is, according to Samuel Hays, the dominant theme of the Populist and Progressive eras.[1] In that response, there was no doctrinaire view as to the proper role of government in economic life. A role for government gradually emerged as the result of compromise.

The thread of this response had several strands. The first was the development of a prescriptive literature, ranging from Henry George's *Progress and Poverty* (1879) which stressed the monopoly of land ownership as the source of America's economic ills, to Edward Bellamy's Utopian tract *Looking Backward* (1882), and Henry Demerest Lloyd's diagnostic *Wealth Against Commonwealth* (1894), which vilified Standard Oil. This tradition continued after 1900, although it took a more extravagant, muckraking tone with Ida Tarbell's *History of the Standard Oil Company* (1904) and Gustavus Myers' *History of the Great American Fortunes* (1910). These studies publicized the existence of great economic inequality in the United States, and warned that political inequality would result from the growing impact of large-scale enterprise on government.

The second strand focused on the role of the individual in an industrial society. Many writers concentrated on the confining and impoverishing forces of industrialism—for example, the declining role of the church and clergy was viewed by some as a sign of social disintegration. On the other hand, some reactions were more positive, among them movements promoting a greater role for women in public and business life and attempts to ameliorate the conditions of the urban poor.

The third strand was the development of a more specific antimonopoly bias. With the emergence of the trusts in the 1880s and the wave of mergers and consolidations around the turn of the century, monopoly power seemed ascendant. Big business was identified with administered prices, market power, and trade associations in place of the competition which had characterized much of the nineteenth century.[2]

These three strands were twisted together in a swelling cry for government regulation of the economy in the "public interest." But the public call for government intervention and social reform did not go unchallenged. Many businessmen continued to espouse the laissez-faire principles of Social Darwinism and the superiority of an economic system run by private businessmen free from government interference.

Reactions to Industrialism

As the dissidents saw it, the most pressing problem in the American economy by the late nineteenth century was how to cope with the impersonal market system and the perversion of it by big business. Farmers and laborers experimented with the formation of countervailing organizations, both economic and political, and pressed government to come to their defense.

Agrarian unrest

"Perhaps no development of the nineteenth century brought greater disappointment to the American farmers than did their failure to realize the prosperity that they had expected from industrialism."[3] Productivity increases like those associated with nineteenth-century manufacturing expansion result in more output to be distributed among the population. But for a particular sector such as agriculture, the share of increased output depends upon relative movements of prices and outputs. Industrialization produced a new set of interdependencies between agriculture and the nonfarm sectors which influenced the flow of income to farmers and their general sense of well-being. In the late nineteenth century, the American farmer came to believe that industrialization had eroded his relative income and dealt a death blow to his way of life. Much of the agrarian unrest that has been stressed by historians originated in the Midwest, and it is upon this area of the country that the following comments are concentrated.

Farmers were discontented largely because they believed that they were exploited by many other groups in the economy: by railroads which charged "excessive" rates; by speculators and land monopolists who took up the "best" available lands; by mortgage lenders who charged "exhorbitant" rates of interest; by falling prices which increased the "burden" of their mortgage debts; by "giant" corporations who were "oppressive," "extortionate," and "tyrannical."[4] A standard interpretation is that farmers sold in competitive markets and purchased in monopolistic markets which produced deteriorating terms of trade for farmers from 1870 to 1900.

The belief that they were exploited gave rise to many farm-based organizations and political movements. These began in earnest with the development in the 1860s and early 1870s of the Grange, which had both an educative role for farmers and a growing political role—lobbying for cheaper, uniform freight rates through railroad regulation, curbing of middlemen's profits, cheaper credit facilities, cooperative stores and marketing associations. In the 1880s the Southern Alliance and the National Farmers Alliance or Northwestern Alliance were formed. Their strategy was to campaign for corrective legislation against antiagrarian forces, and for cooperative marketing and purchasing organizations. These two broadly based groups articulated farmer distrust of middlemen, trusts, railroads, and the national banking system.

Politically, farmer unrest culminated in the 1890s with the Populist movement.[5] Populism was essentially an agrarian movement and represented a direct response to economic injustices, whether real or imagined, suffered at the hands of eastern financial and banking interests and the trunk-line railroad systems. In 1892 the election platform of the new People's Party included free coinage of silver, the graduated income tax, government ownership and operation of railroads, and the abolition of corporate landholding among its planks. By 1896, however, the People's Party was wracked by internal struggles over "free silver" and Populist-Democratic fusion. Partly because of dissension, partly because much of its program of economic reform was usurped by the Democrats, and partly because the return of prosperity after 1896 made farm protests seemingly inappropriate, the Populist movement collapsed by the end of the century.

The years from 1900 to the end of the First World War are regarded as a period of great farm prosperity. They also marked an increasing concern on the part of the federal government with the production, marketing, and financial problems of farmers, ranging from the Commission on Country Life and its representations to Congress in 1908, to improvements in the organization of the United States Department of Agriculture and refinement of its practical research institutions, and the insertion of clauses in the Federal Reserve Act and the Federal Farm Loan Act designed to help solve the problem of long-term farm credit. The years of farm prosperity were followed by unsettled conditions in the 1920s, and a return of agitation for a "fair share" for agriculture.

Did real economic grievances underlie agrarian unrest between 1870 and 1900? First, farmers complained about transportation facilities—the lack of transportation and the alleged monopolistic practices of railroads in setting railroad freight rates. In general, western and southern producers shipped great distances to market and paid high ton-mile rates in comparison with rates over similar distances in the East. Even though nominal freight rates fell considerably between 1870 and 1900, discrimination between regional rates remained and provoked continued complaints by regional farm groups. Of concern too were anomalies in the structure of freight rates caused by the lack of competition.

There was at least a pretence of competition on the trunk lines between East and West with rate wars, long-haul/short-haul discrimination, and rebating, although by the 1870s railroad companies had formed traffic associations and concluded pooling arrangements in an attempt to neutralize competitive pressures. However, local rates in areas where railroads enjoyed some degree of natural monopoly could be raised to compensate for competitive rates on the trunk lines. The condemnation of railroad rate-making policy was compounded by suspicion of railroad grain elevator ownership and pricing policies for storage, and by allegations of undue railroad influence on government policies.

In response, many farm groups protested against railroad rates and argued for government intervention to lower rates. The Grange did so during the 1870s, and Grange-sponsored legislation was passed in several states in an attempt to exercise control over railroad operations. In 1874 the American Cheap Transport Association demanded federal railroad ownership to compete with privately owned lines, and the Windom Committee recommended federal government participation to provide a benchmark for competitive freight rates. It was not until the passage of the Interstate Commerce Act in 1887 that the federal government finally took action on the issue of railroad regulation.

However, the data on freight rates do not confirm that farmers were being exploited by railroads. Certainly, there was a decreasing trend in nominal freight rates from the early 1870s to the late 1890s. However, nominal freight rates are not conclusive; only a comparison of changes in freight rates with changes in the prices of farm products at the farm can determine whether the *real burden* of freight rates was rising, falling, or remaining approximately constant. Robert Higgs[6] has recently found that the real burden of freight rates during this period was not moving adversely for the farmer. He employed data on nominal freight rates and on prices received by farmers for wheat, corn, and cotton (the three major cash crops) to calculate indexes of the purchasing power of farm produce from 1867 to 1915. The three indexes vary considerably from year to year, with movements unfavorable to farmers concentrated in the early 1870s and in the mid-1890s. However, the secular trend over the period from 1867 to 1897 is approximately horizontal, suggesting little or no change in the farmer's purchasing power from wheat, corn, and cotton in terms of their command over freight rates, and there is real improvement in the farm price of wheat, corn, and cotton in the period from 1897 to 1915, the "age of prosperity" for the farmer.

Transport charges were an important part of farmers' costs, and the failure of transport costs to decline could have been a genuine economic source of farm distress in the 1870s and 1890s. The Populists were most active in those states where transport charges tended to bulk large in farm costs—in Kansas, Nebraska, and the Dakotas. Moreover, recent experience gave the farmers of the 1890s no reason to expect an improvement in the relationship of transport costs to farm prices; they believed that their problems arose from high freight rates. The change in trend after 1896 was coincident with and undoubtedly contributed to agrarian prosperity. It coincided as well with the disappearance of Populism as a political protest movement.

Midwestern farmers also complained that the marketing of small grains was concentrated in the hands of elevator companies and was extremely sensitive to changes in the supply of railway box cars, the grading and pricing practices of elevator companies, and the supply of elevators. Charges that monopoly power was exercised by such companies were frequently made. There seems to be some evidence to support these claims: for example, in 1874 the city of Chicago had but fourteen elevators to handle the inspection, grading, and mixing of grains, and these elevators were controlled by nine firms whose apparent collusion on storage charges and pricing practices precipitated action by the local Patrons of Husbandry. Again, the Chicago wheat market was notorious until the 1870s for attempts to corner the market before trading in wheat futures was well developed. Producers had virtually no voice in the marketing of wheat. However, it is difficult to go much beyond impressionistic accounts of the susceptibility of grain farmers to monopolistic marketing practices and estimate the extent of such practices and the resulting costs borne by farmers. Nevertheless, it is their perception that such costs were incurred, which is relevant to the rise of farmers' protest movement and, thus, it is sufficient to acknowledge that farmers complained bitterly about such costs.

A third major factor cited as a cause of agrarian unrest was the supply of credit, both short-term and long-term. The farm sector in the American Midwest was characterized by a shortage of capital and concomitant high interest rates. Indeed, many farmers appear to have been forced to rely upon merchants and implement dealers for short-term loans.

During 1873 to 1895, more and more farmers in the plains states came to hold the Populist view that the mortgage was a sign of economic distress to the farmer and easy profit for the money lender. Moreover, Populists argued that interest rates were high, even on good security, in the Midwest compared with the East, and regarded the American Bankers' Association as synonymous with organized money power, exploitive of the agrarian interest.

Considerable research has been done on the midwestern mortgage market. Allan Bogue has argued convincingly that mortgages were not taken out in periods of distress but were sought by farmers in order to purchase equipment, livestock and land during periods of prosperity.[7] The western farmer who homesteaded his 160 acres, bought his farming equipment, erected farm buildings, hired someone to break 40 acres of prairie sod, fenced it, and sunk a 40-foot well incurred cash costs of about $1,000 and also needed to support his family for at least one year before farming would generate income.[8] If he purchased land, his capital outlay would be even greater. In order to finance these expenditures, many farmers had recourse to borrowing.

Western mortgages were a recognized form of investment in the eastern states as early as the 1850s. Many investors had difficulties in supervising the activities of their western agents which tended to increase the risk associated with western mortgages. Also, investors suffered risk from unpredictable falls in agricultural prices and poor crop years which encumbered the farmer's ability to make mortgage payments. Regional rate differentials between the East and West may have represented conscious discrimination on the part of eastern investors, or more likely the existence of risk differentials between investments in the two areas.

In any case, the trend of interest rates in this area was downwards from 1875 to 1900. From the legal maximum allowed by state usury laws in 1860s and 1870s, interest rates fell by approximately one-half during the period to 1905.[9] Bogue argues that the decrease in rates was attributable in part to competition among lenders. The accumulation of savings in the East and the high demand for credit in the West and the emergence of the western mortgage broker to facilitate the transfer of funds contributed to the more effective functioning of a national capital market. Moreover, nominal interest rates fell because of deflationary pressures over this period. If nominal interest rates were falling, was there a corresponding change in the *real* interest rates to the farmer? Fogel and Rutner's research suggests that there would have been a small, almost negligible, increase in the burden of farmers who had low debt-to-asset ratios.[10] However, in some areas, especially those of quite recent settlement, there tended to be higher ratios of debt to assets, which implied a higher burden of interest charges over time with the declining price level.

These results tend to be corroborated by Nugent's study of Populists in Kansas in which he argues that "mortgage distress was not only real, but particularly severe for the Populists."[11] Populists, as agrarians, often came from a precarious economic situation. Tighter conditions with respect to mortgages, freight costs, or any other economic variable, as occurred in the 1890s, were more severely felt by those whose capital was less extensive and whose operations were more marginal, and whose debt-asset ratios were higher. Such farmers became proponents of Populist reform.

Many historians have argued that the steady downward trend in agricultural prices was the foremost cause of agrarian unrest. To properly assess complaints about agricultural prices, it is necessary to examine the trend of prices paid by farmers for purchased commodities and services as well as the prices received by farmers for their output—that is, changes in the agricultural terms of trade. Most arguments concerning changes in the terms of trade for agricultural products in the late nineteenth century have been founded on an index of wholesale prices in New York, Cincinnati, and Chicago compiled in the Warren-Pearson index. However, this index does not readily yield a comparison of prices for goods purchased and goods sold by the farmer *at the farm*. Only under certain assumptionscould wholesale prices be employed as an index of trends in relative prices paid and received by farmers—for example, that transport charges fell equally rapidly for agricultural and nonagricultural goods.

The data indicate that the wholesale prices of farm products fell only as fast as wholesale prices of nonfarm goods between 1865 and 1897. In fact, nonfarm prices perhaps fell a fraction more, and taken together with quality improvements in nonfarm goods, especially in manufactures, it is possible that the agricultural terms of trade for farmers actually improved a bit over the period. In the period from 1897 to 1917, there is no doubt that farm prices increased relative to nonfarm prices and that the agricultural terms of trade improved substantially.[12]

The real issue, however, does not concern changes in the agricultural terms of trade alone, but also the effect on the relative incomes of farmers—the income terms of trade of farmers up until 1897. Productivity increases in agriculture were substantially less than productivity inreases in the nonfarm sector, as Kendrick's findings attest. Farm income grew less rapidly than nonfarm income over the period, and farmers as a group became relatively worse off compared with nonfarmers. Fogel and Rutner conclude that the average real income of farmers rose at an average rate of 1.3 percent annually from 1849 to 1899, which was substantial but still less than the annual growth in per capita income of 1.6 percent for the nation as a whole. A more revealing statistic, real income per farm worker, grew at 1.0 percent a year compared with a national average of 1.4 percent per worker.[13] After 1897 farm output per man-hour experienced little change, and farm incomes continued to fall behind in spite of improvements in the relative prices of farm versus nonfarm goods.[14]

The relative importance of these factors varied from region to region, from crop to crop, and from farm to farm. But one common cause links them together. Whatever the particular complaint, farmers above all despaired of their increased susceptibility to market forces. Douglass North has argued that ultimately it was the instability of world markets that increased the vulnerability of the farmer.[15] The farmer now found himself competing in world markets in which fluctuating prices combined with vagaries of the weather to create great uncertainty. The international market determined the prices of wheat and cotton, and the farmer in the United States was a price-taker of those world-determined prices. According to North, the nexus ran from high prices as a signal to the expansion of agriculture, which with a time lag brought forth an increased supply of agricultural commodities the world over and, in turn, led to depressed prices in the United States and in world markets. From 1870 to 1896, the increase in the demand for agricultural commodities was met in the United States by surges of movement into new, rich lands of high fertility. Productivity gains tended to be passed on to consumers in the form of low prices and this brought about low returns to farmers. In the period after 1900, on the other hand, supply increases could be met only by adding poorer land to cultivation or by more intensive cultivation of better-quality lands. In either case, the result was increasing real costs of producing agricultural commodities which simultaneously increased rents on better-quality lands and tended to bring about both an increase in farm income in aggregate and an increase in the relative incomes of holders of good land.

Taking a somewhat broader approach, Anne Mayhew interprets agrarian protest as essentially a reaction to the commerialization of agriculture and the objections of farmers to the increased importance of markets.[16] Before 1870, she argues, the farmer was commercially oriented only in the limited sense that he was happy to sell surpluses of agricultural products when given the opportunity to do so. His activities were marked by the absence of any major commercial ties and, consequently, since he was not *obliged* to sell agricultural surpluses because of his high degree of self-sufficiency, changes in the costs of transport and credit and in agricultural prices were not crucial to him.

After 1870, however, farmers in the Midwest responded to the opportunities represented by the construction of railroads, capital flows, and developing markets by specializing and producing for the market. Further, agriculture expanded into areas where there was increased difficulty in maintaining rural self-sufficiency since in many parts of the Midwest only a limited range of crops could be grown. In addition, many farmers borrowed to purchase land in order to approach the optimum size of agricultural unit. Thus, for a variety of reasons, the farmer incurred obligations to buy inputs and to sell a major part of his produce. He was caught up in market forces which represented not just opportunity but also potential difficulty, because they placed a premium on his capacity as a business man as well as farmer. Moreover, in many outlying areas, the farmer was confronted by one supplier of inputs and one buyer of outputs, and consequently the danger of exploitation by rural monopoly power was an additional risk.

Many of these arguments are variations on the theme that agrarian protest was a reaction to the farmer's deteriorating status in a rapidly industrializing American society. As Samuel Hays has argued, the farmer was caught up in a complex industrial system and the transformation of agriculture which this involved.[17] Does this mean, then, that Populism was a movement intended to "save agricultural America from industrialism," anxious for a return to the "good old days"?[18] Clearly not. This "retrogressive" view is contradicted by the readiness of farmers to adopt improved technology and farming methods. Farmers were receptive to mechanization and changes in agricultural practices, and to the necessary role of railroads in the commercialization of agriculture. What agrarians wanted were economic remedies for their economic grievances. Farmers accepted industrialism, but bitterly opposed their vulnerability to some of its forms and, by late century, were ready to join with labor to seek redress.

Industrial Unrest

The growth in the size of industries and of the typical industrial firm implied certain changes in the life-style of American workers: first, a decline in self-employment and worker autonomy, and the rise of a working class; second, the growing impersonality of the employer/employee relationship, compounded by the rise of professional management and the corporate form; third and above all, an increase of insecurity associated with the dangers of unemployment, physical injury, lack of bargaining power, and job security.[19] This growing fear and insecurity was the industrial workers' analogue to the farmers' distrust of market forces. Industrial unrest was manifested in bitter and protracted strikes which occurred periodically from the 1870s until the First World War, and in concerted efforts to establish effective labor unions.[20]

The first large union was the National Labor Union, formed in the late 1860s as a federation of local craft organizations. Its major interest was in social reform, but it did combine with agrarian reformers to engage in political activity. Of more lasting significance was the Knights of Labor, established in 1869. Membership in the Knights of Labor included both skilled and unskilled workers, and it enjoyed substantial popularity in the early part of the 1880s.

The growth of the American Federation of Labor (AF of L) began in the 1880s. The Federation of Organized Trades and Labor Unions had been organized in 1881, and comprised six of the largest craft unions in the United States. In 1886 the AF of L emerged from the old Federation.

Labor unrest was frequently vented in strike action. In the mid-1870s, violent and lengthy strikes occurred in the railroad sector, especially in Pittsburgh in 1877. A threatened general strike in support of the eight-hour day and police intervention in the McCormick strike precipitated the Haymarket Affair on May 4, 1886, in which radicals and anarchists loosely associated with the Knights of Labor were arrested after a bomb explosion at a meeting in downtown Chicago. Their identification with Haymarket and the charge of union irresponsibility helped to bring about the demise of the Knights of Labor. Bitter too was the Homestead Strike of 1892, an attempt by the Amalgamated Association of Iron and Steel Workers to organize the Homestead works of Carnegie Steel. Carnegie management attempted to oust the union with Pinkerton detectives and finally the state militia intervened. This was followed in 1894 by the Pullman Strike and widespread rioting in Chicago. In the 1901 strike called by the Iron and Steel Workers against some of the constituent companies of United States Steel, a principal issue was union recognition. The failure of this strike has been interpreted as a significant victory for antiunion forces, and signalled the beginning of a period of slow union growth. Throughout the last decade of the century, wages appear to have been only part of labor's grievances: union recognition and enforcement of union rules were of equal if not greater importance.[21]

The AF of L emphasized "practical" goals. It was not concerned with Utopian schemes for a better society, but with immediate solutions to the common problems of wages, hours, accidents, unemployment, and recognition. Their tactics were the industrial actions of the strike and boycott and nonpartisan political pressure. By 1900 labor's philosophy, under the leadership of Samuel Gompers, was to pursue political support by working through the established political parties and aggressively support trade agreements and improved working conditions. Taking the lessons of Haymarket and the Pullman Strike to heart, Gompers was concerned that the AF of L operate within the capitalist system and avoid radicalism in order to gain public sympathy.[22]

Labor's organizations were countered after 1900 by organized antiunion activity on the part of business leaders. Whereas antiunion measures were largely ad hoc (for example, vicious strike breaking) in the nineteenth century, after 1900 they took a more group-oriented and legalistic turn. The National Association of Manufacturers formed in 1903 and the American Anti-Boycott Association (1902) lobbied against the development of unions and their attempts at organizing labor. Furthermore, the Sherman Act was invoked against union officials in several boycott cases, among them the Danbury Hatters' case (1908) and the Buck's Stove and Range Company case (1914). The use of the court injunction to prevent boycotts also began.

But, the strategy of political support for labor's "friends" and the punishing of "enemies" by withholding support led to the enactment of some progressive legislation. A federal Department of Labor was established in 1912, and took a more favorable view of union recognition and collective bargaining. The Federation's support for Woodrow Wilson in 1912 was followed by the passing of the Clayton Act of 1914 which exempted labor from prosecution under the antitrust Acts, and promised a softer use of the court injunction.

Labor also participated in the National Civic Federation, established in 1900. This organization brought together employers and workers to lobby against strikes and lock-outs and to provide machinery for mediation and conciliation of labor disputes. It assisted labor in opposing the antiunion propaganda of the National Association of Manufacturers.

Was labor unrest related to adverse changes in the incomes of industrial workers during 1870 to 1914? Historical accounts often imply that incomes of most industrial workers were inadequate to support wage earners and their families at a decent standard of living. Coupled with this was the instability of industrial employment—the likelihood of unemployment and the danger of serious injury. Improvements over the period in reduction of hours worked and child-labor and safer working conditions were few, and were not sufficient for historians to conclude that workers had become distinctly better off during the sixty years after the Civil War. The continued poverty of the working class in the midst of rapidly expanding production was believed in large part to be the result of victimization of workers by employers through the exercise of "monopoly" powers.[23]

However, two studies by Clarence Long and Albert Rees of changes in industrial real wages between 1860 and 1914 have produced a reassessment of the workers' standard of living over this period. Long's study considers the period 1860 to 1890.[24] He found that in nominal terms the average daily wage increased from 1860 to 1890 by about fifty percent for manufacturing and about sixty percent for building trades workers. At the same time, the length of the work day decreased from an average in manufacturing of 10.9 hours per day in 1860 to approximately 10 hours per day in 1890. The most common work day was 10 hours and the next most common 12 hours at the end of the period. The decrease in the average work day combined with the increase of the average daily money wage implies that the percentage increase in hourly wages was even larger (eleven percent more) than in daily wages over the period; that is, manufacturing wages rose by sixty-one percent per hour compared with fifty percent daily.[25]

What about the change in real wages? Long calculated that the increase in the manufacturing worker's daily real wages appeared to be the same as for money wages, approximately fifty percent. There was some increase in real wages in every decade of the period but the increase was uneven, with most of the gain occurring during the 1880s. Real annual earnings of manufacturing workers rose by about forty-six percent from under $300 to more than $425 annually by the end of the period, and building real wages rose somewhat more.[26] The net advance in hourly wages in manufacturing, both nominal and real, averaged about 1.6 percent compounded annually over the period. (Compare this figure with that for 1914 to 1953, when the rate of increase was about 5 percent for nominal wages and 2.8 percent for real wages.)

Long's data also demonstrated large wage differentials among industries and occupations with wages tending on average to be relatively low in the South and for women, children, and youths. According to Long, from 1860 to 1890, in spite of frequent setbacks, labor made definite and significant gains in real earnings. Traditions regarding the length of the working day, however, proved harder to break down and the decrease in the average working day was relatively slight.

Rees' study covers the period from 1890 to 1914.[27] He found both an increase in average hourly earnings from 15.8 cents per hour in 1890 to 22 cents in 1914 (in constant dollars of 1914) and a decrease in average hours worked per day from approximately 10 hours in 1890 to 9.3 hours in 1914. Average hours worked per week fell below 50 with the standard work-week requiring a worker to complete five 9-hour days plus a half-day on Saturday mornings. Some trades had fallen to a 44-hour work-week by 191. The index of real daily earnings rose steadily from 1890 to 1914 but less than the increase in hourly earnings, thereby reflecting the fact that some of the gains in real income were taken by the worker in the form of increased leisure. About seventy-seven percent of the increase in real income represented the increased consumption of goods and services, and the remaining twenty-three percent was increased leisure.[28]

Real hourly earnings of manufacturing workers' rose by a total of thirty-seven percent from 1890 to 1914, or at a compound annual rate of 1.3 percent. This rate of increase is somewhat lower than the one calculated by Long for the period from 1860 to 1890. It is also less than the rate of increase in output per production worker per man-hour in manufacturing found in most productivity studies. This finding suggests a decrease in the wage-earners' share over the period, which may have been due partly to changes in alternative opportunities for workers, including the disappearance of the agricultural frontier by 1890 and the effect of immigration on the wage level.[29]

Overall, it appears that hourly earnings adjusted for the cost of living rose significantly between the Civil War and the First World War compared with the probable growth in income per farm employee. In addition, the gains in better working conditions, shorter work-days, shorter work-weeks, and increased safety of industrial employment mean that the wages and earnings figures tend to understate the increase in the industrial workers' real income.[30]

A broader perspective is provided by the data on annual earnings of all nonfarm employees from 1870 to 1930, summarized in Table 7.1.

Table 7.1 Earnings of Nonfarm Employees, 1870-1930

Year	Real earnings when employed ($)
1870	375
1880	395
1890	519
1900	573
1910	669
1920	714
1930	898

SOURCE: Stanley Lebergott, *Manpower in Economic Growth: The American Record Since 1800* (New York: McGraw-Hill, 1964), pp. 524,528.

They show little increase in real earnings during the 1870s, with substantial increases in the 1880s, a slow-down in the 1890s, and then substantial gains during the 1900s. Real earnings increased relatively slowly from 1910 to 1920 but grew rapidly in the decade of the 1920s.

Do these increases in labor earnings suggest that industrial workers were not "victimized" by the "robber barons"? In fact, the increase in real hourly wages is not sufficient to invalidate the "exploitation" hypothesis. A satisfactory test of this premise requires measuring what the increase in real hourly wages *would have been* if monopoly power had not existed—an unlikely prospect!

It is interesting that only a small percentage of the American labor force were members of unions through this period, the percentage ranging from 2.3 percent of the labor force in 1870 to 2.7 percent in 1900, 12.1 percent in 1920, and 7.4 percent in 1930.[31] Labor's apparent unwillingness to organize in unions is partly explained by the general prosperity of the period, especially after 1900, and by the growing spirit of reform pervading American society.[32] At the same time, these percentage figures perhaps understate the extent of durable union growth in the late nineteenth and early twentieth centuries. The slow organizing of skilled workers into craft unions affiliated with the AF of L gave a firm basis for expansion of the labor movement in the twentieth century.

On the other hand, the increase in real wages and earnings notwithstanding, organized labor certainly proved incapable of restricting the supply of skilled labor to American industry. Attempts to withhold labor supplies led to replacement by immigrants, women, and machinery. Evolving monopsonistic hiring practices by cartels and the effectiveness of the employer's black-list were also instrumental in holding back union organization in industries like steel, characterized by few constituent companies and the easy exchange of information. Finally, manufacturers had access to favorable legal facilities: for example, the issue of injunctions to prevent labor unions from causing work interruptions was frequent in pre-1910 industrial disputes. Unions in this period suffered from a social and political climate of hostility which was only gradually overcome in the postwar years.

With industrialization, both the industrial worker and the farmer lost much of their former self-reliance and independence. Their growing discontent intensified social cleavage in the United States. The gulf between rich and poor seemed to be increasing. It was rationalized by apologists for the "robber barons" in terms of the philosophical doctrine of Social Darwinism and the classical theory of economic competition, both of which implied that success went to the able and denied the existence of a conflict between the public and the private interest. The turmoil of the 1890s with its strikes and marches on Washington, anti-immigrant movements and associations, and the depression from 1893 to 1896, brought matters to a head.

One means of seeking to rectify the economic balance was to organize farm groups and industrial unions as countervailing centers of power—collective efforts to cope with the market system and monopoly. In the Populist era, the farmer saw himself and the laborer as members of the same, oppressed class.[33] But the mutual sympathy of farm and labor groups began to give way in the 1890s to cleavages over the tariff, the monetization of silver, and other issues. The rift was complete by the 1896 election. After the demise of the Populist party, both farm and labor groups adopted nonpartisan political stances and sharp tensions between the two inhibited the development of common reform policies.

A second means involved defining the proper role of government in the economy. The American government had characteristically assisted in the creation of private wealth through the use of public supports to private initiative, including financial aid to railroads, promotion of improved agriculture, and tariff policies to help support manufacturing interests. By 1900 the question was whether government should depart from its customary role and take a more interventionist stance. In part this change was encouraged by sending to Washington "reform" representatives charged with changing the status quo.

Many historians have argued that the unifying theme of American history from 1870 to 1914 was the popular attack against corporate wealth and monopoly. Through local, state, and federal governments, dissident groups sought to curb corporate power and to provide greater economic opportunity for their members. But this view may be overly simplistic. The social, economic and political movements of this period were a reaction, not against the corporation alone but above all against industrialism.[34] The impersonal market economy contained elements disturbing to both the small businessman, the industrial worker, and the farmer. To this element was added the growing discontent of many Americans with the emphasis on "materialism" in American society, and its replacement of older, more "precious" values. Political reform involved coming to terms with the vastly new society which industrialism had wrought.

Government Intervention and Legislative Remedies: A Case Study of Railroad Regulation

The regulation of business firms in the interests of promoting or restoring competition was the lynch-pin of reform. To preserve the benefits of bigness but control its potential for evil was the goal. The case for national regulation of business was predicated on the growth of markets. State legislation could not begin to regulate firms whose activities were conducted over several states in regional or national markets.

National regulation really began with the Interstate Commerce Act (1887). By prohibiting rebates, pooling, and short-haul/long-haul rate discrimination, and by insisting on "reasonable and just" charges by railroads, the act epitomized the belief that competition was necessary within the railroad sector. The Sherman Antitrust Act (1890) was the next legislative attempt to combat the threat to competition by declaring illegal "every contract, combination in the form of trust or otherwise, or conspiracy, in restraint of trade or commerce." A series of decisions by the Supreme Court undermined the effectiveness of both acts, and indeed one—the E. C. Knight Case (1895), which condoned merger activity—helped to precipitate the wave of mergers at the turn of the century. No longer was it necessary for firms to conclude an agreement in order to control markets; after merger or consolidation, they could control markets by virtue of their size.

Vocal criticism of mergers and consolidations during the early 1900s led to increased interest in enforcing the Sherman Act. The first step in 1903 was the Expedition Act, by which suits under the Sherman Act were to be given precedence in the courts in order to reduce delays. But nothing was done to strengthen the legislation until 1914.

During the Roosevelt and Taft administrations, a more vigorous enforcement of the existing law resulted in an increase in prosecutions by the Antitrust Division of the federal Department of Justice, the most significant being the dissolution in 1904 of the Northern Securities Company. However, this decision did not deter businessmen from using the holding company form. Even the successful prosecutions of Standard Oil Company of New Jersey and American Tobacco Company in 1911 left matters in little better state.

In these later cases, the Supreme Court caused great confusion by changing the ground rules. Early on the Supreme Court had not attempted to distinguish between "reasonable" and "unreasonable" restraint of trade; both were declared illegal. In the later cases, however, the Court decided itself to determine whether or not "unreasonable" restraint of trade existed. Reasonable restraint was declared to be acceptable. Moreover, the Court decided that potential monopoly was not sufficient to order dissolution; dissolution required *actual* use of monopoly powers.

Under the Wilson administration, the law was revised. First, the Federal Trade Commission was established in 1914. The commission was designed to prevent the use of unfair methods of competition, and was empowered to investigate mergers and consolidations, to conduct hearings, to issue "cease and desist" orders, and to resort to the courts for enforcement of its decisions. Second, the Clayton Antitrust Act of 1914 forbade price discrimination, intercorporate stock purchases, and interlocking directorates when the result was to lessen competition or bring about monopoly.

The strengthening of antitrust legislation and more successful prosecutions meant that an effective legislative framework for controlling big business appeared to be well in place by the second decade of the twentieth century. Whether this legislation was sufficient to prevent the continued development of large-scale enterprise or, at least, to effectively police it remained to be seen. Let us turn now to the development of regulation of railroads.

The development of railroad regulation

The period immediately after the Civil War was characterized by intense competition among railroads. There were five major trunk lines—the Grand Trunk, the New York Central, the Pennsylvania, the Erie, and the Baltimore and Ohio Railroads—which competed for the through traffic between the West and the East. West of Chicago, several "Granger" roads vied for trade. Fierce competition led to a series of rate wars in the 1870s, which climaxed in the "Great Rate War" of 1876-77.

By the 1870s the railroad companies began to experiment with ways of ending this expensive competition. Purchase of shipping companies, agreements with shippers, and the use of special contracts for exclusive carriage of freight enabled railroads to secure traffic by offering rebates or drawbacks, whether by underbilling, underclassification, or simply by rate reductions from the advertised price.

Most important were voluntary agreements among railroads themselves. These associations or "pools" were designed to obviate competition, in some cases by dividing territories geographically or, more commonly, by agreeing to share traffic or to adjust earnings, allowing traffic to flow along its natural lines. Perhaps the most spectacular was the Northern Trunk Line Pool formed to control grain rates between Chicago and the eastern seaboard.[35] Eventually comprised of the New York Central, Baltimore and Ohio, Pennsylvania, and Erie Railroads, the object was to develop a systematic rate structure and to pool earnings.

The basic deficiency of the pool system was the extreme difficulty of enforcing agreements. Cheating was possible and often profitable, since even a small rate cut could greatly increase revenues and profits at the expense of competitors. Thus, pools tended to be quite unstable: for example, new agreements were regularly made and broken throughout the history of the Northern Trunk Line Pool from 1874 to 1889.

Ultimately, competition was most surely reduced by combining railroads into larger and fewer systems—by leasing branch and competitive lines, by stock-ownership in several railroad companies and subsequent interlocking of directorships, or by actual consolidation. This process peaked in the 1890s and the 1900s with investment bankers' participation in railroad consolidation.

After 1870 many segments of the American population called for a general downward revision of railroad rates, and an end to discrimination in the railroad sector. The passing of general laws of incorporation in many states provided the legislative framework by removing constraints on the formation of new railroad corporations. However, pooling agreements and consolidations more than offset the effects of new lines being built.

If new roads were not the answer, government ownership in the railroad sector was another possibility. The Windom Committee's report in 1874 recommended that the federal government should own or control at least one of the major trunk lines between the eastern seaboard and the Midwest in order to ensure competitive rate making. But government ownership of railroads was not taken very seriously.

Regulation proved to be a more likely alternative. Indeed, state regulation was widely employed. Originally, state regulation was administered by the legislatures through railroad committees, or by specialized railway boards or commissions. But legislatures proved to be cumbersome regulators, largely because of their lack of expertise, and the railway commission became more common. There were only four state commissions by 1860, and 28 by 1897. The regulatory powers of state commissions were influenced by several Supreme Court decisions. In the case of Munn vs. Illinois (1877), the Court ruled that the railroad's charter was subject to the usual limitations on common carriers to charge only "reasonable" rates, and the courts were to decide what was "reasonable." By this decision, the public nature of railroad operations was firmly established and the state regulatory movement encouraged. But in 1886 a second judgment (Illinois vs. Wabash, St. Louis, and Pacific Railroad) exposed the inherent limitations in state regulation—that is, the preponderance of interstate operations by railroads. The application of Illinois' statute preventing short-haul/long-haul discrimination to shipments from Illinois to New York was found to violate federal jurisdiction of interstate commerce. It was this case which brought to public attention the need for national regulation.

The call for federal participation had come even earlier. In 1874 the Windom Committee had argued for national regulation and in the early

1880s the Cullom Committee had done likewise. Agitation had increased throughout the period, both from eastern producers, shippers, and merchants, and from western farmers and shippers. Even the railroads appeared to welcome national regulation as a substitute for the anarchy of separate state jurisdictions—anticipating perhaps, that a national regulatory body would support efforts by the railroads to rationalize competitive pressure and promote stability by recognizing their pooling and rate agreements. The result was the passing of the Interstate Commerce Act in 1887, which prohibited rebates and short-haul/long-haul discrimination while requiring that railroads levy "reasonable and just" charges, and prohibited pooling of freight and earnings. The act established an Interstate Commerce Commission (ICC) of five members to investigate abuses by railroads and, if necessary, resort to the courts to compel compliance to commission orders.

Problems with the interpretation of the ICC's regulatory powers became apparent in judicial decisions in the 1890s. In the "maximum freight rates" case of 1897, the Supreme Court argued that three agencies could be expected to set railroad rates—a railroad company itself, Congress, or some subordinate agency of Congress. According to the Court, Congress had not exercised this right, nor had it assigned its powers in "unmistakable" terms to the ICC. The commission was left with virtually no power to prescribe rates. Again, in 1897 the Court decided that competitive circumstances justified short-haul/long-haul rate discrimination. Although, in the Trans-Missouri Freight Association case, the Supreme Court decided that the Sherman Act did apply to transportation agencies, by the end of the 1890s the development of an effective system of railroad regulation had been thwarted. The right of government to regulate railroads as public enterprises had been affirmed and the railroad commission had been introduced and its powers refined and extended by 1897, but the Supreme Court had undermined the ICC's power to establish reasonable rates and its prohibition of rate discrimination.

After 1900 the railroad problem was becoming more serious: rates had begun to rise, and financial manipulations and struggles in railroad management were the order of the day. Railroads were circumventing the Sherman Antitrust Act by consolidating into larger systems. By 1906 seven large groups controlled over two-thirds of American railroad mileage and about eighty-five percent of railroad earnings.[36] There were some attempts to break up monopoly power—for example, in the Northern Securities case of 1904—and to strengthen the regulatory legislation in 1903 with the Expedition Act and the Elkins Act, an amendment to the Interstate Commerce Act designed to end rebates. In 1904 and again in 1905, Roosevelt declared that railroad legislation had become "a paramount issue." In 1906 the Hepburn Act was passed, raising the ICC's membership from five to seven and extending its power to other common carriers. The act empowered the commission to prescribe "just and reasonable" rates, and established effective government control by providing that orders of the commission were to take effect within thirty days.

The Mann-Elkins Act (1910) gave additional powers to the commission: it could suspend for up to ten months any new rates proposed by carriers and oblige the carrier to demonstrate that the new rates were reasonable. The act also ended ambiguity about short-haul/long-haul discrimination. Finally, the Clayton Antitrust Act (1914) prohibited interlocking directorates and the purchase of stock in competing companies, which reduced the ability of railroad companies to lessen competition through horizontal integration and "voluntary" agreements.

By 1914 the ICC had extensive powers to enforce reasonable rates and prevent discriminatory pricing practices. To the extent that efficiency was to be gained from pooling and consolidations, the legislation perpetuated inefficiency by "forcing" railroads to compete. Some of these problems were solved in the Transportation Act of 1920, which, by permitting railroads to engage in pooling and exempting them from the Clayton Act, recognized the existence of efficiencies of large-scale enterprise in the railroad sector. By the same token, the act recognized that more effective regulation was necessary to ensure that the gains were passed on to the public. For this reason, the commission was increased in number to eleven, and some of its powers were extended still further to include control over security issues and to prescribe "reasonable" rates of return on investment. By 1920 the body of federal railroad regulation seemed complete.

The demand for railroad regulation: an interpretation[37]

The coming of railroad regulation is often represented as the outcome of a struggle pitting dissident groups against the railroad's great economic power. In this interpretation, the "Granger Revolt," the "Great Strike" of 1877, and Populism were attempts to secure economic justice through federal government regulation, a tactic strongly opposed by the railroads.

Gabriel Kolko has reexamined the presumption that the federal government consciously acted to contain railroad interests.[38] Kolko argues that although it appears paradoxical, the intervention of the federal government was welcomed by railroad managements, since the railroads had not been able to achieve lasting and effective control over their own industry.

Kolko's study covers the period 1877 to 1916. Before 1900, conscious that freight rates were declining almost continuously and that fierce competition had disastrous consequences, railroads tried to establish rate stability and to moderate competition. They resorted first to voluntary cooperative solutions culminating in the pool agreements but, when these agreements proved impossible to enforce, turned to government regulation. The failure of the Interstate Commerce Act necessitated a return to voluntary attempts to reduce competition, this time through mergers and consolidations. But the railroad industry remained operationally competitive despite pools and mergers. Only after 1900 was there a final—and eventually successful—resort to a political solution.

Railroads sought stability, and recognized early their dependence on federal government "protection." The failure to develop a stable pool system, and the increased hostility of farmers, labor, and state governments threatened the continued existence of regional and national railroad systems. Railroads saw regulation as a potential cartelizing device, and as insulation from both competitors and the demands of large shippers who often insisted on rebates from published freight rates. Federal regulation was preferred to state regulation because the latter was unpredictable and often harsh—in the Midwest, for example, where state regulation reflected dissident organizations such as the Grange.

However, railroad leaders were not the only group favoring regulation. For different reasons, many other groups, among them shippers and farmers, also favored federal regulation. Nor was there railroad solidarity on legislative measures. In fact, railroads often disagreed on specific points of legislation, and on many points there was the additional complexity of opposition from shippers or farm organizations. But the railroad industry as a whole "consistently accepted the basic premises of Federal regulation since only through the positive intervention of the national political structure could the destabilizing, costly effects of cutthroat competition, predatory speculators, and greedy shippers be overcome."[39]

By the 1920s, consistent with railroad interests, rate regulation came to be guided by the principle that railroads were entitled to a reasonable profit on their investment. The ICC had brought about the maintenance of rates and the abolition of rebates and was in a position to protect the railroads from the attacks of state governments and regulatory commissions, and of shippers and consumers groups. Thus, the severe competition of the pre-1900 period had been replaced by regulation in the railroads' interests. The ICC's primary function became to administer to the needs of the industry which it was ostensibly designed to regulate, rather than to "make the dominant economic forces susceptible to the control and welfare of the large majority of the people".[40]

Kolko's interpretation, if valid, would overthrow the traditional interpretation in American historiography that railroad regulation was an attempt to reduce the balance of economic power in favor of the "public interest" against the monopolistic power and discriminatory tactics of railroads. Kolko has corrected earlier interpretations by demonstrating that many railroads supported the principle of federal regulation. However, that regulation favored railroads at the expense of shippers and consumers is not supported simply by showing that the railroads favored federal regulation.

Kolko's interpretation has been widely questioned.[41] Let us consider one such critique in some detail. Robert Harbeson's criticisms of Kolko's argument are essentially twofold: first, that Kolko has provided an incorrect assessment of the economic characteristics of the railroad industry and, second, that he has mistakenly charged that the ICC had a pro-railroad bias in its interpretation of the Interstate Commerce Act.

Kolko emphasized throughout that the railroad sector was a competitive industry, and in support he cited the decline in railroad freight rates from the 1870s to the late 1890s, the recurrence of rate wars, and the large and increasing number of railroads to 1907. However, these factors are consistent with alternative explanations of the market structure of the railroad industry.[42] The decline in railroad rates, for example, may have reflected, not competitive forces pushing down rates at the expense of profits but a decline in railroad costs which permitted lower rates with constant or even higher profits. During the period, the continuous decline in the aggregate price-level and improvements in railroad technology leading to productivity increase are both consistent with a substantial reduction in operating costs.[43] Falling operating costs may explain much of the decrease in railroad freight rates.

Second, the market structure of the railroad industry was not just a function of the number of individual railroads. Many of the railroads that Kolko included were switching or terminal companies and branch lines, not parts of through railroad systems. Also, competition refers here not to the total number of firms, but to the number of firms in a given market, in most cases a pair of communities. Since most such pairs were serviced by from one to five or six railroads, the correct type of market structure would appear to be monopoly or oligopoly. In any case, price wars are invalid indicators of a competitive market structure, but rather indicate the presence of duopoly or oligopoly, market structures in which there is a recognized interdependence among the firms. In these cases, price competition tends to be sporadic and to be self-corrective, and the price-output solution adopted by the industry is not likely to be the perfectly competitive one.[44]

Some control over railroad rate-making was necessary for protection of public interest. In addition, direct regulation of railroad rates would appear to have been better than a policy of enforced price competition because the railroad industry was characterized by decreasing costs. Decreasing unit costs over a wide range of output of railroad services imply that attempts to enforce price competition would be ineffective. Even if feasible, they would induce wasteful duplication of investment and prevent cost reductions associated with economies of scale.

Harbeson also addresses Kolko's charge that the ICC had a pro-railroad bias.[45] In concluding that the railroads strongly supported federal regulation because the commission shaped its administration of the act to meet railroad interests, Kolko relied on (i) the nature of the commission's procedures, with their heavy reliance upon informal settlement of complaints through investigation and advice to the railroads, (ii) the commission's administration of the short-haul/long-haul clause, and (iii) the commission's policies with respect to the rate-increase cases, 1910-1917.

Harbeson demonstrates that the commission was given broad discretion to develop its procedures by the act and that its reliance on informality conformed to the statute. Moreover, he argues that informality in procedures did not obviously prejudice shippers and favor carriers, as Kolko argued. On the contrary, the interests of shippers were advanced by the use of informal procedures because delays and expenses were less with the informal method as compared with formal litigation. The provision in the 1887 Act which required the commission to rely on the courts for enforcement of its decisions was prejudicial to its ability to regulate effectively, and the Hepburn Act of 1906 corrected this situation.

The short-haul/long-haul clause prohibited railroads from charging more for a shorter than for a longer distance (the shorter being included within the longer) "under substantially similar circumstances and conditions," unless special application had been approved by the ICC. The commission published guidelines which indicated the circumstances under which it would approve applications: competition from water carriers, foreign or interstate railroads not subject to the act, and "rare" cases of competition with railroads subject to the act where a danger of "destruction of legitimate competition" existed. In the 1897 Alabama Midland case, the Supreme Court held that competition between carriers subject to the act justified discriminatory pricing. Thereafter, the clause remained moribund until it was made effective in the 1910 Mann-Elkins Act. Thus, the ICC's failure to impose this clause before 1910 was not a case of pro-railroad bias, but resulted from a loophole in the Interstate Commerce Act which the Supreme Court prevented the commission from effectively closing.

Because the commission emphasized the financial needs of the railroads in determining the reasonableness of proposals for rate increases, Kolko concluded that the "commission had now formally become a guarantee of relative security and profits" to the railroad sector.[46] But a change in freight-rate levels is no guarantee of profits, because profits depend, among other things, upon the level of earnings which reflects the volume of traffic as well as rate levels. Moreover, the commission lacked authority to control the building of new lines and to prescribe minimum freight rates. Added to this were the prohibition of pooling and the susceptibility of railroad consolidations to antitrust legislation after the Clayton Act was passed.

Since all of these factors affected profit making, it becomes difficult to substantiate an indictment of the commission for its interpretation of the rate-increase cases. Moreover, circumstances had changed. There had been significant increases in the price level between 1897 and 1914, and even more rapid increases from 1914 to 1920. Productivity increases in the railroad sector simply were not great enough after 1900 to offset the effects of price increases on railroad costs. There was a *prima facie* case for valid increases in rates reflecting increased costs. In fact, the commission refused to grant all of the requested rate increases, a fact which is inconsistent with Kolko's thesis of a pro-railroad bias. His rationale for this—"the principle enunciated, not each particular application of that principle"—is not convincing.[47]

Harbeson agrees with Kolko that the railroads supported the principle of federal regulation but cannot agree that regulation was peculiarly beneficial to the railroads. "The important fact is that the public interest *was* served by federal railway regulation, at first very imperfectly, but slowly and painfully with increasing effectiveness over the period."[48] By 1920 regulation of the railroad sector was intended to ensure a level of railroad earnings sufficient to provide an adequate railroad system, a goal both in the public interest and in the interest of the railroad companies.

This conflict of interpretation over the essence of railroad regulation arises in part from the inherent nature of a methodology which is nontheoretical and nonquantitative. While the main view remains that regulation is instituted primarily for the protection and the benefit of the public or some large subgroup of the public, in this case for the benefit of shippers and consumers, and to the detriment of the railroads, George Stigler has recently argued that regulation is often "acquired" by an industry, and is designed and operated primarily for the industry's benefit.[49]

State regulation can provide many benefits to an industry. When the powers of the state are delegated to the regulatory body, including the power to coerce through taxation or through direct order, this provides the industry with the possibility of increasing its profits. There are many examples. The industry may gain control over the entry of new rivals. Stigler argues that the Civil Aeronautics Board and the Federal Deposit Insurance Corporation have made it extremely difficult for new entrants into the commercial aviation and banking fields. Or, the regulatory body might seek powers affecting substitute and complement goods and services—in the case of the railroad, control over other carriers. Finally, there is the possibility of price fixing—for example, price controls administered by a regulatory body with coercive powers.

On the other hand, there are some limitations on the exercise of cartel policies by a regulated industry. Often procedural delays occur because of the law or the bureaucracy of regulation; for example, there were long lapses between the time when the ICC first heard rate cases and their final resolution by the Supreme Court. Again, regulation often involves "outsider participation." Because of the political process, many regulated industries are under pressure to service small industries or small communities; in the railroad sector, the abandonment of unprofitable lines is politically difficult.

Even so, industries are able to acquire regulation in their own interests because of the nature of the political process. The industry which seeks regulation must go to the appropriate seller of those services — the political party and political representatives — and pay for regulation with its votes and its resources through campaign contributions and services.[50]

The burden of railroad regulation: an estimate

Was the net effect of regulation on the railroad industry onerous or beneficial? The railroads were in favor, at least in principle, of federal regulation, and Stigler has provided a theoretical rationale for that position. A recent analysis of the need for effective regulation in the early history of the ICC has been provided by Spann and Erickson.[51] They begin with the period of the "voluntary" agreements among railroad companies in the 1870s and the 1880s, when railroads were faced with high fixed costs of operation and increasing competition from new roads, and attempted to maintain high freight rates through cartel arrangements. Such arrangements are basically unstable since one firm in the cartel can usually profit by breaking the agreement, and the trunk line cartels of the 1870s and 1880s were inherently unstable.

The need for regulation of the railroad industry rests implicitly on the assumption that there were decreasing costs in the industry.[52] But Spann and Erickson argue that railroad costs were not decreasing; in fact, most large railroad companies were operating as though they had nondecreasing marginal costs, and by implication nondecreasing long-run average costs.[53]

In an industry subject to decreasing costs (or increasing returns) one expects to observe mergers rather than cartels, because the large firm will have lower costs and, consequently, greater profit-making potential. In the period under consideration, horizontal combination does not appear to have occurred as much as cartel formation. It is true that the New York Central, Pennsylvania, and Erie systems were formed by mergers of smaller roads; however, once formed, they established the Northern Trunk Line Cartel together with the Baltimore and Ohio Railroad. There was no attempt at merger among any subset of these companies in order to enjoy unrealized economies of scale. Second, a rapid expansion in the size of firms is expected in decreasing-cost industries. In the 1880s many contemporary observers were complaining of "over-investment" in the railroad sector, suggesting rapid rates of growth of assets. However, in Spann and Erickson's examination, the growth rates in total assets for the largest roads were not high relative to the growth rates of all railroads. Third, it appears, too, that many new railroads, smaller than the existing railroads, were entering competition in the area controlled by the trunk-line cartel roads in the 1870s and the 1880s. This would not be expected behavior if the original large roads were subject to increasing returns.[54] Finally, cost and output data, particularly for the trunk line cartel railroads, suggest that average costs were decreasing over a range and became constant at larger outputs of railroad services.[55] Spann and Erickson conclude that the railroad industry was not subject to decreasing costs, but was a constant-cost industry in an unstable cartel situation. Consequently, the formation of the ICC represented a response to the demand for regulation by railroads in order to stabilize cartel practices.

What effects did the formation of the ICC have on the cartel's activities? One effect was to alter the structure of rates on the trunk-line cartel in accordance with the Commerce Act by lowering short-haul rates by fifteen to thirty percent, and slightly increasing long-haul rates. The basic impact was to stabilize the cartel and to prevent long-haul rates from decreasing to competitive levels.[56] Since pooling was illegal, new methods of cooperating among the member railroads were found in the price system. The cartel, in effect, fixed long-haul rates and the ICC ratified and enforced those rates. The short-haul rates were fixed indirectly by the long-haul rates because of the short-haul/long-haul discrimination clause. If one railroad in the cartel had less traffic than its share, it could reduce rates to regain its share. The ICC reduced the potential profit from cheating, however, because a rate cut on long-haul traffic had to be extended to all traffic on the railroad because of the regulations, and immediate announcements of rate changes permitted other cartel members to make rate cuts if they so wished. The result was an increase in the profits and the stability of the railroad industry between 1887 and 1893, a stability which was decreased in the subsequent era by Supreme Court decisions undermining the authority of the commission.[57]

But the ICC's regulatory function probably had net social benefits at least in the short run. Social benefits from short-haul rate reduction outweighed social losses from long-haul rate increases which implied certain losses for shippers and users, especially in the grain trade from the Midwest to the Atlantic seaboard. ICC regulation had net benefits of approximately $9 million in 1890 with estimated gains from short-haul regulation of $26.8 million and estimated losses on long-haul regulation of $17.8 million.[58] The regulatory powers of the ICC stabilized the trunk-line cartel in long-haul traffic, lowered prices for short-haul traffic, and limited monopoly pricing in local markets by linking long-haul and short-haul rates. This was not entirely advantageous, since regulation did impose costs on the competitive sector, although these were outweighed by the benefits gained in the noncompetitive sector.

The Spann-Erickson and Zerbe studies cast some light on the ICC's early years from 1887 to 1893, but there have as yet been no similar attempts to discern the impact of regulation and changes in the powers and effectiveness of the commission over the period from 1893 to 1920. The railroads appear to have favored federal regulations but, aside from the period 1887 to 1893, it is not yet clear whether regulation most benefited the railroads or their users.

Conclusion

The late nineteenth and early twentieth century were remarkable for the growth of American industrialism. They were remarkable, too, for the emergence of big business and the frightening spectre of monopoly power which accompanied the corporation and the holding company, this in a nation hitherto regarded as the bastion of competition and individualism. The great American business leaders came to be portrayed as predators who preyed upon the powerless. The image was accentuated as the Populist movement broadened into Progressivism, and became after 1900 a full-scale national debate over trusts and monopolies, and the truth of the muckrakers' revelations.[59]

The emergence of noncompetitive forces was instrumental in fomenting agrarian and industrial unrest. Even more so, industrialism—of which the rise of big business was simply a manifestation—brought with it the subordination of agrarian and industrial workers alike to a system which combined the promise of prosperity with the increased insecurity of market forces. They found a convenient scapegoat in the belief that "robber barons" and corporate leaders were taking advantage of the unorganized.

The reaction was twofold — the formation of countervailing groups to force a better bargain, and growing interest in government intervention in the economy, especially in federal regulation of business, in order to further the public interest. Ironically enough, the industries which regulation was designed to curb may have benefited most from it.

8

The Market Economy: Prosperity and Prostration

Introduction

Before 1930 most Americans viewed the private enterprise economy as essentially self-regulating. They believed that most economic problems were temporary and would be corrected by the interplay of the market forces of demand and supply, provided that the potentially harmful economic power of large organizations -- governments, monopolistic and oligopolistic corporations, banks, and trade unions -- was carefully circumscribed. Until the 1920s this goal appeared to have been achieved although there were already problems in "Paradise." Agrarian unrest, trade union activity, and the exercise of market power by giant corporations each occupied a place on the American stage before the First World War. Government's economic role was limited to establishing the basic legal framework of the economy, to selective intervention in such areas as tariff legislation, and to a broadly defined regulatory function which ranged from transportation to food and drug standards and antitrust legislation. Essentially, the federal government's role was to encourage private enterprise which was to be constrained by government's regulatory powers only when excessive market power threatened the public well-being.

The Great Depression of the 1930s changed public perceptions of the economic role of government. Clearly, there was a pressing need for government economic leadership and intervention, which began as an ad hoc palliative for current problems and culminated by the end of the Second World War and the passing of the Employment Act of 1946 in general acceptance of the government's ultimate responsibility for the economic state of the nation. In this sense, the 1930s can be viewed as a watershed in American economic history.

A Brief Overview

Table 8.1 presents a summary of several important macroeconomic variables which describe the course of the economy during the 1920s and 1930s.

Real GNP grew steadily after the recession of 1921 until 1929, although short recessions occurred in 1924 and 1927. Even so, the period from 1923 to 1929 is regarded as one of the most prosperous in American history, so prosperous in fact that George Soule entitled his famous monograph on the period, *Prosperity Decade*. Total consumption expenditures increased by twenty-five percent from 1923 to 1929 and show a similar pattern to GNP, but gross investment remains fairly stable and picks up the recessions of 1924 and 1927 more clearly than the other series. The index of industrial production shows an eighty-eight percent gain by 1929 from its low point in 1921 (and a thirty percent gain over 1923), and Standard and Poor's index of common stock prices increased about four fold during the same period. Unemployment averaged only 3.8 percent during 1923 to 1929, after the high rates of 1921 and 1922. The money supply grew more rapidly in the first half of the decade than in the later years.

For most observers of the "New Era," the collapse of the stock market in October 1929 signalled the end of the prosperous 1920s. Often overlooked is the fact that some economic indicators had already begun to turn downwards in early summer. The collapse of the stock market followed and greatly exacerbated this turndown. But the stock market panic and Black Thursday remain the symbol of the Depression's beginnings.

The indicators in Table 8.1 record the depth of the fall from 1929 to 1933. Real GNP plummetted from $104.4 billions in 1929 to $74.2 billions in 1933, a fall of some thirty percent. The decline in aggregate demand is evident in real consumption expenditures which fell by almost twenty percent, and real investment expenditures, the more volatile component, which virtually disappeared, falling from over $16 billion in 1929 to only $300 million in 1933. Moreover, the other indicators kept pace. The index of industrial production fell by more than eighty percent to a low of 100.5 in 1932, and unemployment reached a peak of almost

Table 8.1 Selected Economic Indicators, 1920-1941

Year	GNP (billions of $ 1929)	Total consumption expenditures (billions of $ 1929)	Gross investment expenditures (billions of $ 1929)	Index of industrial production (1913 = 100)	Index of common stock prices (1941-43 = 10)	Civilian unemployment (%)	Money supply (billion)
1920	73.3	52.7	12.8	124.0	7.98	4.0	34.80
1921	71.6	56.1	7.4	100.1	6.86	11.9	32.85
1922	75.8	58.1	10.6	125.9	8.41	7.6	33.72
1923	85.8	63.4	15.6	144.4	8.57	3.2	36.60
1924	88.4	68.1	12.4	137.7	9.05	5.5	38.58
1925	90.5	66.1	16.4	153.0	11.15	4.0	42.05
1926	96.4	71.5	17.1	163.1	12.59	1.9	43.68
1927	97.3	73.2	15.6	164.5	15.34	4.1	44.73
1928	98.5	74.8	14.5	171.8	19.95	4.4	46.42
1929	104.4	79.0	16.2	188.3	26.02	3.2	46.60
1930	95.1	74.7	10.5	155.6	21.03	8.7	45.73
1931	89.5	72.2	6.8	129.9	13.66	15.9	42.69
1932	76.4	66.0	0.8	100.5	6.93	23.6	36.05
1933	74.2	64.6	0.3	119.9	8.96	24.9	32.23
1934	80.8	68.0	1.8	129.9	9.84	21.7	34.36
1935	91.4	72.3	8.8	149.1	10.60	20.1	39.07
1936	100.9	79.7	9.3	178.3	15.47	16.9	43.48
1937	109.1	82.6	14.6	194.5	15.41	14.3	45.68
1938	103.2	81.3	6.8	152.3	11.49	19.0	45.51
1939	111.0	85.9	9.9	188.0	12.06	17.2	49.27
1940	121.0	90.5	14.2	213.9	11.02	14.6	55.20
1941	138.7	96.4	18.9	275.5	9.82	9.9	62.51

SOURCE: GNP — John W. Kendrick, *Productivity Trends in the United States,* N. B. E. R., General Series, no. 71 (Princeton: Princeton University Press, 1961), pp. 294-295; Consumption — United States Bureau of Economic Analysis, *Long Term Economic Growth, 1860-1970* (Washington, D.C.: Government Printing Office, 1973), ser. A23, p. 184; Investment — *Long Term Economic Growth*, ser. A27, p. 186; Industrial Production — *Long Term Economic Growth*, ser. A15, p. 184; Common Stock Prices — *Long Term Economic Growth*, ser. B84, p. 224; Unemployment — United States Bureau of the Census, *Historical Statistics of the United States* (Washington D.C.: Government Printing Office, 1975), ser. D47, p. 73; Money Supply — *Long Term Economic Growth,* ser. B111, pp. 230-231.

twenty-five percent in 1933. Fully one-quarter of the labor force was unemployed in the depths of the Depression. The collapse of stock prices was complete by 1932.

Recovery from this low point was slow. Even though the 1929 levels of GNP, consumption, and industrial production were restored by 1937, investment expenditures continued to lag as did stock prices. More importantly, unemployment remained close to fifteen percent. The recession of 1937–38 plunged the economy downwards again, and recovery remained weak until the new, powerful stimulus imparted to investment, industrial production, and employment by the burgeoning war economy in 1940 and 1941.

This brief review cannot begin to portray the immense social cost and dislocation of a catastrophe like the Great Depression which destroyed the hopes and aspirations—indeed, the very lives—of so many Americans. Moreover, while the picture presented by these broad statistical aggregates is a correct one, the data do not reveal many differential effects of the Depression among the various sectors of production and income groups. Nor do the data help us very much in trying to pinpoint some of the more critical components of consumption and investment expenditures that might help us to better understand the causes of the Depression.

To do so, we can disaggregate total investment expenditures to see whether the constituents yield useful additional information about the course of the economy in the 1920s and 1930s. Table 8.2 presents data on private new construction, private producers durable expenditures, and changes in business inventories. We can now see that the collapse in total investment was based in each of its components. The largest single component, private new construction, appears to have peaked in 1926 and declined slowly thereafter until 1929, when the decline became more rapid, reaching the trough in 1933. On the other hand, expenditures on producers' durables rallied after the recession of 1927 to peak in 1929, before their fall to a 1933 trough. If one is to look for a "cause" of the Depression in the investment sector, perhaps one should concentrate on nonresidential and residential construction where the downturn occurred as early as 1926.

Again, we can disaggregate total consumption expenditures in Table 8.3 into expenditures on consumer perishables, semidurable commodities, durable commodities, and services. Each of these components grew during the 1920s, with expenditures on services and on durable commodities growing most rapidly. During the collapse from 1929 to 1933, the most volatile component was durables expenditures which fell by more than sixty percent from their 1929 peak. Why were durables expenditures more responsive than the other components of consumption?

Table 8.2 Gross Private Components of Domestic Investment, 1920-1941

Year	Gross private new construction	Gross private producers durables	New private const. and equipment	Change in business inventories	Gross private domestic investment
1919	4.42	3.89	8.31	4.05	12.4
1920	5.38	4.75	10.1	7.36	17.5
1921	4.80	2.95	7.75	0.06	7.81
1922	6.34	3.22	9.55	0.53	10.1
1923	8.11	4.58	12.7	2.99	15.7
1924	8.90	4.28	13.2	-0.94	12.2
1925	9.76	4.65	14.4	1.75	16.2
1926	10.5	5.05	15.5	1.52	17.0
1927	9.99	4.66	14.6	0.41	15.1
1928	9.52	4.96	14.5	-0.38	14.1
1929	8.91	5.60	14.5	1.71	16.2
1930	6.35	4.26	10.6	-0.35	10.3
1931	4.07	2.70	6.77	-1.15	5.62
1932	1.95	1.49	3.44	-2.48	0.96
1933	1.49	1.47	2.97	-1.56	1.40
1934	1.91	2.16	4.07	-0.74	3.33
1935	2.43	2.90	5.34	1.07	6.41
1936	3.25	3.97	7.23	1.26	8.49
1937	4.38	4.87	9.24	2.54	11.8
1938	3.92	3.47	7.39	-0.91	6.48
1939	4.88	3.97	8.85	0.41	9.26
1940	5.69	5.26	11.0	2.18	13.1
1941	6.86	6.58	13.4	4.47	17.9

SOURCE: J. A. Swanson and S. M. Williamson, "Estimates of National Product and Income for the United States Economy, 1919–1941," *Explorations in Economic History* 10 (Fall 1972), p. 70.

In part, the explanation lies in the peculiar nature of durables: one consumes the services of a durable good over a period of time, and once an initial purchase has been made, the replacement of the durable can be postponed. A prospective buyer can avoid paying the high initial price of the replacement good by repairing the existing one and continuing to consume its services. On the other hand, the consumption of durables was favorably affected by a significant qualitative change in purchase arrangements in the 1920s—the development of installment buying. How critical was the behavior of consumer durables' expenditures to the continuing prosperity of the late 1920s and to the onset and deepening of the Depression?

Table 8.3 Components of Consumption Expenditures, 1920-41

Year	Perishable commodities	Semidurable commodities	Durable commodities	Services	Total consumption expenditures
1919	23.9	8.70	5.72	15.0	53.3
1920	26.4	10.1	6.59	19.7	62.8
1921	21.4	8.20	5.33	23.4	58.3
1922	20.7	8.46	5.81	22.5	57.4
1923	22.3	9.56	7.39	24.7	63.9
1924	22.9	9.04	7.41	28.4	67.8
1925	24.5	9.47	8.42	24.9	67.3
1926	26.1	9.90	8.78	28.3	73.1
1927	25.8	10.1	8.38	28.5	72.7
1928	26.4	10.2	8.60	29.9	75.0
1929	27.3	10.4	9.21	31.9	78.8
1930	25.1	8.91	7.16	29.6	70.8
1931	21.3	7.70	5.49	26.7	61.1
1932	17.1	5.64	3.65	22.7	49.1
1933	17.0	5.21	3.47	20.5	46.2
1934	20.4	6.32	4.21	20.9	51.8
1935	22.6	6.73	5.11	21.8	56.2
1936	25.5	7.40	6.30	23.4	62.6
1937	27.5	7.76	6.93	25.1	67.2
1938	26.3	7.61	5.69	25.0	64.6
1939	27.0	8.11	6.67	25.8	67.6
1940	28.5	8.52	7.77	26.9	71.7
1941	32.0	10.1	9.65	28.9	80.7

SOURCE: Swanson and Williamson, "Estimates of National Product," p. 69.

Another variable which fits into the aggregate demand side of the basic model is government expenditures. Government spending increased in the 1930s as the economy began its agonizing recovery from the depths of 1933. Did these expenditures alone indicate a greater commitment on the part of the government to intervention in the economy? Was the federal government a successful practitioner of expansionary fiscal policy during the 1930s? To these issues we now turn.

The 1920s

The decade of the 1920s has been characterized by George Soule as "the flowering of private enterprise" in the United States, as a period of great prosperity with a minimum of government interference and a maximum of government encouragement.[1]

The recovery from the postwar depression in 1922 was led by the private sector of the economy, and was carried through the early boom from 1923 to 1926 by rising consumption expenditures, particularly on services and durable goods like automobiles and household appliances, and by the dramatic expansion in residential construction. There were rapid increases in labor productivity in the manufacturing sector, with the renewed development and diffusion of mass-production methods, many involving the electric motor. Meanwhile, the federal government maintained a low profile, with a persistent, annual budgetary surplus, a deaf ear to agitation for farm relief and new labor legislation, and a reluctance to enforce antitrust laws against business in a vigorous way.

Portents of Doom

In brief, 1922 to 1929 is normally viewed as a long period of sustained growth, real GNP having risen by thirty-eight percent and industrial production by fifty percent, with striking advances in key capital-intensive industries like construction, automobiles, electricity and electrical equipment.

But this portrait of prosperity hides many blemishes. In agriculture, for example, the 1920s was alleged to be a period of declining real incomes, primarily because the growth in demand for farm produce failed to keep pace with the gains in farm productive efficiency. The resultant "overproduction" and falling prices led during the 1920s to repeated demands for government assistance, particularly in the areas of stabilizing agricultural prices (the notion of prewar "parity" prices was commonplace) and farm credit.

Another potential problem in the 1920s lay in the labor movement, where union membership fell dramatically. The traditional craft emphasis of the AFL found no foothold in the new mass-production industries, and the relative increase in the employment of unskilled laborers had serious, adverse implications for labor unions, which would not be remedied until the establishment of the Committee for Industrial Organization (CIO) in 1935. Meanwhile, nothing seemed to encumber the growth of large corporations through renewed merger activity. The 1920s saw the abandonment of the trust-busting policy developed in the Sherman and Clayton Acts, after the Supreme Court decision in 1920 against the dissolution of United States Steel. The Court's finding that "good behavior" rather than "large size" was the vital criterion for deciding trust cases helped to promote the new merger movement and to undermine the effectiveness of the Federal Trade Commission as a watch dog against collusion and price fixing. The laxness of antitrust policy combined with the weakness of the labor movement helped to make the 1920s the age of *corporate* prosperity.

In the financial sector, the banking system remained highly decentralized, and unit banks were liable to incur liquidity problems, especially where farm or business borrowers encountered economic difficulties. Easy credit policies fed the speculative boom from 1927 on, but the Federal Reserve's restrictive policy in 1928 caused interest rates to rise and helped to bring about liquidity problems and decline in aggregate demand in 1929. The speculative upward spiral of stock prices finally peaked in September 1929, but it was built upon a delicate fabric of margin purchases and unfounded expectations of continued price rises, a fabric that was to be purged in the October crash and the subsequent deflation, and was to be rebuilt in sturdier form with the establishment of a new regulatory framework in the Securities and Exchange Commission in 1935.

Foreign sector commodity trade and capital flows were complicated by increasingly restrictive American and foreign tariff policies on the one hand, and by the emergence of the United States as a leading creditor nation after the First World War, and by the reparations issue on the other. The reduction of American foreign lending in mid-1928 brought further distress to the world economy.

Thus, the fundamental image of American prosperity concealed many portents of doom in the 1920s. Notwithstanding these areas of concern, many writers continue to emphasize consumption and investment expenditures as the most likely sources of the Great Depression, suggesting that the economy was moving towards a state of "underconsumption" in the late 1920s.[2] Some recent work on income distribution, the consumption of durable commodities, and residential construction during the 1920s sheds light on these issues.

Changes in Income Distribution, 1920s

Conventional wisdom concludes that the 1920s was a period of prosperity. Were the benefits of prosperity widely distributed?

Many economic historians have argued that the 1920s saw structural changes in the United States economy which had adverse implications for sustained growth. They have pointed out that the 1920s saw an increase in monopoly and oligopoly power among corporations and a rapid rate of technological change which led to increases in profits relative to wages (since technological changes led to lower production costs, market power led to diminished downward flexibility in prices, and weakened labor unions, which lost bargaining strength).[3] These developments, they concluded, favored owners of capital, and created an "imbalance" between consumption and investment. There was an increase in funds available for investment relative to consumption. Moreover, since consumption expenditures could not keep pace—a tendency towards underconsumption developed—there were declining investment opportunities to absorb the available investment funds. The result was declining aggregate demand in the household and business sectors.

Two recent studies of income distribution in the 1920s have cast light on this argument. Robert Keller's study of factor income distribution attempts to put the changes in the 1920s into perspective by comparing the experience during 1923–1929 with an earlier period, 1899–1907, and a later period, 1948–1957.[4] The success of his attempt depends in large part on whether his assumption that these are three comparable periods of sustained expansion is convincing.

Keller begins by estimating national income originating in three sectors—mining, manufacturing, and transportation and other public utilities. These three sectors contain about one-third of total national income originating, and Keller's presumption is that changes in these three sectors are indicative of economy-wide changes. For each sector, Keller finds (1) labor income, defined as wages, salaries, and other employee compensation, and (2) capital income, defined as corporate profits after tax and net interest payments. He then expresses each as a ratio of national income originating by sector.

Capital's share in the three sectors rose from 19.6 percent in 1923 to 25.5 percent in 1929, whereas labor's share declined from 77.9 percent in 1923 to 72.9 percent in 1929.[5] The data for the earlier and later periods suggest a contrary result: labor's share increased and capital's share decreased during 1899–1907 and 1948–1957. Keller concludes, then, that the increases in capital's share in the 1920s appears to be unique. This is an interesting result and, if valid, would have implications for the relevance of the underconsumption thesis. Notwithstanding some concerns about extrapolating results for these three sectors to the national economy and about the comparability of the three time periods, the fact remains that, at the least, factor income distribution in three important sectors of the economy favored capital relative to labor during the "prosperity" of the 1920s.

Next, Keller examines the reasons underlying this change. He proposes that the growth of capital-intensive sectors is the most obvious explanation; that is, capital's share likely increased because sectors with high capital-intensity in production grew more rapidly than sectors with a small capital share. In fact, he is able to provide firm estimates that about one-half of the change in capital's share is explained by the relative growth of capital-intensive sectors, a point that had previously been overlooked. The other half of the growth in capital's share results in large part from monopoly power in metals industries, electric utilities, and changes in government regulations permitting an increase in the maximum rate of return allowed railroads. A second important factor is the reduction in fuel expenditures in electric utilities, railroads, and metal industries in the presence of output price rigidity. And, third, there were large increases in factor productivity in the 1920s which led to cost reductions and increased returns to capital. Even with its limitations, Keller's finding of changing factor income distribution in the 1920s suggests that prosperity was not shared between capitalists and laborers.

Another recent study of income distribution in the 1920s by Charles Holt confirms the inference drawn from Keller's work.[6] Holt begins with Kuznets' data which showed that per capita current-dollar income increased by ten percent during 1923–1929, but that an increasing share of income flowed to upper-income groups.[7] The share of income received by the top one percent increased from thirteen percent in 1923 to nineteen percent in 1929, that is, by thirty-five percent during the seven-year period, whereas the share of the lower ninety-five percent increased by only five percent. Indeed, the lower ninety-five percent of *nonfarm* population showed no increase during 1923 to 1929,and the lower ninety-three percent actually suffered a slight decrease in per capita income! Meanwhile, the incomes of the farm population increased by twenty-one percent.[8]

Holt then adjusts Kuznets' estimates (based on income received in a given year) to allow for income *status* over a longer period, which results in estimates of per capita income for *permanent* members of the upper and lower income groups. Again, Holt's findings confirm that the 1920s was a period of prosperity for the few. Nonfarm upper-income groups and farmers received the gains; nonfarm lower-income groups actually lost ground. The changes in real disposable income per capita are summarized in Table 8.4. Briefly, the top one percent of nonfarm population

Table 8.4 Changes in Disposable Income Per Capita, 1923-1929.

Series	Per Cent Change, 1923-29
1. Entire Population	13
2. *Nonfarm Population*	
a) Entire Nonfarm Population	9
b) Top 1 percent	63
c) 2nd - 7th percentiles	23
d) lower 93 percent	-4
3. *Farm population*	
a) Entire Farm Population	21

SOURCE: Charles F. Holt, "Who Benefited From the Prosperity of the Twenties?" *Explorations in Economic History* 14 (Summer 1977), p. 283.

enjoyed a sixty-three percent increase in real per capita income, made possible largely by capital gains. On the other hand, the lower ninety-three percent suffered a four percent decline in real income.

The traditional emphasis on the "troubled farmer" during the 1920s may have to be reconsidered, for Holt's data show a twenty-one percent increase in farm per capita income. This rise occurred in spite of the litany of standard farm problems—rural bank failures, farm mortgage foreclosures, and falling agricultural prices. Holt's findings reinforce the notion that the farmer's poverty must be viewed in the context of agriculture's halcyon days before World War I and not from the perspective of 1920s experience alone.

Thus, the prosperity of the 1920s was not widely distributed. Any increase in real consumption expenditures during 1923–1929 must have been fairly narrowly based among upper-income earners and farmers, since over ninety percent of the nonfarm population actually saw their real incomes deteriorate.

Automobiles, Housing and Market Saturation, 1920s

One component of consumption expenditures to receive considerable attention is consumer durables. Of major concern has been the notion that consumer durables' markets—as well as the market for residential housing—had become saturated or beset by excess supply by the late 1920s.

To begin with, many writers believe that the structure of consumer preferences changed in favor of durable goods during the twentieth century, and that these changes were probably concentrated during the 1920s. This impression has been reinforced by both qualitative and quantitative evidence pertinent to the 1920s—the growth of installment buying, output data for automobiles and electric appliances. Recently, Harold Vatter has attempted to determine whether the notion of a consumer durables' "revolution" is valid.[9]

In fact, Vatter's data suggest that consumers did not devote a much greater proportion of consumption expenditures to durables between the 1870s and mid-twentieth century. In Table 8.5, the ratio of durables expenditures to GNP varies over the period from 6.9 to 8.9 percent, displaying at best a "gentle upward drift."[10] With high income elasticity of demand for durables, the essential stability of durables consumption as income has increased over the past century is explained by Vatter through the notion of saturation purchase rates in each income bracket, beginning with the upper-income brackets and eventually diffusing throughout the economy as a whole.

For the 1920s, Vatter finds no evidence of a marked shift in durables' consumption, although he acknowledges that certain

Table 8.5 Durables Outlays, Consumer Expenditures, and GNP 1869-1879 to 1944-1953

Decade	Ratio, durables to total consumer flow	Ratio, Durables to GNP
1869-1878	8.94	6.92
1874-1883	8.75	6.77
1879-1888	9.43	7.33
1884-1893	10.39	7.83
1889-1898	10.24	7.63
1894-1903	9.73	7.30
1899-1908	9.43	7.20
1904-1913	9.24	7.16
1909-1918	9.39	7.26
1914-1923	9.58	7.49
1919-1928	10.93	8.59
1924-1933	10.50	8.67
1929-1938	9.12	7.85
1934-1943	9.06	7.47
1939-1948	9.07	7.33
1944-1953	11.02	8.92

SOURCE: Harold G. Vatter, "Has There Been a Twentieth-Century Consumer Durables Revolution?" *Journal of Economic History,* 27 (March 1967), p. 5.

NOTE: The percentages are based on figures in real $ 1929.

qualitative changes—the diffusion of the automobile and electrification— did occur, and these phenomena may explain a slight upward drift. New durables products may have been diffused rapidly through the higher income groups during the 1920s, accounting for the increased ratios. Some short period increases (or decreases) can be explained by institutional changes like the development of installment credit or by the peculiar nature of durables goods themselves (the postponement of purchases, the increasing importance of replacement purchases with widespread adoption of the good, the development of second-hand markets). Vatter's conclusion that the 1920s did not witness a durables revolution and that durables' expenditures have been stable over the long run, are not inconsistent with the short-term relative expansion of durables' expenditures in the 1920s.

Even so, saturated markets may have been developing for key durables-producing industries by the late 1920s. There are several possible interpretations of saturation, each of which connotes, in either static or dynamic form, the impression of excess supply or deficient demand.[11] Consumption of a durable good complicates the issue somewhat, since the use of a durable good extends over several time periods. Consequently, new purchases of a durable good depend upon the desired stream of services and the stock of the durable good currently held by consumers. Actual stock and desired stock are adjusted to each other according to a set of behavioral relationships (usually involving data on prices, income, depreciation rates, and so forth).

Mercer and Morgan analyzed production of a major consumer durable, the automobile, to determine whether the market for automobiles was saturated in the late 1920s. The American automobile industry became commercially viable at the turn of the century, and its first significant growth and the emergence of large corporations occurred after 1907. Production increased from some 65,000 units in 1908 to 200,000 in 1911, to almost 900,000 in 1915, and averaged more than one and one-half million units during the rest of the decade. Production averaged well over 3 million cars annually during 1923–1926, and reached a prewar peak of 4 million cars in 1929. Some authors have argued, however, that a new phase began in the mid-1920s when the industry began to mature and had to meet the new worries of exhaustion of their potential market. The shift to lighter, cheaper cars, installment purchases, and the extension of the road network all had a positive effect on the demand for cars, but by the late twenties the industry clearly faced the problem of adjusting production to a more stable demand. Competition for market shares rather than the continued growth of the market became a major concern. During the 1920s the number of replacement buyers compared with first-time purchasers increased from about one-fifth in 1921 to almost sixty percent in 1929. Although the number of new car registrations increased from 1921 to 1929, the percentage increase tended to decline (with the exception of 1929), and there was even a decrease in new car production in 1927.

To test for market saturation, Mercer and Morgan estimate two sets of automobile demand functions, one for auto registration stock and one for new car equivalents (based on a weighting of all automobiles according to their age). Mercer and Morgan found evidence of static saturation in 1921, 1924–1927, and 1930–1932, but conclude the automobile market was not saturated in the crucial years of 1928 and 1929.[12] Their preferred estimates are for the definition of dynamic saturation: here, they find that the market was saturated in 1924–1927 and from 1929–1932, although not for 1928.[13] They conclude that the strength of automobile demand in the late 1920s was declining, and the market was moving toward a state of saturation. Thus, the dynamic saturation measures indicate that conditions in the automobile market exacerbated the decline in the growth of aggregate demand in the late 1920s, and that the slowdown in the growth of this component of consumer durables' spending was communicated to the rest of the economy by the multiplier-accelerator mechanism.

The question which must be addressed, however, concerns whether the saturation results are sufficiently robust to permit such a strong conclusion. The Mercer and Morgan automobile demand functions have been respecified by George and Oksanen to include, first, a combined stock adjustment and adaptive expectations scheme and, second, a Friedman-type permanent income series, which performs very well.[14] As with Mercer and Morgan's paper, George and Oksanen's demand function does not indicate static saturation for the late 1920s (with the exception of some tentative findings for 1927). However, the dynamic saturation tests are less similar: George and Oksanen corroborate the existence of dynamic saturation from 1924–1927, and confirm 1928 as a year of nonsaturation. But they cannot confirm Mercer and Morgan's claim of dynamic saturation for 1929. The evidence on saturation for 1929 is inconclusive at best. Given the weakness of the findings for 1929 and that1928 was clearly nonsaturated, there is now considerable doubt that conditions in the automobile market amplified the decline in the growth of aggregate demand. Hence, there appears to be a lack of support for the underconsumption thesis in this market at least.

A similar controversy has emerged in the literature on residential construction, a component of gross investment expenditures. Here, the issue is whether there was overbuilding (saturation) in residential construction during the late 1920s. The stock of residential housing was insufficient after the First World War, and this led to an increase in the rate of construction in the early 1920s to meet pent-up demand. However, the rate of population growth decreased by the mid-1920s, partly because of immigration restrictions after 1924. By the late 1920s overbuilding appears to have set in and to have reinforced the decline in residential construction initiated by reduced family formation and population growth.

Bolch, Fels, and McMahon have examined these issues, and found evidence for a housing surplus in the 1920s.[15] From 1917–1921, net household formation exceeded housing starts: thus excess demand in the housing market signalled an increase in the supply of residential construction. But from 1922–1930 housing starts exceeded net household formation, and there were excessive dwelling units after 1926 even though residential construction began to decline after 1926. They conclude that the housing industry was slow to adjust to demographic changes in the 1920s.

Mercer and Morgan have corroborated Bolch, Fels, and McMahon's results using an alternative technique based on concepts of saturation.[16] Briefly, they found continuous state saturation for

1921–1938, and dynamic saturation in the industry from 1925–1931. Clearly, desired housing stock was growing less rapidly than actual stock during the late 1920s. The decline in residential construction was offset by buoyant demand in other sectors until 1929, when the deflationary impact of the housing surplus aggravated the severity of the recession.

Does the evidence on income distribution and durables' consumption support the underconsumption thesis? Changes in income distribution likely favored the upper-income groups, and consumption expenditures might have grown more rapidly in the 1920s if the increases in income had been more widely distributed. The evidence on durables' expenditures is mixed. While there was some increase in the ratio of durables' expenditures to GNP, no consumer durables' "revolution" occurred in the 1920s. Saturation in the automobile market was probably not a factor in dampening consumption, but in residential housing, a component of investment expenditures, there was excess supply after 1926 which did adversely affect aggregate demand and help to bring on the Depression.

The Crash and Its Aftermath: The 1930s

Stock prices began to fall rapidly in October and November 1929, after the September peak. The collapse of the stock market reinforced the decline in aggregate economic activity which had begun in June 1929, partly by contributing to reduced consumption demand directly through the reduced wealth of households and partly by contributing to reduced investment demand by adversely affecting business expectations about the profitability of new investment.

We have already reviewed some of the major indicators of the Depression's magnitude.[17] Briefly, real GNP fell by some thirty percent between 1929 and 1933, and gross investment fell by some ninety percent, with major collapses in residential construction and producers' durables production. Although there were significant sectoral differences in employment and real income losses, the fact remains of an overwhelming deterioration in mining, manufacturing, and agriculture. The collapse of the banking system and of the international economy was the final blow.

Economic historians have emphasized both the magnitude of the Depression and the slowness of economic recovery. Why was the Depression so severe? As noted earlier, two classes of explanations have been categorized and analyzed in detail by Peter Temin: the monetary hypothesis, whose main proponents have identified the collapse of the banking system as the primary cause, and the spending hypothesis where the fall in aggregate demand, especially autonomous components within consumption, investment, and the foreign sector, are identified as primary causes.

The monetarist position was developed by Milton Friedman and Anna Jacobson Schwartz who, believing that the chain of economic events runs from changes in the money supply to changes in income, concluded that the Great Depression originated in financial markets.[18] They argued that an initial decline in the money stock in 1929–1930 became a sharp decrease about twenty-five percent) in 1931–1933 because of bank failures and the Federal Reserve's abdication of its responsibility to support the monetary base and provide liquidity to the banking system. The Federal Reserve's failure to use its powers effectively converted a serious recession into the Great Depression! On the other hand, strict adherents to the spending hypothesis hold that money had no independent role in the onset of the Depression, that changes in the money supply were merely responses to changes in income brought about by falling aggregate demand.[19]

The search for a "unique" cause of the Great Depression has been rekindled by Temin's indictment of the money hypothesis.[20] Undoubtedly, the best assessment of the contentious issues has been provided by R. J. Gordon and J. A. Wilcox who, after rejecting the "hard-line" monetarist and nonmonetarist explanations, conclude that a synthesis of the money and spending hypotheses provides the most convincing explanation.[21] Nonmonetary factors (construction, consumption expenditures, and international events) initiated the contraction in 1929, and the failure of the Federal Reserve to offset the deflationary impact of bank failures in 1931–1933 exacerbated the situation. A more effective monetary policy after 1931 could have prevented the economic collapse to the depths of 1933.

To this point, we have emphasized components of expenditure as possible areas of disturbance in the 1920s helping to bring on the Depression. To housing, consumer durables, and changing income distribution can be added the effect of the stock market crash on investment and consumption spending, and the international collapse which undoubtedly exaggerated the problems emanating from the domestic economy. The two competing hypotheses can be partly reconciled by focusing on connecting elements like the stock market which reverberated on both the real and financial sectors. In particular, we will focus on consumption expenditures, since the underconsumption thesis has traditional roots and since Temin's recent study and the studies on market saturation have given it new life.

Consumption and the Depression

According to Temin,[22] the Depression began in 1929 for a combination of reasons, among them tight financial imbalances in various markets like housing. But he emphasizes falling consumption expenditures as crucial, and points to three identifiable deflationary forces on consumption. First, the stock market crash in October 1929 led to reduced personal wealth and hence to reduced consumption expenditures. Second, a poor harvest in 1929 led to lower agricultural output and lower farm income, and hence to reduced consumption expenditures by farm familes. Third, a still further fall in consumption expenditures for both durables and nondurables is, as yet, largely unexplained. Effective expansionary economic policies were not employed by the government, and by 1931 the Depression was endemic and worldwide.

Temin's selection of consumption expenditures for a crucial role in the onset of the Depression results from his comparison of the recession in 1929–1930 with the recessions in 1920–1921 and 1937–1938. The 1929–1930 recession was different from the others in its drastic decline in consumption and in construction, private construction falling by some $2 billion from 1926 to 1929. Temin concludes that the fall in consumption is larger than can be expected from the fall in income alone, and turns to the stock market crash as a potential causal factor. His chain of reasoning is straightforward: falling stock prices had an adverse impact on personal wealth and, consequently, led to reduced personal consumption expenditure through this wealth affect. Moreover, the collapse of the stock market may have led to generally pessimistic expectations about future deterioration of wealth (and possibly income too), and this change in expectations may have further reduced consumption spending. Only part of this stock market effect can be captured by Temin's estimation technique. Hence, much of the fall in consumption remains antonomous or, more accurately, "unexplained."[23]

This nexus has been examined in an interesting recent study by Frederic Mishkin.[24] Mishkin looks at changes in the household balance sheet as a transmission mechanism for relating deflationary events and policies from the financial sector to aggregate demand. In particular, he argues that the large buildup of household liabilities in 1929 and the price deflation from 1929 to 1933 increased the real burden of debt, and the effect of the stock market crash and of the continuing decline in stock prices reduced the value of household financial assets. Both reinforced the decline in consumption.

Consumption depends on more than current income; that is, it depends on current and past income, expectations about future income, the household's net wealth, and so forth.[25] But, according to Mishkin, a household's net wealth portfolio is not comprised of homogeneous holdings. Instead, one ought to consider a "liquidity" hypothesis version which stresses the composition of the household balance sheet: the consumer's holdings of financial assets and his liabilities. The liquidity thesis concentrates on the imperfect capital markets for tangible assets like residential housing and consumers' durables which cause these assets to be illiquid. When a consumer faces financial distress, he prefers to hold highly liquid financial assets rather than illiquid assets. As financial distress increases, as it did during the Depression, the demand for illiquid assets decreases.

The composition of a consumer's balance sheet determines the probability of his suffering financial hardship. When his indebtedness is high (as it was in the beginning of the Depression), large contracted debt service payments increase the probability of hardship. (The severe price deflation during the early years of the Depression further amplified this source of hardship by increasing the real burden of debt payments.) Again, when the value of financial asset holdings decreases (as did households' holdings of stocks and bonds during 1929–1933), the consumer is more likely to suffer distress. The demand for illiquid assets, then, can be interpreted as depending directly on the value of financial asset holdings and inversely on holdings of liabilities. This framework is particularly relevant to the analysis of consumer durables' spending and residential housing construction.

Data on household liabilities, household financial asset holdings, and household net worth are presented in Table 8.6. The correspondence between changes in the household balance sheet and aggregate demand during the Depression is striking. During 1929–1930, for example, the financial position of the American consumer deteriorated rapidly. Household liabilities increased by twenty percent, and the value of financial assets decreased by four percent. Usually, the growth in household liabilities corresponds with a growth in assets and net worth. But not so in 1929 and 1930. The value of financial assets decreased because of the stock market crash, and precipitated a decrease in aggregate demand. Moreover, the increase in household debt during the 1920s had been widespread and the deflation of the early 1930s led to increases in the real burden of household debt which were felt by many. This helped bring about a continuing decline in household net worth amounting to about $100 billion between 1929 and 1934.[26]

Mishkin offers a similarly convincing exposition of the correspondence between the consumer's deteriorating financial position and the recession of 1937–1938. The downturn in the stock market in 1937

Table 8.6 Household Balance Sheets, 1929-1941

Year	Household liabilities ($ 1938 billions)	Household financial asset holdings ($ 1938 billions)	Household net worth ($ 1938 billions)
1929	65.3	637.8	844.1
1930	78.1	613.0	828.9
1931	79.5	578.6	801.0
1932	81.0	533.7	755.1
1933	75.9	545.3	752.7
1934	67.5	548.2	745.5
1935	65.1	562.2	758.8
1936	65.5	617.3	811.9
1937	64.9	604.6	810.5
1938	66.1	557.4	783.3
1939	66.2	581.2	816.0
1940	65.9	594.5	832.8
1941	65.5	582.0	827.9

SOURCE: Frederic S. Mishkin, "The Household Balance Sheet and The Great Depression," *Journal of Economic History* 38 (December 1978), p. 920.

NOTES: 1. Household liabilities include security loans, mortgages, consumer credit, and other liabilities.

2. Financial assets include currency plus demand deposits, time and savings deposits, corporate and government bonds, corporate equity, life insurance, and other miscellaneous assets.

reversed the improvement in household net worth of the mid-1930s, and the financial restrictions of 1938 further decreased the value of financial assets. Aggregate demand declined as a result.

The liquidity hypothesis provides a theoretical framework for linking the household's balance sheet to changes in aggregate demand, and Mishkin's examination of changes in the balance sheet and in the aggregate economy from 1929 to 1939 establishes the temporal correspondence of their movements. Next, Mishkin attempts to estimate precisely the extent of balance sheet changes on aggregate demand by using parameter estimates obtained from postwar data in studies which confirm that balance sheet changes have powerful effects on consumer durables and residential housing expenditures.[27] Increased indebtedness and falling values of household financial assets, as happened in the early years of the Depression, would have shifted consumer demand significantly away from illiquid assets.

Admittedly crude, Mishkin's estimates suggest that the balance sheet changes explain more than two-thirds of the twenty percent decline in consumer durables expenditures and the forty percent fall in residential construction in 1930. In addition, the drop in net wealth from 1929 to 1930 further depressed demand. The collapse of the economy from 1930 to 1933, in particular the continued decline of the consumer durables and residential housing sectors, can be explained by the further deterioration of household balance sheets in 1931 and 1932 and by the continued fall of consumer net wealth. Finally, changes in balance sheets and net wealth provide convincing explanations of the recovery from 1933 to 1935 when consumers' financial positions improved steadily along with expanding demand for consumer durables and residential housing, and for the recession of 1937–1938 when households' financial positions were weakened by the stock market's difficulties and the demand for tangible assets declined once again.

It is possible that Mishkin's reliance on postwar parameters is not strictly appropriate for his study of the Depression period. The economy may have experienced some structural transformation between the 1920s and the post-1945 era; alternatively, the parameters for demand functions for consumer durables and residential housing in the postwar period may be quite appropriate for studies of the Depression economy. Notwithstanding this possible source of bias, Mishkin's study represents a very important piece of work, for he successfully links the Keynesian emphasis on shifts in aggregate spending in the key sectors of consumer durables and residential construction to the monetarist emphasis on events in the financial sector as a major element underlying the decrease in aggregate demand.

Government Economic Policy in the 1930s: Effective or Inconsequential?

The economic collapse of the 1930s, writes Peter Temin, "shattered people's faith in the ability of the economy to run smoothly without interference . . . the stage was set for a major expansion of the role of government in the economy."[28] But, a principal reason for the severity of the Depression and for the protracted and uncertain nature of recovery was the absence of a systematic, well-conceived expansionary macroeconomic policy. Built-in stabilizers designed to make countercyclical policy partly automatic were not yet well developed, nor was an aggressive, discretionary fiscal and monetary policy mix introduced.

The Hoover and Roosevelt administrations are usually characterized as "inactive and complacent" on the one hand and "radical and interventionist" on the other. These are undoubtedly exaggerated labels to apply in either case.

President Hoover's first step in November 1929 was to rely on tactics of moral suasion and reassurance. He convened a series of conferences with leading businessmen to try to promote industry agreements to maintain employment and wages in the hope that their example would permeate through the economy. But the economy soon degenerated into real collapse and by mid-1931, marked by a series of bank failures, the wage maintenance agreements had disintegrated and the "voluntary system" appeared to be a failure. From the fiscal point of view, Hoover's administration was able to maintain a budgetary surplus through the fiscal year ending June 30, 1930. Deficits in the succeeding years were incurred because of decreased revenues rather than increased expenditures. But this was no forerunner of deficit spending to promote economic recovery. Far from it! President Hoover stated, "We cannot squander ourselves into prosperity,"[29] and economic orthodoxy and public opinion alike were on his side. Latter-day Social Darwinists like Andrew Mellon, Secretary of the Treasury, argued that government should not interfere with the "natural process of liquidation."

This does not mean that the Hoover administration was inactive or indifferent. In fact, circumstances forced the administration to move toward a more interventionist stance than philosophical considerations alone would have tolerated. The traditional policy response to tariff increases was embodied in the Smoot-Hawley Tariff of 1930. More importantly, however, the Hoover administration began to take more positive action: the Reconstruction Finance Corporation was introduced in early 1932 with an initial capitalization of $1.5 billion. Later in 1932 the Emergency Relief and Construction Act empowered the RFC to lend some $1.8 billion to states for relief and public works. But, by and large, Hoover's actions were "too little, too late."

President Roosevelt assumed office on March 4, 1933. With the Depression at its nadir, Roosevelt set about revitalizing the domestic economy.[30] The First Hundred Days saw a number of decisive policy measures: a return to autarchy with immediate withdrawal from the World Economic Conference in London and departure from the gold standard in April 1933; an immediate return to financial stability by promulgation of a bank holiday from March 5–13, followed by passage in June of the Glass-Steagall Banking Reform Act, which revamped the Federal Reserve System and established the Federal Deposit Insurance Corporation; the Agricultural Adjustment Act (AAA) and the Farm Credit Administration, expected to bolster sagging agricultural fortunes; and the National Industrial Recovery Act (NIRA) and the National Recovery Administration to provide aid to industry. Several measures were intended to promote employment and relief, such as the Federal Emergency Relief Act and Administration, the Civilian Conservation Corps (CCC), and the Public Works Administration (PWA).[31]

Subsequently, the Roosevelt administration began to capitalize on the growing public conviction that the federal government should be more active in promoting the restoration of economic activity by introducing the New Deal legislation with which it has come to be identified. But the path was fraught with difficulties. Both the NIRA and the AAA were declared unconstitutional by the Supreme Court in 1935, and only a confrontation with the administration pressured the Court to cooperate with the passage of New Deal legislation.

The second stage of the New Deal marked a shift in policy from a preoccupation with short-run recovery to long-term reform—new commitments to provide lifelong economic security, to recognize labor union organizations and collective bargaining, and to curb the worst excesses of economic power by the "economic royalists." The Social Security Act of 1935 provided for a basic system of unemployment and old age assistance. Building on the Norris-La Guardia Act of 1932, the National Labor Relations (Wagner) Act of 1935 established the National Labor Relations Board (NLRB) and gave workers unequivocally the right to unionize and bargain collectively while prohibiting employers from engaging in unfair labor practices, and the Fair Labor Standards Act of 1938 introduced the minimum wage and the forty-hour week. Both greatly encouraged the growth of union membership. The tentative attempts at central planning under the NIRA (which suspended the antitrust laws and encouraged industry to form cartels to promote price, output, and employment stability in the public interest) were abandoned after the act was declared unconstitutional, and antitrust policy to promote competition and reduce economic power was applied vigorously under the Sherman Act after 1937. Finally, the Securities Exchange Act, 1934, established the Securities Exchange Commission to regulate trade in securities and correct some of the more glaring abuses which contributed to the stock market collapse of 1929. Improved efficiency in agriculture, reforms in banking, and a renewed commitment to meet the pressing needs of the unemployed were other features of New Deal policy.

In essence, perhaps the longest standing impact of the Depression and the New Deal has been the education of the American public to the importance of economic leadership and power of government to influence the economy for good or ill. The New Deal also gained widespread acceptance of the principle of ultimate federal government responsibility for the economic state of the nation, which culminates in the Employment Act of 1946, the definitive, albeit vague, statement of government's economic responsibilities.

The long-run impact of the New Deal notwithstanding, there remains a question of its short-run efficiency as a recovery device in the 1930s. There have been several attempts to assess government policy during the Depression, and two of these attempts are of particular interest: first, E. Cary Brown's classic examination of the effectiveness of fiscal policy in promoting economic recovery and, second, John Kirkwood's policy simulations with a macroeconomic model of the economy for the Depression period.[32]

Brown's Appraisal of Fiscal Policy. To assess the effectiveness of fiscal policy in promoting economic recovery, Brown developed a measure of the contribution of fiscal policy to aggregate demand. Government expenditures increase demand, and taxes decrease demand for output. The critical concept is the measurement of the net effect of government activity at some *particular level* of income—here full-employment income. This specification is necessary, because measuring the shift in demand from any observed level of income leads to a confusion between shifts in the demand schedule (because of legislative changes in tax schedules, for example) and movements along given schedules (in response to income changes). Measuring shifts in aggregate demand at full employment income yields a "pure" measure of changes in the expansiveness of fiscal activity as the vertical shift in the aggregate demand schedule. The question at issue is whether fiscal policy is more or less expansionary from year to year. To avoid the confusion introduced by the variable incomes actually observed, the full-employment level of income is specified as the basis for comparison. Brown assesses, then, whether full-employment aggregate demand is increased or reduced by *net* fiscal activity.

Brown's conclusion is very revealing. The trend of the direct effects of fiscal policy on full employment aggregate demand during the 1930s was downward. Federal fiscal policy was only mildly expansionary until 1937–1938, but state and local government policies were deflationary and more than offset the federal policy, so that the net effect was contractionary.[33] The results are summarized in Table 8.7.

The federal government's fiscal activities were somewhat more expansionary in the 1930s than in 1929. The government's surplus led to fiscal drag in the late 1920s; policy was expansionary in 1931 and 1932, less so in 1933 because of the large tax increase in the Revenue Act of 1932, became more expansionary in 1934 through 1936, and dropped sharply in 1937 and 1938. State and local governments were expansionary through 1932, but decreasingly so partly because there were legal and practical limits in their ability to incur deficits; their activities fell below the 1929 level in 1932, and remained distinctly nonexpansionary from 1933 onwards. The combined effect saw the federal government's expansionary activity barely offsetting the contractionary effects of state and local government activity. Taking 1929 as a benchmark, the combined effect was far stronger in 1931, 1936, and 1939 (taking 2.0 percent as a dividing point) and a little stronger in 1930, 1932, 1934, and 1935 (taking the 1929 level of 1.4 percent as the benchmark). But, overall perfor-

Table 8.7 Effect of Fiscal Policy on Full Employment Aggregate Demand, 1929-1939

	Net Shift in Demand as Percent of Full Employment GNP		
Year	**All Governments**	**Federal Government**	**State and Local Governments**
1929	1.4	-0.4	1.8
1930	1.9	0.0	2.0
1931	3.6	1.7	1.8
1932	1.8	1.0	0.9
1933	0.5	0.5	0.1
1934	1.5	2.0	-0.4
1935	1.6	1.9	-0.3
1936	2.6	2.5	0.2
1937	0.2	0.1	0.1
1938	1.2	1.2	0.0
1939	2.0	1.4	0.5

SOURCE: E. Cary Brown, "Fiscal Policy in the Twenties: A Reappraisal," *American Economic Review* 46 (December 1956), p. 865.

mance was weak in 1933, and 1937–38, respectively the years of the Depression's nadir and the sharp recession which put an end to recovery. Expansionary effects were stronger early in the decade.[34]

Thus, Brown concludes that fiscal policy was unsuccessful in the 1930s, primarily because it was not employed in any meaningful sense. The full potential of fiscal policy was only to be realized with the huge expenditures by government during the Second World War. To be fair, however, it is important to keep in mind that government was confronted in the 1930s with a collapsed economy, a unique situation. Indeed, Alvin Hansen has stressed the salvaging nature of the task with which government was faced; it was not a matter of aiding in a "normal" recovery of a strong economy from a "normal" recession.[35] The President was handicapped by prevailing notions of fiscal orthodoxy which continued to press for balanced budgets, and led to increases in tax rates during the depths of the Depression. By today's standards, this constitutes to most economists a bad error in fiscal policy. Even so, deficit financing was employed; current dollar deficits increased from $1.3 billion in 1933 to $2.9 billion in 1936,[36] which constituted peacetime deficit financing on a hitherto unprecedented scale. Given the prevailing fiscal orthodoxy, could more have been expected?

Kirkwood's Policy Simulations: An Appraisal. Although econometric studies of the Depression are still relatively rare, Kirkwood has estimated an interesting model designed explicitly to analyze the United States economy during this period. He employs the model to assess the causes of the Depression and to analyse the efficiency of alternative policies which might have been followed.

Most of the equations work reasonably well according to the usual criteria, and the model yields historical simulations which closely track the behavior of the economy during the period in question (the years 1929 through 1960 with the war years excluded). Changes in exogenous variables are specified as policy instruments (for example, an increase in government expenditures, or an increase in high-powered money).

Nowadays few economists would dispute that simulation exercises are an important aspect of judging the efficacy of a model. Moreover, *hypothetical* exercises, designed to permit an exploration of the potential effects of alternative choices assumed to be open to policy makers, are also of importance in the analysis of economic policy. Does it follow from this that the use of such simulations to conduct exercises in "hypothetical history" is justifiable?

An investment function is at the heart of Kirkwood's model, not only in the usual sense that private investment is an important determinant of aggregate demand or in the sense that the presence of an interest rate in his investment function connects the monetary and expenditure sectors, but *because the investment function is specified to include stock market prices* as an exogenous variable, and stock market prices are assigned a leading role by Kirkwood in causing the Great Depression. The investment function used in the model works well according to conventional criteria.

For estimating this model, it was clearly worrisome to employ a sample size of a dozen or so years (the prewar period of Kirkwood's model) and this led Kirkwood to use additional observations for the postwar years through 1960.[37] It is, of course, sometimes argued that, in order to analyze a particular period such as the Great Depression, it is necessary to study the behavior of the economy over longer periods which include a variety of experiences. On the other hand, it might be argued that there is reason to expect a complex structural shift to have taken place in certain sectors of the economy following the Second World War and that models incorporating both prewar and postwar experience ought to make allowance for the possibility of such shifts. In any event, there remains the question of why 1960 was selected as a terminal point for the estimation of the model. Why not 1950? Or 1959? Surely the argument is not that along with the end of the Republican years in the White House the structure of the economy underwent a change.[38]

Kirkwood's findings can be summarized briefly. First, he concludes that "capital saturation" could not have been a preeminent "cause" of the depression on the basis of a simulation wherein it is assumed that the economy started with an appreciably lower capital stock than in fact existed in 1929. It emerges that the course of the Depression, as measured by the behavior of GNP, would not have been radically different from that which actually occurred.

Kirkwood bases another simulation exercise on the assumption that the stock market crash did not occur, but that stock prices increased at eight percent a year from 1929 onwards. The result is a strong recovery in the economy beginning in 1933. It appears that the stock prices term in the investment system provides the critical connection. The increase in income appears to have been generated mainly by investment, which is assumed to increase beginning in 1929 at four percent annually. Thus, the collapse of the stock market is held responsible by Kirkwood for the sharp decline in investment expenditures.

Third, he tests and refutes the suggestion that if the monetary authorities had followed a course of continual growth in the money supply, rather than allowing it to contract severely early in the Depression and then allowing it to undergo a very large increase in the 1930s, the decline in GNP would have been appreciably attentuated.

Then, through use of another simulation, he demonstrates that a continuing ten percent increase in government expenditures would have effected a very significant continuing increase in GNP. But even so, only an enormous increase in the rate of government expenditures would have sufficed to close the gap between "potential" and actual GNP in the worst period of the Depression.

What is begged by this analysis is precisely that which is of most interest to students of political economy, namely the "likely" reaction of Congress to policy proposals consistent with the assumptions made in Kirkwood's analysis.[39] Moreover, is there any reason to believe that private decision-makers would have continued to behave, in the face of such public policies, in a manner consistent with the estimated parameters in the model? Is it impossible to conceive that the reaction to legislation even more "radical" than that proposed during the "first New Deal" would have created massive uncertainty in the business community? And would not such uncertainty create a parametric shift in the investment function (to say nothing of other behavioral relations)?

The rather ambiguous performance of econometric models in forecasting the contemporary economy is well known, but at least those models are, presumably, in a continuous process of change and improvement as new data become available to permit comparisons of predictions with actual events. However, in the case of econometric models designed to analyze profoundly complex events in a purely historical context, such processes of revision and improvement are ruled out. It is consequently too great a burden upon such models to expect that they could be of any significant use in explaining events of the pervasiveness and complexity of the Great Depression. Some of these issues are summarized by Murphy:[40]

> If we think of the person who tests a counterfactual as manipulating an "instrument" variable in order to influence a "target" variable, we are more likely to ask questions which represent conceivable and feasible policy changes. We will be able, so to say, to perform an operation or experiment on the economy. Furthermore, due recognition of "boundary conditions" is important. A set of targets and instruments can be mathematically compatible but can violate boundary conditions. . . . To take (Milton) Friedman's counterfactual, it may well be that the Federal Reserve Board might have influenced matters differently historically, but was it ever a feasible choice that it could have acted differently than it acted? Such reservations are not in order if we wish to take lessons from history, because boundary conditions may have changed—which is to say that we may be legitimately critical of the government today for failing to do something which it did not do yesterday, but we may be making perfectionist criticisms to speak about yesterday in the same tone of voice.

Surely the foregoing problems are accentuated when one attempts to use macroeconomic models, as Kirkwood does, to assess the prospects for the "peaceful" evolution of capitalism. He concludes that "sensible behavior by our economic policy-makers would have brought capitalism out of the Depression, not left it stagnant."[41] It is clearly questionable to use observations drawn from post-War experience to test such a proposition. Would anyone dispute that post-War developments in the United States economy were appreciably influenced by the existence of the War? One need mention only the stimulus given by the War to research and development activities to refute any such claim.

Macroeconometric models may be useful in providing tentative answers to historical questions involving, for example, the relative potency of fiscal policy as opposed to monetary policy during a particular historical period. On the other hand, their application is fraught with profound and perhaps insuperable difficulties when the events in question entail as complex and pervasive an interaction between economic and non-economic phenomena as characterized the Great Depression.

Conclusion

The legacy of the Great Depression is the New Deal—the first, decisive intervention of the federal government into the operation of the national economy which gained acceptance for the principle of ultimate government responsibility for the economic state of the nation. This responsibility was expanded during the Second World War, and refined and articulated in general terms in the Employment Act of 1946.

Could the Great Depression happen again? Most economists would answer with an emphatic no. There have been critical changes in the state of economic knowledge. There have been improvements in economic institutions. And government has developed and refined the policy instruments available to it—both discretionary weapons and automatic stabilizers. Finally, the increased size of the government sector, together with general agreement as to its economic responsibilities, have made the task all the more manageable.[42] To these developments in the postwar economy we now turn.

9

World War Two and Its Aftermath: The Ascendancy of the Mixed Economy

Introduction

The Great Depression marked the beginning of a fundamental change in the composition of economic activity in the United States between the public and private sectors, a change that has matured into the "mixed economy" of the present. Not only has the relative size of the government sector increased greatly, but also government has involved itself in new areas like social security and welfare and economic stabilization, as well as continuing to meet its responsibilities in traditional areas like national defense and education. Combined with "big" business and "big" labor, which were already on the scene, the emergence of "big" government, in the space of a few years, has completed the transformation of the American market economy begun by the forces of industrialism in the nineteenth century into a mixed economy.

The Changing Government Sector

Since 1929 there have been two major developments in the economic role of government—the greatly increased size of the government sector, and the government's assumption of responsibility for economic stabilization policy.

Table 9.1 Growth of Government Expenditure
Selected Years, 1902-1970

Year	Total Expenditure ($1958 billions)	Percent of GNP
1902	4.6	7.3
1913	8.6	7.8
1929	21.1	10.4
1940	40.0	17.6
1950	82.4	23.1
1960	132.1	27.0
1970	232.2	32.2

SOURCE: Richard A. Musgrave and Peggy B. Musgrave, *Public Finance in Theory and Practice,* 2d (New York: Mc Graw-Hill, 1976), p. 133.

As Table 9.1 shows, the government sector has grown considerably. At the beginning of this century, total government expenditures (by federal, state, and local governments) comprised about seven percent of GNP, and remained less than ten percent of GNP into the 1920s. Then, government expenditures began to rise during the 1930s with new obligations assumed during the Great Depression, jumped again during World War Two because of national defense commitments, and continued to rise in the postwar era, exceeding thirty percent of GNP by 1970.

There have been simultaneous changes in the types and sources of government expenditure as well. Defense-related expenditures have increased from about one-fifth of total government activity in the early 1900s to about fifty percent during the Second War, and stabilized between thirty-five and forty percent during the 1950s and 1960s. Defense costs were twenty-eight percent of GNP in 1970.[1] Thus, part of the growth in the relative size of government has been based on the upward shift in military spending, initially because of American involvement in World War Two and subsequently because of the continuing priority placed on national defense.

Civilian expenditures also increased significantly from 1900 to 1940, and again from 1950 to 1970. Transfer payments to support personal income levels have been of increasing importance since the Depression. Social welfare expenditures—including social security and welfare, health and hospitals, housing and community development—have grown from less than ten percent of civilian expenditures prior to 1930 to over thirty percent. Expenditure on education, on the other hand, has been roughly constant between twenty and twenty-five percent since 1900.

There has been a significant redistribution towards expenditures by the federal government compared with state and local governments. Taking intergovernmental grants at their point of origin (i.e., at the federal government level), federal expenditures were about one-third of total government expenditures prior to 1930, increased sharply with expanded defense commitments during the war, and have represented about two-thirds of government expenditures since 1950. State and local expenditures have fallen correspondingly.[2]

Thus, the relative importance of government economic activity has increased from less than ten percent of GNP in 1900 to about one-third of GNP at present. Why has there been such a substantial increase in the size of the public sector? One explanation is Wagner's law of increasing state activity, which states that the relative growth of the public sector is inherent in industrialized countries whose citizens opt for social progress. Another is the displacement effect, which proposes that government expenditures increase in a step-wise fashion, growing primarily during periods of major social disturbances (like the Great Depression and World War Two) and necessitating larger government budgets which soon become permanent. Both explanations are predicated on the high income elasticity of demand for public goods—growing needs for transportation and education, the development and expansion of social security and welfare programs, defense expenditures, and so forth.

The level of American GNP has come to depend more and more on the level of government spending. At the same time, government has assumed ultimate responsibility for macroeconomic stabilization policy. Before the Second World War, the federal government had few explicit economic policy targets and instruments. When the federal government assumed a greater economic role during the Depression, it did so as an economic "godfather" of last resort because of the obvious inability of private-sector decisions to raise the economy from the abyss, rather than as the architect of a coherent, consistent stabilization policy. As with the earlier movement towards regulation, the shift towards government intervention in the 1930s was precipitated by the obvious deficiencies of the market system, of which mass unemployment was the most calamitous.[3] The New Deal soon came, with the benefit of hindsight, to receive credit as a successful experiment in good economic management, and helped to push the federal government to the formal assumption of responsibility "to promote maximum employment, production, and purchasing power" in the Employment Act of 1946. By establishing the Council of Economic Advisers and the Joint Committee on the Economic Report, the act provided for the continuous monitoring of economic affairs by Congress.[4] The framework for government management of the national economy was in place.

Since then, the federal government has developed a clear set of economic goals—full employment, price stability, rapid economic growth, and balance of payments equilibrium—and a more refined set of policy instruments—automatic stabilizers, and discretionary fiscal and monetary weapons—to help achieve these aims. The process has not been an easy one: the goals often conflict, and monetary and fiscal policies can interfere with one other unless properly coordinated. While the government's stabilization record has been far from perfect, the result has been a more stable national economy since World War Two than before.[5]

To achieve its policy goals, the federal government has benefited from the growth in the share of government spending which has provided it with additional leverage over aggregate output, and from the continuing refinement of its arsenal of automatic stabilizers (for example, the progressive income tax structure, and unemployment and welfare systems, which insulate personal income in times of recession) and discretionary policies (for example, the tax cuts of 1962 and 1964 which, by helping to reduce unemployment, were heralded as a triumph of the "New Economics"). Put simply, we know more about the operation of the economy now than we did in the 1930s, and the larger government sector and new economic institutions have made government's stabilization functions more practicable.

Not only in the sphere of stabilization policy is government expected to produce antidotes to market defects. The development of social security legislation and its requirement of public transfer payments was a governmental response to the economic insecurity of industrialism made manifest by the Great Depression. Since then, public consciousness of the market system's failures has heightened, and the demand for government intervention to solve these problems has led to federal action on a broad front—environmental problems of pollution and urban blight, income redistribution programs like the War Against Poverty, indeed a host of areas that would have been considered unthinkable only a generation ago. In part, these actions reflect changes in social philosophy, in part changes in the balance of political power among various groups in the population. But, in essence, the public has encouraged the government sector to increase in size, and to expand the scope of its intervention. The upshot has been a persistent public demand for "large, usually in part deficit-financed, G (government expenditures) to sustain economic growth."[6] This is the single most significant development in the postwar economy.

The Private Sector and Government: Uneasy Truce?

In earlier chapters, we saw that economic and social forces combined to promote concentrations of power in the corporate sector and among labor unions. Since World War Two there have been further adjustments in the private sector.

The structure of American industry has changed relatively little since 1945.[7] The dominance of large corporations continues, whether concentration of power is measured by value added, total assets, or sales. As we have seen, the first merger movement at the turn of the century led to significant concentration in some manufacturing industries, and less conspicuous intercorporate links through family connections, financial houses, and interlocking directorates probably reinforced the trend towards concentration.

However, there seems to have been little trend toward increased concentration since then, although average concentration ratios, however measured, show modest increases since 1945.[8] Whatever the measures used, it is clear that oligopoly is prevalent in about one-half of American manufacturing industry, and that there remain sharp distinctions in concentration levels among industries.

This does not mean that there have been no recent changes in the corporate sector. While there is no discernible trend towards horizontal and vertical integration which characterized earlier merger movements, there was a postwar merger wave which peaked in 1968 and which saw an emphasis on diversification, that is, the creation of conglomerates. Conglomerates are formed by the merger of corporations when there is no clear relationship between product lines, markets, or buyers and sellers.[9] Postwar developments in antitrust legislation and subsequent judicial interpretations have encouraged the formation of conglomerates. The Celler-Kefauver Act of 1950 limited the attractiveness of traditional types of merger by restricting mergers leading to significant shifts in market shares. Thus, there has been a marked decrease in horizontal mergers aimed at market dominance, and a greater interest in diversification through the establishment of conglomerates.

Greater legislative restrictions were also placed on the labor movement after the favorable legislation of the New Deal and the wartime employment setting led to a rapid rise in membership. Union membership reached its low point in 1933, but the National Labor Relations Act, improving employment conditions, and the establishment of the Congress on Industrial Organization (CIO) in 1938 saw membership climb dramatically from a little over three million in 1930 to almost nine million in 1940, and about sixteen million in 1950. Since then, union membership increased steadily to reach twenty million in 1970, and now represents about one-third of employees in nonagricultural employment.[10]

The major question confronting the labor movement prior to World War Two was whether to organize by occupation or by industry. The AFL had been successful in reaching skilled craftsmen, but had made little progress in manufacturing industries where mass production was carried out by semi-skilled and unskilled workers. The Committee of Industrial Organization was established by six member unions of the AFL in 1935 to promote industrial unionism. Expelled from the AFL, they founded the CIO in 1938. The CIO spearheaded the organization of mass-production industry, where most new union members were to be found. From 1936 to 1941, for example, the CIO unionized many giant manufacturing industries, among them automobile makers (Ford, GM, and Chrysler), producers of electrical equipment (GE, Westinghouse), rubber manufacturers (Goodrich, Goodyear, and Firestone), US Steel, oil companies, and meat-packers. The CIO was able to take swift advantage of the previous vacuum in industrial unionism and the favorable environment provided by the NLRA. By the early 1950s, the rivalry between the two major unions had quieted: a joint committee to discuss amalgamation was established in 1952, and the AFL-CIO merger was completed in 1955. Since then, the unity of the labor movement has occasionally been shaken (by the expulsion of the Teamsters in 1957 and the withdrawal of the United Auto Workers in 1968, for example) and the scope for further expansion appears to be limited, but the AFL-CIO still represents the principal voice of labor on public policy issues.

Even so, there has been a change in public attitudes toward labor unions, for they now seem to bear some of the scrutiny and criticism that used to be directed almost exclusively towards big business. This is reflected in the most important labor legislation since the war. Whereas the NLRA was distinctly pro-labor, postwar legislation has tried to redress the balance between unions and employers. The Taft-Hartley Act (1947), an amendment to the NLRA, defined unfair labor practices of unions as an analogue to the unfair practices of firms specified in the earlier legislation. And the Landrum-Griffin Act (1959) provided for federal regulation of internal union business amid allegations about the corruption of certain union leaders. The NLRA and these amendments constitute the prevailing labor legislation in the United States today.

Labor and business have maintained a relatively quiescent status quo since 1945. But both have been confronted with the dramatic upsurge in government activity. The expanding power of government has had an articulate spokesman in the person of John Kenneth Galbraith. Galbraith began by urging that, when concentrations of power arise, they stimulate the growth of countervailing concentrations of power. Thus, "big" business spawned "big" labor and the development of a political farm bloc, and both have produced "big" government in the postwar era.[11] For Galbraith, the devil has always been the giant corporation, which has perverted the market economy: it controls the output side of its operations through market power, based on a large market share and large expenditures on advertising, and controls the input side as a monopolistic buyer of suppliers' output. Thus, market forces are relegated to agriculture and the services sector in Galbraith's scheme of things. In fact, in *The New Industrial State*, even government has been corrupted by giant enterprise: no longer is government the public's protector, but is now in league with corporate power.[12]

Galbraith's work has touched a sympathetic—possible paranoiac—chord in the public by postulating that giant enterprises subvert government efforts to regulate them in the public interest. Friedman, on the other hand, believes that government has promoted the growth of giant corporations and concentration of economic power by its regulatory efforts.[13] These are important empirical and philosophical questions which remain to be settled. Clearly, countervailing groups are not always on different sides—big business and big labor may have common economic interests at the expense of the consumer. But, given the existence of big business and big labor, how does one ensure that considerations of the public interest remain in the forefront? Should we naively dismantle government regulation and reduce government economic activity in the *hope* that firms and unions will reduce their market power voluntarily? Given the existing concentrations of economic power, government appears to be the only conceivable countervailing influence that can act as guardian of the public interest. It may be imperfect; it may flirt with private economic power; it may even be subverted on occasion. But, in the end, government is the only practicable alternative. Surely, government's joining with business and labor in an "unholy trinity" safeguards the public interest more than abandoning the field of battle to private hands alone![14]

Epilogue: Prospect and Retrospect

Between the Civil War and the Great Depression, the United States was transformed from a predominantly agricultural economy into a great industrial nation. From a position in manufacturing output third to Great Britain and Germany in 1870, the United States emerged by 1900 as the world's leading industrial power, and increased her lead to one of commanding proportions during the twentieth century.

We have analyzed the transformation of the American economy from the vantage point of the market system. The growth of the national market is often singled out as the crucial demand factor. Transportation improvements lowered real costs of transporting freight and passengers and the geographic concentration of population—increasing population density and urbanization—helped to lower distribution costs. Rising output and incomes per capita together with increasing population created a large, growing, national market.

Significant changes in the structural composition of output accompanied the development of the American economy. The agricultural sector fell in relative size as per capita incomes rose because the income elasticities of demand for foodstuffs are typically low. The share of manufacturing output increased because the income elasticities of manufactured goods are typically high. As a result, the structure of commodity output changed in favor of industrial products.

The growth of output resulted partly from the growth in quantity and quality of factor supplies—in population and the labor force, land and natural resources, and the stock of capital. The capital-output ratio increased substantially in the manufacturing sector as the process of capital-deepening and the substitution of capital for labor occurred. In agriculture, the most significant gains in capital intensity occurred in a short burst around the Civil War, and then again in the 1920s and after the Second World War. Moreover, the growing stock of real reproducible capital embodied the fruits of technological progress and contributed in the manufacturing sector to the substitution of machinery for handicraft skills, the development of producers' goods industries, the use of new power sources, organizational changes including standardization of products and parts, machine-manufacture of parts, and the assembly line. In agriculture mechanization of farm equipment was vital in releasing farm labor to the expanding manufacturing and services sectors.

Whereas the agricultural sector continued to rely upon the owner-operator for the direction of farm operations, the organization of the manufacturing sector was revolutionized. The emergence of big business was accompanied by profound changes in the structure of industrial enterprise, particularly the rise of the factory and growing dependence on the corporate form. By 1900 the owner-operated, small-scale manufacturing firm had been relegated to a minor position and the manufacturing sector was dominated by large enterprises producing for regional or national markets. In many cases, these giant firms resulted from the businessman's search for production and marketing efficiency, but in other cases the search for market control and the destruction of competition provided the major stimulus. By 1900 the shift towards managerial rather than proprietorial control of the business firm was in full swing. As the large firm's affairs came to be supervised by professional, bureaucratic management, the triumph of big business was complete.

The nineteenth century United States was a classic case of a market economy in which private ownership of the means of production and distribution and private initiative in business affairs was the norm. Business leaders of the time believed in a self-regulating capitalist economy in which the proper role for government was narrowly constrained to the provision of political and legal order. They believed, too, that the operation of "natural laws" enabled men of capacity and industry to succeed. In other words, a man's chances of material success were self-determined. Moreover, society was benefited by the free play of economic forces and individual actions without government interference.

But the industrialization of America was not without its costs, and agrarian and industrial unrest became a major social and economic issue. The industrial worker feared the growing insecurity of employment, the monotony of repetitive work tasks, and his growing dependence upon an impersonal employer. The American farmer lamented his increased susceptibility to the play of market forces. Both the industrial worker and the farmer had lost much of their former self-reliance and independence. Many independent, small businessmen joined in the demands for reform.

The discontent of farmers and industrial workers as they tried to come to grips with the new society produced by industrialism intensified a growing social cleavage in the United States. The gulf between rich and poor seemed to be increasing. The spectre of monopoly power was raised in a nation which had prided itself as the bastion of competition and individualism. The turmoil of the 1890s brought matters to a head.

The development of the modern economy changed unalterably the old economic and political order. The dissidents first tried to rectify the economic balance by organizing into countervailing groups—farmer organizations, labor unions, and other associations. But these attempts had limited success. More lasting in its impact was the redefinition of the proper role of government in the economy. In response to growing public agitation, the federal government shifted from its earlier limited emphasis on development to a new, expanded role. Although the public outcry for government intervention did not go unchallenged, by 1900 government had enacted antitrust legislation, and was attempting to regulate business in the public interest. As the 1920s dawned, the political reforms of the Progressive era seemed to have contended successfully with the vastly new society which industrialism had wrought.

Complacency was checked abruptly by the cataclysm of 1929. The Great Depression pointed out glaring weaknesses in the American economic system and government's economic role as popularly conceived. Before 1930 most Americans believed economic problems were temporary and self-correcting, and that government intervention should be directed at potentially harmful concentrations of economic power. But the Great Depression of the 1930s changed perceptions of the desirable economic role of government; the public demanded government economic leadership and intervention and got the New Deal -- the first, comprehensive intervention of the federal government into the operation of the national economy. What began as tentative ad hoc solutions to the economic crisis culminated in the Employment Act of 1946 and general acceptance of the government's ultimate responsibility for the economic state of the nation. Moreover, the Great Depression precipitated rapid growth in the share of economic activity originating in the public sector. Together they have resulted in our contemporary mixed economy.

Will there be any retreat from the mixed economy? Not likely in view of the continuing problems plaguing the American economy. The problems of the 1970s—critical shortages in energy resources, a drastic slow-down in productivity growth, uncertainty about the continued pace of technological change, chronic unemployment and persistent inflation, balance of payments problems, poverty in the midst of abundance—are still with us, and will undoubtedly persist well into the 1980s. The inability of the market economy to deal effectively with such basic problems has necessitated the rise of government first as arbiter, then as healer, and finally—and reluctantly—as economic overlord. The mixed economy is here to stay.

BIBLIOGRAPHIC NOTE

In writing this book, I have drawn upon the published research accomplishments of many scholars. I am greatly indebted to them. Their work is acknowledged in the footnotes of each chapter. Rather than replicate here the references cited in the body of the book, I have chosen to prepare a brief bibliographic note to introduce the reader to some of the most significant textbook and reference sources which will prove useful in providing background or supplementary information to the issues raised in each chapter. It will be clear to the reader that I have not written a comprehensive account of the economic development of the United States, but a series of interpretive essays intended to introduce and assess some important themes in the literature on post-Civil War manufacturing and agricultural growth and their dramatic economic and social consequences. The reader will find little mention of such traditional topics as money and banking, immigration, trade, transportation and communications, to name but a few, or to the currently fashionable emphasis on resource depletion or the environmental impact of economic growth. I hope that the bibliographic note will help to remedy this deficiency by pointing the reader towards appropriate sources to broaden and deepen his knowledge of American economic history.

There are many fine, standard textbooks that give thorough coverage of the whole span of American economic history from the colonial beginnings to the present. Among the best of these are: Ralph Gray and John M. Peterson, *Economic Development of the United States*, rev. ed. (Homewood: Richard D. Irwin, 1974); Gerald Gunderson, *A New Economic History of America* (New York: McGraw-Hill, 1976); Albert W. Niemi, Jr., *U. S. Economic History*, 2d ed. (Chicago: Rand McNally, 1980); Sidney Ratner, James H. Soltow, and

Richard Sylla, *The Evolution of the American Economy: Growth, Welfare, and Decision Making* (New York: Basic Books, 1980); Ross M. Robertson and Gary M. Walton, *History of the American Economy*, 4th ed. (New York: Harcourt, Brace, Jovanovich, 1979); and Harry N. Scheiber, Harold G. Vatter, and Harold Underwood Faulkner, *American Economic History,* 9th ed. (New York: Harper & Row, 1976). Two books that try to outline current developments in the "new" economic history— which emphasizes the formal use of economic theory and the statistical testing of economic models—are Douglass C. North, *Growth and Welfare in the American Past,* 2d ed. (Englewood Cliffs, N.J.: Prentice-Hall, 1974), and Susan Previant Lee and Peter Passell, *A New Economic View of American History* (New York: W. W. Norton, 1979). North is particularly thought-provoking, although brief and somewhat sketchy. Lee and Passell is the more detailed of the two, and provides excellent in-depth coverage of many important topics, along with an annotated bibliography at the end of each chapter. Finally, a superb reference text which is organized topically is Lance E. Davis, R. A. Easterlin, William N. Parker, et al., *American Economic Growth: An Economist's History of the United States* (New York: Harper & Row, 1972).

The principal journals for the publication of research in American economic history are the *Journal of Economic History* and *Explorations in Economic History*. Both will richly reward close study. Another excellent periodical containing many items of interest is the *Business History Review*. The reader should also consult the annual volumes edited by Paul Uselding entitled *Research in Economic History* (Greenwich, Conn.: JAI Press). There are some anthologies of published research papers which make suitable complements to the texts mentioned above. Two which feature papers in quantitative economic history are Robert W. Fogel and Stanley L. Engerman, eds., *The Reinterpretation of American Economic History* (New York: Harper & Row, 1971), and Peter Temin, ed., *New Economic History: Selected Readings* (Harmondsworth, Eng.: Penguin, 1973). Somewhat older, but still useful is Ralph L. Andreano, ed., *New Views on American Economic Development* (Cambridge, Mass.: Schenkman, 1965). Although a bit dated, all of the essays in Harold Williamson, ed., *The Growth of the American Economy*, 2d ed. (Englewood Cliffs, N.J.: Prentice-Hall, 1951) are accessible to the general reader, and many are still well worth reading. Some of the research publications of the National Bureau of Economic Research are of particular interest to economic historians, such as *Output, Employment, and Productivity in the United States After 1800*, NBER, Studies in Income and Wealth, Volume 30 (New York: Columbia University Press, 1966), and *Trends in the American Economy in the Nineteenth Century,* NBER, Studies in Income and Wealth, Volume 24 (Princeton: Princeton University Press, 1960).

In this book, I have tried at all times to blend the findings of traditional historical scholarship with some characteristic examples drawn from the "new" economic history. A good review of several alternative methodological foci or unifying themes in American economic history is contained in George R. Taylor and Lucius F. Ellsworth, eds., *Approaches to American Economic History* (Charlottesville, Va.: University Press of Virginia, 1971). For readers interested in pursuing some of the methodological underpinnings of "cliometrics," I recommend, as a starting point, either P. J. George and E. H. Oksanen, "Recent

Methodological Developments in the Quantification of Economic History," in *Histoire Sociale-Social History* 3 (April 1969), pp. 5-31, or A. H. Conrad and J. R. Meyer, "Economic Theory, Statistical Inference, and Economic History," *Journal of Economic History* 17 (December 1957), pp. 524-544. Of considerable interest too is J. D. Gould, "Hypothetical History," *Economic History Review* 22 (August 1969), pp. 195-207. Readers who wish to pursue some of the more challenging epistemological questions would do well to consult Peter D. McCelland, *Causal Explanation and Model Building in History, Economics, and the New Economic History* (Ithaca, N.Y.: Cornell University Press, 1975). A nuts-and-bolts introduction to the methods of the quantitative economic historian is presented in Roderick Floud, *An Introduction to Quantitative Methods for Historians* (Princeton: Princeton University Press, 1973). A good review of the accomplishments of the "new" economic history is Donald N. McCloskey, "The Achievements of the Cliometric School," *Journal of Economic History* 38 (March 1978), pp. 13-28.

Finally, there are two compendia of historical statistics which the reader will find invaluable, both published by the United States Bureau of the Census. They are the *Historical Statistics of the United States* (Washington, D.C.: Government Printing Office, 1975), and *Long Term Economic Growth 1860 - 1970* (Washington, D.C.: Government Printing Office, 1973).

Notes

1. An Overview of American Growth; 1840–1960

1. See, in particular, Douglass C. North, *The Economic Growth of the United States, 1790-1860* (Englewood Cliffs, N.J.: Prentice-Hall, 1961).

2. Diane Lindstrom, *Economic Development in the Philadelphia Region, 1810-1850* (New York: Columbia University Press, 1978).

3. Gallman has developed comprehensive estimates for Gross National Product and Net National Product and for commodity output in the United States from 1834 onwards. Easterlin has prepared National Income estimates and has presented these estimates by geographic region in the United States from 1840 to the present. Kuznets has, of course, completed monumental researches involving the formulation of national income accounting and capital formation data for the American economy. Two readily accessible reference sources are Lance E. Davis, R. A. Easterlin, William N. Parker, et al., *American Economic Growth: An Economist's History of the United States* (New York: Harper and Row, 1972), chap. 2-6, 8, 9, and Robert W. Fogel and Stanley L. Engerman, eds., *The Reinterpretation of American Economic History* (New York: Harper and Row, 1971), esp. pp. 14-49 where articles by Kuznets, Gallman and Howle, and Easterlin are reproduced.

4. The debate is effectively summarized by Stanley Engerman in "The Economic Impact of the Civil War," *Explorations in Entrepreneurial History* 3 (Spring/Summer 1966), pp. 176-199.

5. Douglass C. North, "Comments on Stuart Bruchey's Paper," *Explorations in Entrepreneurial History* 1 (Winter 1964), p. 160.

6. Broude provides a succinct statement of the dimensions of government intervention in the nineteenth-century economy. See Henry W. Broude, "The Role of the State in American Economic Development, 1820-1890," in Hugh G. J. Aitken, ed., *The State and Economic Growth* (New York: Social Science Research Council, 1959), pp. 4-25.

2. The Sources of Growth

1. The characteristic method of supply analysis in the study of economic growth involves the use of an aggregate production function in which output is written as some function of the quantity and quality of productive inputs. This procedure allows for partitioning the contributions to the growth of output of increases in the supply of each input. Total factor productivity increases whenever output grows more rapidly than the weighted increase in the factors of production. This difference is usually identified with technological change, although because of its residual nature it is also often referred to as a measure of our "ignorance." Both increases in factor supplies and improved factor productivity have contributed to the growth of American output. For a useful technical discussion, see Robert M. Solow, "Technical Change and the Aggregate Production Function," *Review of Economics and Statistics* 39 (August 1957), pp. 312-320.

2. Stanley Lebergott, "Labor Force and Employment, 1800-1960," in *Output, Employment, and Productivity in the United States after 1800,* N. B. E. R., Studies in Income and Wealth, vol. 30 (New York: Columbia University Press, 1966), p. 118.

3. Simon Kuznets, *Capital in the American Economy: Its Formation and Financing*, N. B. E. R., Studies in Capital Formation and Financing, no. 9 (Princeton: Princeton University Press, 1961), pp. 64-65. All figures are expressed in constant $1929.

4. Edward F. Denison, *The Sources of Economic Growth in the United States* (New York: Committee for Economic Development, 1962); John W. Kendrick, *Productivity Trends in the United States,* N. B. E. R., General Series, no. 71 (Princeton: Princeton University Press, 1961) and *Postwar Productivity Trends in the United States, 1948-1969,* N. B. E. R., General Series, no. 98 (New York: Columbia University Press, 1973); Moses Abramovitz and Paul A. David, "Reinterpreting Economic Growth: Parables and Realities," *American Economic Review,* 63, no. 2 (May 1973), pp. 428-439.

5. Abramovitz and David, "Reinterpreting Economic Growth," p. 431.

6. Kendrick, *Productivity Trends in the United States,* p. 79, and *Postwar Productivity Trends*, p. 41.

7. Kendrick, *Productivity Trends in the United States,* pp. 136, 148, and *Postward Productivity Trends,* pp. 86-88, 92.

8. See Robert E. Gallman, "Changes in Total U. S. Agricultural Factor Productivity in the Nineteenth Century," *Agricultural History* 46, no. 2 (Summer 1972), pp. 191-210.

9. Kendrick, *Productivity Trends in the United States,* pp. 136, 148, and *Postwar Productivity Trends*, pp. 86-88, 92.

10. Kendrick, *Productivity Trends in the United States*, p. 121, and *Postwar Productivity Trends,* p. 72. Empirical studies suggest that the coefficient of substitution of capital for labor is less than one and, consequently, although labor input has decreased, its share of income has risen.

11. The primary sector includes agriculture, forestry and fishing, and mining—all activities involving exploitation of the natural resources base. Usually, by far the largest component of this sector is associated with agricultural output. Often, mining will be combined with manufacturing to provide a contrast between agricultural and mining-manufacturing variables, since mining is regarded as the extractive industry most nearly like manufacturing in its employment and output characteristics.

12. Stanley Lebergott, "Labor Force and Employment, 1800-1960," pp. 117-210. The percentages cited here are from p. 119, but do not add to 100 per cent because some service employment is excluded.

13. Gallman and Howle, "Trends in the Structure of the American Economy since 1840," pp. 27-28.

14. For a succinct and readily accessible introduction, see William J. Baumol, *Economic Theory and Operations Analysis,* 4th ed. (Englewood Cliffs, N.J.: Prentice-Hall, 1977), chap. 10, esp. pp. 238-245.

15. This section is based on Harold F. Williamson, Ralph L. Andreano, and Carmen Menezes, "The American Petroleum Industry," in *Output, Employment, and Productivity in the United States After 1800,* pp. 349-402.

16. Ibid., pp. 355, 377.

17. Ibid., p. 378.

18. Ibid., p. 382.

19. Ibid., p. 384.

20. Robert W. Fogel and Stanley L. Engerman, "A Model for the Explanation of Industrial Expansion during the Nineteenth Century: With an Application to the American Iron Industry," *Journal of Political Economy* 77, no. 3 (May/-June, 1969), pp. 306-328. Reprinted in Fogel and Engerman, eds., *The Reinterpretation of American Economic History,* pp. 148-162. A more general treatment of the iron and steel industry is Peter Temin, *Iron and Steel in Nineteenth-Century America: An Economic Inquiry* (Cambridge, Mass.: M.I.T. Press, 1964). Chapters 2 and 3 provide an excellent discussion of probable demand and supply shifts, drawn largely from literary and qualitative sources, and are a good supplement to Fogel and Engerman's paper.

21. For more detailed discussion of this procedure and some difficulties inherent in it, see Fogel and Engerman, Ibid.; Gavin Wright, "Econometric Studies of History," in Intriligator, Michael D., ed., *Frontiers of Quantitative Economics* (Amsterdam: North-Holland, 1970), pp. 449-453; and Paul L. Joskow and Edward F. McKelvey, "The Fogel-Engerman Model: A Clarifying Note," *Journal of Political Economy* 81, no. 5 (September/October 1973), pp. 1236-40.

22. See Nathan Rosenberg, *Perspectives on Technology* (New York: Cambridge University Press, 1976), pp. 204-205.

3. Technological Change in Manufacturing

1. Jacob Schmookler, *Invention and Economic Growth* (Cambridge, Mass.: Harvard University Press, 1966).

2. Edwin Layton, "Mirror-Image Twins: The Communities of Science and Technology in 19th-Century America," *Technology and Culture* 12 (October 1971), pp. 562-580.

3. Nathan Rosenberg, "Factors Affecting the Diffusion of Technology," *Explorations in Economic History* 10, no. 1 (Fall 1972), pp. 3-34. Reprinted in *Perspectives on Technology* (New York: Cambridge University Press, 1976), pp. 189-210.

4. In a world of perfect foresight, even a slight lowering of costs with a new technique compared with the old is sufficient to induce widespread diffusion of the new. In fact, however, there are risks and uncertainties influencing calculations of the profitability of new techniques and, the greater are these risks, the greater will be the expected differential in favor of the new technique required for diffusion to occur.

5. See, for example, H. J. Habakkuk, *American and British Technology in the Nineteenth Century* (Cambridge: The University Press, 1962), pp. 4-5, where commentary by Michael Chevalier, E. G. Wakefield, Richard Cobden, E. W. Watkin, and various groups of visiting English technicians is described. Also see John E. Sawyer, "The Social Basis of the American System of Manufacturing," *Journal of Economic History* 14, no. 3 (September 1954), pp. 361-379, for a more extensive discussion.

6. *American and British Technology in the Nineteenth Century.*

7. Nathan Rosenberg cites two very good examples of this with respect to the "wasteful" use of wood: in the development of both American wood-working machinery and the balloon-frame house, cheap wood tended to be substituted for expensive labor. See Nathan Rosenberg, *Technology and American Economic Growth* (New York: Harper and Row, 1972), pp. 27-31.

8. The emphasis is important. In fact, Habakkuk subtitled his book "The Search for Labor-Saving Inventions," which is surely indicative of his train of thought.

9. Moses Abramovitz and Paul A. David, "Reinterpreting Economic Growth: Parables and Realities," *American Economic Review,* 63, no. 2 (May 1973), pp. 428-439, and "Economic Growth in America: Historical Parables and Realities," *De Economist,* 121, no. 3 (May/June 1973), pp. 251-272. David had earlier collaborated in a study covering the period from 1899 to 1960; see Paul A. David and Th. van de Klundert, "Biased Efficiency Growth and Capital-Labor Substitution in the U. S., 1899-1960," *American Economic Review* 55, no. 3 (June 1965), pp. 357-394.

10. E. Asher, "Industrial Efficiency and Biased Technical Change in American and British Manufacturing: The Case of Textiles in the Nineteenth Century," *Journal of Economic History* 32, no. 2 (June 1972), pp. 431-442. Both studies are predicated on the assumption that "well-behaved" constant-elasticity-of-substitution production functions with factor-augmenting technological change can be employed to depict the technology of the aggregate American economy and of the textile industries of the United States and Great Britain, respectively.

11. As we saw in chapter 2, there appears to have been capital-deepening technological change in the nineteenth century American economy which increased the capital-labor ratio in production. In terms of efficiency units, however, the ratio of capital to labor inputs was lowered, which implies in turn that capital was becoming the increasingly scarce input in efficiency terms. This finding "explains" the fact that the total gross share of property (reproducible capital plus land) in Gross Domestic Product was forty-six percent during 1890 to 1905, compared with thirty-two percent in the 1800 to 1855 period, despite the rise in the ratio of capital to Gross Domestic Product over the century.

12. One especially interesting feature of Asher's results in his finding that the labor-saving bias in technological change was greater in Great Britain than in the United States. This is, of course, contradictory to the implications of Habakkuk's thesis, and indicates the need for more comparative American-British research at the industry level.

13. Peter Temin, "Labor Scarcity and the Problem of American Industrial Efficiency in the 1850's," *Journal of Economic History* 26, no. 3 (September 1966), pp. 277-298, and "Labor Scarcity in America," *Journal of Interdisciplinary History* 1, no. 2 (Winter 1971), pp. 251-264.

14. The theoretical bases of Habakkuk's and Temin's positions are neatly summarized in E. Asher, "Relative Productivity and Factor-Intensity in the Manufacturing Sectors of the U. S. and the U. K. During the Nineteenth Century," *De Economist* 119, no. 4 (July/August 1971), pp. 441-446. Also, on this point, see Robert W. Fogel, "The Specification Problem in American Economic History," *Journal of Economic History* 27, no. 3 (September 1967), pp. 299-308.

15. W. D. G. Salter, *Productivity and Technical Change* (Cambridge: The University Press, 1960), chap. III.

16. Rosenberg, *Technology and American Economic Growth*, pp. 50-57.

17. Paul A. David, "Labor Scarcity and the Problem of Technological Practice and Progress in Nineteenth-Century America," in *Technical Choice, Innovation and Economic Growth* (New York: Cambridge University Press, 1975), pp. 19-91. The following discussion draws heavily on pp. 62-68.

18. Ibid., p. 66.

19. Ibid., pp. 89-90.

20. For example, David does not attempt to deal with differences in determinants and rates of technical change among sectors, industries, or commodities. For a discussion of some of the limitations of David's theoretical framework, see Jeffrey G. Williamson, "Technology, Growth, and History," *Journal of Political Economy* 84 (August 1976), pp. 809-820.

21. Schmookler, *Invention and Economic Growth*, passim.

22. Rosenberg, *Technology and American Economic Growth*, p. 47.

23. In a recent paper, Rosenberg has criticized Schmookler for neglecting supply considerations: "Science and technology progress in some measure along lines determined either by internal logic, degree of complexity, or at least in response to forces independent of economic need. . . This sequence in turn imposes significant contraints or presents unique opportunities which materially shape the direction and the timing of the inventive process . . . as a result, the costs of invention differ in different industries," (p. 95) He goes on to argue that "the allocation of inventive resources has in the past been determined jointly by demand forces which have broadly shaped the shifting payoffs to successful invention, together with supply side forces which have determined both the probability of success within any particular time frame as well as the prospective cost of producing a successful invention." (p. 103) See "Science, Invention and Economic Growth," *Economic Journal* 84, no. 333 (March 1974), pp. 90-108. Reprinted in *Perspectives on Technology* (above, note 3), pp. 260-279.

24. Layton, "Mirror-Image Twins," passim.

25. W. Paul Strassman, *Risk and Technological Innovation: American Manufacturing Methods During the Nineteenth Century* (Ithaca, N.Y.: Cornell University Press, 1959).

26. A. Kelley, "Scale Economies, Inventive Activity, and the Economics of American Population Growth," *Explorations in Economic History* 10, no 1 (Fall 1972), pp. 35-52, and Simon Kuznets, "Population Change and Aggregate Output," in *Demographic and Economic Change in Developed Countries,* N. B. E. R., Special Conference Series, vol. 6 (Princeton: Princeton University Press, 1960), pp. 324-339.

27. New industries often emerge to produce inputs for firms in established industries by taking over some production previously undertaken by the older firm. The resulting increase in productivity is attributed to specialization by the new industry, and the external economies reaped by the older industry. For an interesting exposition of this development, see George J. Stigler, "The Division of Labor is Limited by the Extent of the Market," *Journal of Political Economy* 59, no. 3 (June 1951), pp. 185-193.

28. Alan Pred, *The Spatial Dynamics of U. S. Urban-Industrial Growth, 1800-1914* (Cambridge, Mass.: The M.I.T. Press, 1966), esp. chap. 3.

29. Irwin Feller, "The Urban Location of United States Invention, 1860-1910," *Explorations in Economic History* 8, no. 3 (Spring 1971), pp. 285-303; Robert Higgs, "American Inventiveness, 1870-1920," *Journal of Political Economy* 79, no. 3 (May/June 1971), pp. 661-667.

30. John E. Sawyer, "The Social Basis of the American System of Manufacturing" (above, note 5), pp. 361-379.

31. A more extensive discussion of these points can be found in Rosenberg, "Factors Affecting the Diffusion of Technology" (above, note 3), pp. 3-34.

32. See Robert W. Fogel, and Stanley L. Engerman, "A Model for the Explanation of Industrial Expansion During the Nineteenth Century: With an Application to the American Iron Industry," *Journal of Political Economy* 77, no. 3 (May/June 1969), pp. 306-328, reprinted in Fogel and Engerman, eds., *The Rein-*

terpretation of American Economic History (New York: Harper and Row, 1971), pp. 148-162.

33. For a useful discussion of these developments, see Albert Fishlow, "Productivity and Technological Change in the Railroad Sector, 1840-1910," in *Output, Employment, and Productivity in the United States After 1800,* N. B. E. R., Studies in Income and Wealth, vol. 30 (New York: Columbia University Press, 1966), pp. 583-646.

34. This section is based on Nathan Rosenberg, "Technical Change in the Machine Tool Industry, 1840-1910," *Journal of Economic History* 23, no. 3 (September 1963), pp. 414-443, which is reprinted in *Perspectives on Technology,* pp. 9-31. Ross M. Robertson, "Changing Production of Metal Working Machinery, 1860-1920," and Duncan McDougall, "Machine Tool Output, 1861-1910," in *Output, Employment, and Productivity in the United States After 1800,* (above, note 33), pp. 479-517, present studies based on company records, trade publications, and government records.

35. Machine tools shape metal through cutting, whereas other metal-working machinery employs means other than cutting tools such as pressing, stamping, forging, bending, etc.

36. Rosenberg, "Technical Change in the Machine Tool Industry" (above, note 34), pp. 422-423.

37. This section is based principally on Irwin Feller, "The Draper Loom in New England Textiles, 1894-1914: A Study of Diffusion of an Innovation," *Journal of Economic History* 26, no. 3 (September 1966), pp. 320-347, and "The Diffusion and Location of Technological Change in the American Cotton-Textile Industry, 1890-1970," *Technology and Culture* 15 (October 1974), pp. 569-593. Another interesting paper is Lars Sandberg's assessment of the factors responsible for the differential rates of adoption of ring and mule-spinning in the United States and Great Britain. See "American Rings and English Mules: The Role of Economic Rationality," *Quarterly Journal of Economics* 83, no. 1 (February 1969), pp. 25-43.

38. Irwin Feller, "The Draper Loom," p. 327.

39. Feller, "The Diffusion and Location of Technological Change," p. 581.

4. The American Industrial Entrepeneur

1. Joseph A. Schumpeter, "The Creative Response in Economic History," *Journal of Economic History* 7, no. 2 (November 1947), pp. 149-159.

2. An excellent discussion of these issues is presented in W. T. Easterbrook, "The Entrepreneurial Function in Relation to Technological and Economic Change", in B. F. Hoselitz and W. E. Moore, eds., *Industrialization and Society* (Mouton: UNESCO, 1963), pp. 57-73.

3. John E. Sawyer, "The Social Basis of the American System of Manufacturing," *Journal of Economic History* 14, no. 3 (September 1954), pp. 361-379, and Easterbrook, "The Entrepreneurial Function in Relation to Technological and Economic Change," pp. 57-73. A succinct discussion of the interaction between values and social structure in antebellum America is contained in Stuart

Bruchey, *The Roots of American Economic Growth, 1607-1861* (New York: Harper and Row, 1965), chap. 3 and 8. Finally, for a general discussion, see Arthur H. Cole, *Business Enterprise in Its Social Setting* (Cambridge, Mass.: Harvard University Press, 1959).

4. Social Darwinism, usually associated with Herbert Spencer, involved a wholesale transfer into the area of social philosophy of Charles Darwin's theory of natural selection through competitive struggle. Accordingly, social progress was thought to be advanced by individual's acting in their own self-interests and not by the state's attempting to regulate or direct society along certain lines.

5. See Henry W. Broude, "The Role of the State in American Economic Development, 1820-1890," in Hugh G. J. Aitken, ed., *The State and Economic Growth* (New York: Social Science Research Council, 1959), pp. 4-25.

6. David C. McClelland, *The Achieving Society* (Princeton, N.J.: Van Nostrand, 1961). A summary of the book appears as "The Achievement Motive in Economic Growth," in Hoselitz and Moore, eds., *Industrialization and Society,* pp. 74-96.

7. Some comments on American child-raising are contained in Bruchey, *The Roots of American Economic Growth, 1607-1861,* pp. 188-191. A comparison of the probable effects on economic development of differences in child-rearing and family life in the United States and Latin America is presented in Thomas C. Cochran, "Cultural Factors in Economic Growth," *Journal of Economic History* 20, no. 4, (December 1960), pp. 515-530.

8. These points are well-made in J. R. T. Hughes, "Eight Tycoons: The Entrepreneur and American History," *Explorations in Entrepreneurial History* 1, no. 3 (Spring/Summer 1964), pp. 213-231.

9. In certain instances, idealism appears to have been a powerful motivating force. See Jonathan Hughes' discussion of William Penn and Brigham Young in his *The Vital Few: American Economic Progress and Its Protagonists* (Boston: Houghton-Mifflin, 1966), pp. 15-116. In addition, some "ruthless" business entrepreneurs were very idealistic: both Andrew Carnegie and J. P. Morgan believed in the inevitability of social progress, and Carnegie, in particular, devoted his later years to charitable works.

10. See the classic statement of the Horatio Alger legend in Charles A. Beard and Mary Beard, *The Rise of American Civilization* (New York: Macmillan, 1930), pp. 166-210, or the brief review in Bernard Sarachek, "American Entrepreneurs and the Horatio Alger Myth," *Journal of Economic History* 38 (June 1978), pp. 439-56.

11. See Frances W. Gregory and Irene D. Neu, "The American Industrial Elite in the 1870's," and William Miller, "American Historians and the Business Elite," which appeared in William M. Miller, ed., *Men in Business* (New York: Harper and Row, 1962), pp. 193-211, 309-337.

One may question whether samples of business leaders in the 1870s and 1900s can be considered representative of the entrepreneurial class, for the increasing reliance on the corporate form in manufacturing had, as one of its corollaries, the removal of the entrepreneurial function from the classic owner-operator of the mid-nineteenth century firm to the professional management of the large corporation. As far as McClelland is concerned, the entrepreneurial role depends not on type of business position or occupation, but on certain key attributes of the role — risk-taking, innovative activity, individual responsibility, and knowledge of the results of one's actions; that is, the individual either does or does not behave in an entrepreneurial way (*The Achieving Society,* pp. 207-233).

12. Data on business leaders by type of career are as follows: lawyers twelve percent, independent entrepreneurs fourteen percent, family connections twenty-seven percent, and bureaucratic careers forty-seven percent. See Miller, "The Business Elite in Business Bureaucracies," in *Men in Business*, p. 290.

13. Gabriel Kolko, "Brahmins and Business, 1870-1914: A Hypothesis on the Social Basis of Success in American History," in Kurt H. Wolff and Barrington Moore, Jr., eds. *The Critical Spirit: Essays in Honor of Herbert Marcuse* (Boston: Beacon Press, 1967), pp. 343-363.

14. Jocelyn Maynard Ghent and Frederic Cople Jaher, "The Chicago Business Elite, 1830-1930: A Collective Biography," *Business History Review* 50 (Autumn 1976), pp. 288-328.

15. John N. Ingham, "Rags to Riches Revisited: The Effect of City Size and Related Factors on the Recruitment of Business Leaders," *Journal of American History* 63 (December 1976), pp. 615-637.

16. Ibid., p. 637.

17. Sarachek, "American Entrepreneurs and the Horatio Alger Myth", (above, note 10), passim.

18. His entrepreneur either created a new enterprise, brought a moribund one back to prosperity, or developed a large firm by expanding a smaller one or by consolidating several smaller ones. It is the Schumpeterian figure who interests Sarachek, not the career corporate executive. Ibid., p. 440.

19. Ralph Andreano, "A Note on the Horatio Alger Legend: Statistical Studies of the Nineteenth Century American Business Elite," in Louis P. Cain and Paul J. Uselding, eds., *Business Enterprise and Economic Change* (Kent, Ohio: Kent State University Press, 1973), pp. 227-246.

20. Socioeconomic factors, particularly family and educational background, appear to be the most important determinants of "success" in present-day America. Recent work by Christopher Jencks indicates that being born into the "right" family, and achieving high academic test scores in primary school and, above all, completing a university or college degree are the roads to success, measured in his study as earned income and occupational status. See Christopher Jencks et al., *Who Gets Ahead? — The Determinants of Economic Success in America* (New York: Basic Books, 1979).

21. Excellent interpretive essays on these and other American entrepreneurs are contained in Hughes, *The Vital Few: American Economic Progress and Its Protagonists*. Also see John Chamberlain, *Enterprising Americans* (New York: Harper and Row, 1961). They have also been the subject of innumerable personal and business biographies, a few of which are listed below.

22. The concept of a "vital few" has been questioned by Robert Paul Thomas in "The Automobile Industry and Its Tycoon," *Explorations in Entrepreneurial History* 6, no. 2 (Winter 1969), pp. 139-157. Thomas believes that entrepreneurial historians have seldom faced up to the problem of evaluating the contributions of their subjects, but have chosen instead to weave a narrative around their

achievements. "The implicit assumption of this approach . . . is that the entrepreneur concerned has made a unique contribution." (pp. 139-140). Indeed, he argues, individual entrepreneurs simply are not important, because "the supply of entrepreneurs throughout American history, combined with institutions that permitted. . . intense competition, was sufficiently elastic to reduce the importance of any particular individual." (p. 141). If, as Thomas argues, innovations are not the result of individual genius but of general economic forces, then biographical studies of "great" entrepreneurs are of little or no use in the study of the process of innovation.

23. There are several good biographies of Edison, among them Matthew Josephson, *Edison: A Biography* (New York: McGraw Hill, 1959), and Ronald William Clark, *Edison: The Man Who Made The Future* (London: Macdonald and Jane's, 1977). There is a useful section on Edison in Harold C. Passer, *The Electrical Manufacturers, 1875-1900* (Cambridge: Harvard University Press, 1953), pp. 176-191.

24. These firms signed an agreement in 1897 to share their patents, and successfully prevented the emergence of competitive producers of lighting and electrical equipment.

25. Excellent biographies of Carnegie are Joseph F. Wall, *Andrew Carnegie* (New York: Oxford University Press, 1970), Louis M. Hacker, *The World of Andrew Carnegie 1865-1901* (Philadelphia: Lippincott, 1968), and Burton J. Hendrick, *The Life of Andrew Carnegie* (London: Wm. Heinemann, 1933). A brief lively account of Carnegie's career is Harold C. Livesay's *Andrew Carnegie and the Rise of Big Business* (Boston: Little Brown, 1975).

26. See the first two volumes of Allan Nevins' monumental history of Ford Motor Company: Allan Nevins with F. E. Hill, *Ford: The Times, the Man, the Company* (New York: Scribner's, 1954) and *Ford: Expansion and Challenge, 1915-1933* (New York: Scribner's, 1957). A recent psychohistory of Ford is Anne Jardim's *The First Henry Ford: A Study in Personality and Business Leadership* (Cambridge: MIT Press, 1970).

27. Thomas argues that this development had little to do with Ford's genius, but resulted from intense competitive pressure within the industry which, after the adoption of a standard design, made the introduction of the low-price automobile inevitable. Even if this had not occurred, he continues, the increasing availability of used cars would have accomplished the same end. See Thomas, "The Automobile Industry and Its Tycoon", (above, note 22), p. 143.

28. Cited in Harold U. Faulkner, *The Decline of Laissez-Faire, 1897-1917* (New York: Harper and Row, 1968), p. 121. Italics added.

29. Among the standard biographies of Pierpont Morgan are Frederick Lewis Allen, *The Great Pierpont Morgan* (New York: Harper and Row, 1965), John K. Winkler, *Morgan the Magnificent: The Life of J. Pierpont Morgan, 1837-1931* (New York: Vanguard Press, 1930) and George Wheeler, *Pierpont Morgan and Friends: The Anatomy of a Myth* (Englewood Cliffs, N.J.: Prentice Hall, 1973).

30. Stock-watering is the term applied when securities are issued in an amount not warranted by the assets of the corporation. The organization of the United States Steel Company is a good example. The corporation's assets were valued at $682 million when organized, and the corporation was capitalized at $1.4 billion.

About fifty percent of the capitalization represented "water." Even so, the corporation was so successful that it was able to absorb the water and pay annual dividends (with only two exceptions) on its common stock from 1901 to 1929. See Faulkner, *The Decline of Laissez-Faire, 1897-1917*, p. 167.

31. The existence of a "Money Trust" belatedly came under public scrutiny with the investigations of the Pujo (House Banking and Currency) Committee in 1912-1913. The Committee highlighted the concentration of financial power in a few investment banking houses (among them: Morgan; Kuhn, Loeb; Lee, Higginson; Kidder, Peabody) achieved through consolidations of competitive banks and trust companies, interlocking directorates and stockholdings, and the use of influence. Morgan was singled out as the leader because of his conspicuous involvement with the National City Bank and First National Bank of New York, the Bankers' Trust and Guaranty Trust Companies, and the Mutual of New York, New York Life, and Equitable insurance companies. Morgan and his associates held 341 directorships in 112 corporations with assets of more than $22 billion. A useful discussion is presented in Thomas C. Cochran and William Miller, *The Age of Enterprise: A Social History of Industrial America* (New York: Macmillan Co., 1942), pp. 192-202.

32. For an elaboration, see William J. Baumol, "Entrepreneurship in Economic Theory," *American Economic Review* 58 (May 1968), pp. 64-71.

5. Organizational Change in Manufacturing

1. One estimate is that about thirty-two percent of income originating in manufacturing was accounted for by "monopolistic" industries in 1899, that is by industries whose concentration ratios — the share of output contributed by the four largest firms — exceeded one-half. Within the manufacturing sector, the relative extent of monopoly was significant in many industries, among them rubber products, iron and steel products, paper, transportation equipment, tobacco products, petroleum and coal products, nonferrous products, machinery, and foods. See G. Warren Nutter and Henry Adler Einhorn, *Enterprise Monopoly in the United States: 1899-1958* (New York: Columbia University Press, 1969), pp. 50-51.

2. The early history of the corporation is described in Oscar Handlin and Mary F. Handlin, "Origins of the American Business Corporation," *Journal of Economic History* 5, no. 1 (May 1945), pp. 1-23. See also George Heberton Evans, Jr., *Business Incorporations in the United States, 1800-1943,* N. B. E. R., no. 49 (New York: N. B. E. R., 1948), pp. 10-30.

3. Although all such combinations are loosely referred to as mergers, there are two distinct forms of amalgamation — mergers, narrowly defined, and consolidations. The former refers to the acquisition by an existing corporation of other existing corporations and does not normally require the creation of a new corporation, whereas the latter does involve the creation of a new corporation and the dissolution of the old, constituent firms.

4. This discussion is drawn primarily from the monumental work on the growth of American large-scale enterprise by Alfred D. Chandler. See, inter alia,

Alfred D. Chandler, Jr., "The Beginnings of Big Business in American Industry," *Business History Review* 33, no. 1 (Spring 1959), pp. 1-31, his *Strategy and Structure: Chapters in the History of Industrial Enterprise* (Cambridge, Mass.: M.I.T. Press, 1962), esp. chap. 1, and his *The Visible Hand: The Managerial Revolution in American Business* (Cambridge, Mass.: Harvard University Press, 1977), esp. pts. IV and V.

5. Much of the information contained in this section can be found in Ralph L. Nelson, *Merger Movements in American Industry, 1895-1956,* N. B. E. R., General Series, no. 66 (Princeton: Princeton University Press, 1959). On the later period, see as well Carl Eis, "The 1919-1930 Merger Movement in American Industry," *Journal of Law and Economics* 9 (October 1969), pp. 267-296.

6. Nelson, *Merger Movements in American Industry, 1895-1956,* p. 43.

7. A good example is the formation of United States Steel Corporation, discussed earlier in chapter 4. Carnegie's steel works, valued at some $400 million at the time of consolidation, were held entirely in partnerships without recourse to the capital market. The amalgamation of Carnegie Steel with other firms involved the issue of $1.4 billion par value of common and preferred stock and bonds, some of which were transferred to the owners of the constituent firms, the remainder being offered in the capital market.

8. Nelson's attempt to test, statistically, the traditional causal explanations of the first merger wave has been attacked by Ralph Andreano. In particular, Andreano drew attention to Nelson's failure to assess the role of "conditions of entry" in achieving market control. The example of Standard Oil of New Jersey suggests that barriers to entry were not great in the petroleum industry, since Standard was unable to prevent the entry of new vertically integrated firms after 1911 in spite of its resort to predatory pricing and collusive tactics. See Ralph L. Andreano, ed., *New Views on American Economic Development* (Cambridge, Mass.: Schenkman, 1965), pp. 15-19.

9. George J. Stigler, "Monopoly and Oligopoly by Merger," *American Economic Review* 39, no. 3 (May 1949), pp. 23-34.

10. The interested reader is referred to the attempt to develop a quantitative index of the extent and growth of monopoly power in the United States from 1899 to 1958 by Nutter and Einhorn, *Enterprise Monopoly in the United States: 1899-1958.* Unfortunately, estimates of the extent of monopoly do not indicate the importance of its effects on resource allocation and, consequently, on real incomes in the economy.

11. Stigler has described this later movement as "merger for oligopoly." According to him, the scenario was as follows. The dominant firm (usually the merger firm of the early period) did not continue its previous merger program to retain its monopoly position. Thus, its output share declined relative to the industry as a whole. Instead, new mergers were undertaken by smaller companies, and had the effect of transforming these industries from near-monopoly to oligopoly structures. Stigler, "Monopoly and Oligopoly by Merger," pp. 23-34.

12. By the end of the century, funds were being mobilized for manufacturing enterprises in the capital market. See Thomas R. Navin and Marian V. Sears, "The Rise of a Market for Industrial Securities, 1887-1902," *Business History Review* 29, no. 2 (June 1955), pp. 105-138. Lance Davis suggests that J. P.

Morgan's successful shift into manufacturing had a "demonstration effect," creating the impression that manufacturing securities were safe and profitable. In the period after 1900, many more investment-banking houses were established, and they had increasing success in marketing new industrial issues. See Lance E. Davis, "The Investment Market, 1870-1914: The Evolution of a National Market," *Journal of Economic History* 25, no. 3 (September 1965), pp. 386-387. See also Nelson, *Merger Movements in American Industry, 1895-1956,* pp. 89-100.

13. The following section follows closely on the path-breaking work of Profesor Alfred D. Chandler, Jr. See his *Strategy and Structure,* esp. chap. 1 and 6, and case studies of developing administrative structures for Du Pont, General Motors, Standard Oil of New Jersey, and Sears, Roebuck and Company in chap. 2 through 5. See also Chandler's *The Visible Hand,* particularly pts. IV and V.

14. See Alfred D. Chandler, Jr., "The Railroads: Pioneers in Modern Corporate Management," *Business History Review,* 39, no. 1 (Spring 1965), pp. 16-40.

15. See Joseph A. Litterer, "Systematic Management: The Search for Order and Integration," *Business History Review* 35, no. 4 (Winter 1961), pp. 461-476, and "Systematic Management: Design for Organizational Recoupling in American Manufacturing Firms," *Business History Review* 37, no. 3 (Fall 1963), pp. 369-391.

16. For a brief account of an early use of cost accounting techniques, see H. Thomas Johnson, "Accounting for Internal Management Control: Lyman Mills in the 1850's," *Business History Review* 46, no. 4 (Winter 1972), pp. 466-474.

17. For a detailed study, see Samuel Haber, *Efficiency and Uplift: Scientific Management in the Progressive Era* (Chicago: University of Chicago Press, 1964). A comparison of "systematic" and "scientific" management is contained in Daniel Nelson, *Managers and Workers: Origins of the New Factory System in the United States 1880-1920* (Madison: University of Wisconsin Press, 1975), pp. 48-78. For a critical appraisal of the social implications of "Taylorism," see David F. Noble, *America by Design: Science, Technology, and the Rise of Corporate Capitalism* (New York: Alfred A. Knopf, 1979), esp. pp. 264-278. The way in which "scientific management" undermined the workers' control of production is described in David Montgomery, *Workers' Control in America: Studies in the History of Work, Technology, and Labor Struggles* (New York: Cambridge University Press, 1979), chap. 1, 4, and 5.

18. Chandler, *The Visible Hand,* (above, note 4), p. 463.

19. This section is based largely on Chandler, *Strategy and Structure,* chap. 2, and Ernest Dale, "Du Pont: Pioneer in Systematic Management," *Administrative Science Quarterly* 2, no. 1 (June 1957), pp. 25-29. The most comprehensive treatment of Du Pont's development is Alfred D. Chandler, Jr. and Stephen Salsbury, *Pierre S. Du Pont and the Making of the Modern Corporation* (New York: Harper and Row, 1971).

20. New techniques of management accounting were essential to provide top management with data to evaluate company-wide performance and plan future company policy. Many of these techniques — annual operating forecasts, sales reports, flexible budgets, and uniform performance criteria among divisions —

were introduced at General Motors in the 1920s and soon diffused to other multidivisional enterprises. These techniques permitted increased autonomy for divisional managers while ensuring that top management could monitor and plan for divisional operations and coordinate divisional operations with company-wide policy. See H. Thomas Johnson, "Management Accounting in an Early Multidivisional Organization: General Motors in the 1920's," *Business History Review* 52 (Winter 1978), pp. 490-517.

21. The basic historical work on American multinational enterprise is Mira Wilkins, *The Emergence of Multinational Enterprise: American Business Abroad from the Colonial Era to 1914* (Cambridge: Harvard University Press, 1970) and *The Maturing of Multinational Enterprise: American Business Abroad from 1914 to 1970* (Cambridge: Harvard University Press, 1974). For a succinct discussion, see Raymond Vernon, *Sovereignty at Bay: The Multinational Spread of US Enterprise* (New York: Basic Books, 1971), esp. chap. 2 and 3. The broader context of American imperialism is outlined in Robert B. Zevin, "An Interpretation of American Imperialism," *Journal of Economic History* 32 (March 1972), pp. 316-360.

22. Wilkins, *The Emergence of Multinational Enterprise,* p. 35.

23. For an excellent discussion, complete with examples, see Wilkins, *The Emergence of Multinational Enterprise,* chap. 3.

24. Ibid., chap. 7.

25. Vernon shows that in 1967, a high proportion of American foreign direct investment emanated from 187 firms on Fortune's list of the 500 largest industries. These firms had at least six major manufacturing or raw materials-producing subsidiaries abroad. See Vernon, *Sovereignty at Bay*, chap. 1.

26. In Canada, for example, American enterprises control approximately sixty percent of Canadian manufacturing and raw materials production. Kari Levitt, *Silent Surrender: The Multinational Corporation in Canada* (Toronto: Macmillan, 1970) is the best of several critiques of American direct investment in Canada. For data on American control of Canadian manufacturing and raw materials production, see p. 60 and the Appendix, pp. 137-185.

27. Chandler, *The Visible Hand*, p. 1.

6. Technological and Organizational Change in Agriculture

1. The relative importance of the various sources of output growth and their effect on labor productivity can be examined under partitioning techniques, whereby the impact on output growth of the availability of new lands alone or improved technological knowledge alone is isolated. An example of this kind of analysis is presented later in this chapter in the case of small-grain agriculture in the Midwest.

2. *Historical Statistics of the United States*, ser. K265-273, pp. 296-297, and ser. K298-306, pp. 301-302.

3. Ibid., ser. K195-212, pp. 289-290.

4. General discussions of this process are presented in Fred A. Shannon, *The*

Farmer's Last Frontier: Agriculture, 1860-1897 (New York: Holt, Rinehart and Winston, 1945), chap. 11, and Harold U. Faulkner, *The Decline of Laissez-Faire, 1897-1917* (New York: Harper and Row, 1968), chap. 13.

5. Richard Hofstadter, *The Age of Reform: From Bryan to F. D. R.* (New York: Alfred A. Knopf and Random House, 1955), pp. 43, 46.

6. Irwin Feller, "Inventive Activity in Agriculture, 1837-1890," *Journal of Economic History* 22, no. 4 (December 1962), pp. 560-577.

7. Among the most useful discussions of mechanical inventions are Wayne D. Rasmussen, "The Impact of Technological Change in American Agriculture, 1862-1962," *Journal of Economic History* 22, no. 4 (December 1962), pp. 578-591, and Allan G. Bogue, *From Prairie to Corn Belt: Farming on the Illinois and Iowa Prairies in the Nineteenth Century* (Chicago: University of Chicago Press, 1963), chap. 8. For the pre-1870 period, the single best account is Clarence H. Danhof, *Change in Agriculture: The Northern United States, 1820-1870* (Cambridge, Mass.: Harvard University Press, 1969), chaps. 8 and 9.

8. Paul David's study of the diffusion of the reaper in the late 1840s and early 1850s is a classic illustration of the application of microeconomic theory to historical analysis. See Paul A. David, "The Mechanization of Reaping in the Ante-Bellum Midwest," in Henry Rosovsky, ed., *Industrialization in Two Systems: Essays in Honor of Alexander Gerschenkron* (New York: John Wiley, 1966), pp. 3-39. The article is reprinted in Fogel and Engerman, eds. *The Reinterpretation of American Economic History* (New York: Harper and Row, 1971), pp. 214-227. David may have underestimated the extent to which design improvements and sharing and contracting of machine services increased the rate of diffusion in the 1850s. See Alan L. Olmstead, "The Mechanization of Reaping and Mowing in American Agriculture, 1833-1870," *Journal of Economic History* 35, no. 2 (June 1975), pp. 327-352.

9. Bogue, *From Prairie to Corn Belt,* p. 164.

10. See the comments of Faulkner, *The Decline of Laissez-Faire, 1897-1917,* pp. 355-358. The percentage of farms operated by tenants increased from 15.6 percent in 1880 to 35.3 percent in 1910, and 38.1 percent in 1920. In the West Northcentral region, which includes the Prairie and Plains states, the figures rose from 20.5 percent in 1880 to 34.2 percent in 1920. By far the largest percentage of tenant-operated farms was in the South throughout the period. In any case, higher tenancy rates in themselves indicate nothing about changes in farmers' welfare.

11. "Bonanza" farms are discussed in Shannon, *The Farmer's Last Frontier: Agriculture, 1860-1897,* chap. 7. For a discussion of the development of corporate farming in the twentieth century, see Philip M. Raup, "Corporate Farming in the United States," *Journal of Economic History* 33, no. 1 (March 1973), pp. 274-290.

12. Extensive discussions of these information sources are contained in Danhof, *Change in Agriculture: The Northern United States, 1820-1870,* chap. 3, and Bogue, *From Prairie to Corn Belt,* chap. 10. See also Richard T. Farrell, "Advice to Farmers: The Content of Agricultural Newspapers, 1800-1910," *Journal of Agricultural History* 51 (January 1977), pp. 209-217.

13. William N. Parker and Judith L. V. Klein, "Productivity Growth in Grain

Production in the United States, 1840-60 and 1900-10," in *Output, Employment, and Productivity in the United States After 1800,* N. B. E. R., Studies In Income and Wealth, vol. 30 (New York: Columbia University Press, 1966) pp. 523-580, and William N. Parker, "Productivity Growth in American Grain Farming: An Analysis of Its Nineteenth Century Sources," in Fogel and Engerman, eds., *The Reinterpretation of American Economic History,* pp. 175-186.

14. This partitioning technique allows for the estimation of the differential effects of westward expansion, regional specialization, and technological change. A useful heuristic account of the partitioning approach is presented in William A. Parker, "Sources of Agricultural Productivity in the Nineteenth Century," *Journal of Farm Economics* 49, no. 5 (December 1967), pp. 1455-68. A more technical account is contained in Parker and Klein, "Productivity Growth in Grain Production in the United States, 1840-60 and 1900-10."

15. Fred Bateman, "Improvement in American Dairy Farming, 1850-1910: A Quantitative Analysis," *Journal of Economic History* 28, no. 2 (June 1968), pp. 255-273, and "Labor Inputs and Productivity in American Dairy Agriculture, 1850-1910," *Journal of Economic History* 29, no. 2 (June 1969), pp. 206-229.

16. Some reservations about Bateman's estimation of labor productivity are raised in Gerald Gunderson, "Issues in the Measurement of Efficiency of American Dairy Farming, 1850-1910: A Comment," *Journal of Economic History* 29, no. 3 (September 1969), pp. 501-506, and are answered in Bateman's "Reply", Ibid., pp. 506-511.

17. Griliches, Zvi, "Hybrid Corn: An Exploration in the Economics of Technological Change," in *Econometrica* 25, no. 4 (October 1957), pp. 501-522. An abridged version was published as "Hybrid Corn and the Economics of Innovation," in *Science,* no. 132 (July 29, 1960), pp. 275-280, and is reprinted in Fogel and Engerman, *The Reinterpretation of American Economic History,* pp. 207-213.

18. The S-pattern summarizes large bodies of data in terms of three parameters: the origin, which signifies the date of initial adoptions or the beginning of diffusion; the slope of the curve, which indicates the relative speed of diffusion; and the ceiling of the curve, which represents the final level of diffusion among corn acreage.

19. Zvi Griliches, "Research Costs and Social Returns: Hybrid Corn and Related Innovations," *Journal of Political Economy* 66, no. 5 (October 1958), pp. 419-431.

20. An excellent survey of recent contributions to the economic and social history of the postbellum South is Harold D. Woodman, "Sequel to Slavery: The New History Views the Postbellum South," *Journal of Southern History,* 43 (November 1977), pp. 523-554.

21. Roger L. Ransom and Richard Sutch, *One Kind of Freedom: The Economic Consequences of Emancipation* (New York: Cambridge University Press, 1977). Ransom and Sutch deal with a subregion, the "Cotton South," and some of their conclusions based on evidence for this area may have limited applicability to the southern region as a whole.

22. The development of tenancy systems in the postwar period is discussed in Ransom and Sutch, *One Kind of Freedom*, pp. 87-104.

23. See Gavin Wright, *The Political Economy of the Cotton South: Households, Markets and Wealth in the Nineteenth Century* (New York: Norton, 1978), chap. 4. Wright's basic proposition is that the South's low growth rate is not explained by economic and social institutions but by trends in world cotton demand. High cotton prices in the late 1860s pushed the South deeper into cotton and new institutions reinforced this commitment. Subsequent stagnation in world demand had adverse effects on an economy so geared to cotton profitability.

24. Both black and white tenant farmers suffered under these arrangements. However, blacks invariably had less capital, smaller farms, smaller amounts of uncultivated land, and consequently were even more dependent on purchased supplies and hence even more susceptible to exploitation. See Ransom and Sutch, *One Kind of Freedom*, chap. 9.

25. Robert Higgs, *Competition and Coercion: Blacks in the American Economy, 1865-1914* (New York: Cambridge University Press, 1977).

26. Higgs, *Competition and Coercion,* p. 125.

7. Industrialism, Unrest, and Reform; The Coming of Government Regulation

1. Samuel Hays, *The Response to Industrialism, 1885-1914* (Chicago: University of Chicago Press, 1957).

2. Antimonopoly positions were not unique to farmers and industrial workers. Robert Wiebe believes that the decline of the independent, small businessman in the face of emerging monopoly meant that businessmen also were participants in the "search for order." The business community was comprised of members with varied opinions and degrees of influence on the content of new economic regulations. See Robert H. Wiebe, *Businessmen and Reform: A Study of the Progressive Movement* (Cambridge, Mass.: Harvard University Press, 1962), and *The Search for Order, 1877-1920* (New York: Hill and Wang, 1967).

3. Theodore Saloutos, "The Agricultural Problem and Nineteenth Century Industrialism," *Agricultural History* 23, no. 3 (July 1948), p. 156.

4. See the interesting paper by Louis Galambos entitled, "The Agrarian Image of the Large Corporation, 1879-1920: A Study of Social Accommodation," *Journal of Economic History* 28 (September 1968), pp. 341-362. Galambos studied several agrarian publications and analyzed the image of "big business" presented in them. He found that farmers' grievances were reduced after 1900 by the increase in farm incomes, the implementation of various reform measures including the Hepburn Act of 1906 and the Mann-Elkins Act of 1910, and the apparent change in business leadership from the "colorful and outspoken" owner-entrepreneurs of the late nineteenth century to the new generation of "anonymous" administrative officers. Also see his *The Public Image of Big Business in America, 1880-1940: A Quantitative Study of Social Change* (Baltimore: The Johns Hopkins University Press, 1975), which also analyzes the attitudes toward "big business" of professional and labor publications.

5. The seminal study of Populism is Lawrence Goodwyn's *Democratic Promise: The Populist Movement in America* (New York: Oxford University Press,

1976). For a somewhat narrower treatment of Populism as intellectual history, see Norman Pollack, *The Populist Response to Industrial America* (New York: W. W. Norton, 1966).

6. Robert Higgs, "Railroad Rates and the Populist Uprising," *Agricultural History* 44 (July 1970), pp. 291-297.

7. A sample of 102 counties in 1890 indicated that only 9 percent of mortgages outstanding in that year were taken under distress conditions, and more than 90 percent were taken for productive purposes, many in order to finance the purchase of additional real estate.

Allan G. Bogue, *Money at Interest: The Farm Mortgage on the Middle Border* (Ithaca: Cornell University Press, 1955), p. 271.

8. Ibid., p. 4.

9. Ibid., p. 269. See also the data for mean mortgage rates in three Iowa townships, 1852-1896, in Bogue, *From Prairie to Corn Belt: Farming on the Illinois and Iowa Prairies in the Nineteenth Century* (Chicago: University of Chicago Press, 1963), p. 178.

10. Robert W. Fogel and Jack Rutner, "The Efficiency Effects of Federal Land Policy, 1850-1900: A Report of Some Provisional Findings," in William Aydelotte, et al., eds., *Dimensions of Quantitative Research in History* (Princeton: Princeton University Press, 1972), pp. 390-418.

11. Walter T.K. Nugent, "Some Parameters of Populism," *Agricultural History* 40 (October 1966), p. 264.

Bogue used data on the mortgage foreclosure rate to conclude that the 1870s was a relatively poor period compared with the 1880s and the 1890s. See Allan Bogue, *From Prairie to Corn Belt,* p. 179.

12. George F. Warren and Frank A. Pearson, *Prices* (New York: Wiley, 1933), pp. 26-27.

In another study, Fogel and Rutner have pointed out that from 1870 to 1900, the wholesale price index declined even more rapidly than wheat and corn prices, which suggests that the real prices of farm products were increasing. They show an average annual decline in agricultural prices of 1.7 percent from 1869 to 1899. Wholesale prices fell by an estimated 2.0 percent annually, and farm consumer prices by 1.4 percent. There was considerable variation between decades: for example, the data show a 3.8 percent average annual decline in farm prices for the 1870s compared with a 4.1 percent decrease in wholesale prices and a 2.5 percent decrease in farm consumer prices. Farmers were undoubtedly more conscious of declines in the prices received for farm products than in the prices of goods which they purchased. See Fogel and Rutner, "The Efficiency Effects of Federal Land Policy, 1850-1900," pp. 393-394.

13. Ibid., pp. 395-396.

14. To a certain extent, these losses may be offset by capital gains to farmers. Increases in the value of agricultural land reflect increases in expected farm incomes. Bowman's work on midwestern land values from 1860 to 1900 tends to support the belief that farm incomes, reflecting changes in land values, decreased in the 1870s, increased in the 1880s, and experienced little change in the 1890s. However, county-by-county variations in farm land values make generalization difficult.

See John D. Bowman, "An Economic Analysis of Mid-Western Farm Land Values and Farm Land Income, 1860 to 1900," *Yale Economic Essays* 5, no. 2 (Fall 1965), pp. 317-359.

15. Douglass C. North, *Growth and Welfare in the American Past: A New Economic History,* 2d ed. (Englewood Cliffs, N.J.: Prentice-Hall, 1974), pp. 136-137.

16. Anne Mayhew, "A Reappraisal of the Causes of Farm Protest in the United States, 1870-1900," *Journal of Economic History* 32, no. 3 (September 1972), pp. 464-475.

17. Hays, *The Response to Industrialism,* passim.

18. Pollack, *The Populist Response to Industrial America,* p. 3.

19. The development of working-class consciousness and the study of "the worker and not only his institutions" are featured themes in recent contributions to the "new" labor history. In particular, David Montgomery has argued that skilled craft workers made a conscious attempt to resist the subordination of labor resulting from the principles and methods of "scientific management" by reasserting traditional forms of workers' controls over production. The participation of craft workers in labor strife was a response not to economic conditions but to the social implications for the workplace of changing styles of business management. On the other hand, unskilled labor was moved by more mundane issues — wages and employment. Ultimately, craft-based unionism was one of the casualties of the rise of mass-production industries. See David Montgomery, *Workers' Control in America: Studies in the History of Work, Technology, and Labor Struggles* (New York: Cambridge University Press, 1979), esp. chap. 1. Also see David Brody, *Workers in Industrial America: Essays on the Twentieth Century Struggle* (New York: Oxford University Press, 1980), esp. chap. 1.

20. Trade union growth is usually ascribed to the expectation that employees will receive net economic benefits by joining a union, and to the role of unions in articulating labor's grievances during periods of social unrest. For an attempt to assess the relative importance of those factors, see Orley Ashenfelter and John M. Pencavel, "American Trade Union Growth: 1900-1960," *Quarterly Journal of Economics* 83 (August 1969), pp. 434-448. A more general discussion is contained in Albert A. Blum, "Why Unions Grow," *Labor History* 9 (Winter 1968), pp. 39-72.

For a comprehensive account of union development before 1900, see Lloyd Ulman, *The Rise of the National Trade Union* (Cambridge, Mass.: Harvard University Press, 1955).

21. Montgomery, *Workers' Control,* pp. 18-24.

22. There was a vigorous radical element in labor which argued strongly for direct political action based on a working-class movement. The Socialist Party of America made repeated attempts at AF of L conventions to overthrow Gompers and to redirect the Federation towards political action. Other radical groups combined in 1905 to establish the Industrial Workers of the World who advocated greater labor militancy and reliance on the general strike to achieve reform. See Brody, *Workers in Industrial America,* pp. 32-39, for a good, brief discussion.

23. The AF of L was not opposed to "bigness" per se, but was concerned about the performance of large corporations in key areas like wages, hours,

employment, and labor relations. For example, like the farm press, labor publications showed considerable hostility to "big business" in the 1890s, again featuring the use of pejoratives. But, where farmers agitated about pricing policies, labor emphasized labor relations, and wages and hours policies. See Louis Galambos, "The AFL's Concept of Big Business: A Quantitative Study of Attitudes toward the Large Corporation, 1894-1931," *Journal of American History* 58 (March 1971), pp. 847-863. See also his *The Public Image of Big Business in America 1880-1940.*

24. Clarence D. Long, *Wages and Earnings in the United States, 1860-1890,* N. B. E. R., General Series, no. 67 (Princeton: Princeton University Press, 1960).

25. Ibid., pp. 13, 35, and 38.

26. Ibid., p. 68.

27. Albert Rees, *Real Wages in Manufacturing, 1890-1914,* N. B. E. R., General Series, no. 70 (Princeton: Princeton University Press, 1961).

28. Ibid., p. 122.

29. Ibid., p. 25.

30. For example, contrary to popular belief, factory work does not appear to have adversely affected the occupational mortality of industrial workers. See Paul Uselding, "In Dispraise of the Muckrakers: United States Occupational Mortality, 1890-1910," in Uselding, ed., *Research in Economic History*, vol. 1 (Greenwich, Conn.: JAI Press, 1976), pp. 334-371.

31. Davis, Easterlin, Parker, et al., *American Economic Growth*, p. 230.

32. A more enlightened business management played a significant role in these reforms, partly for philanthropic reasons and partly out of self-interest. Employee benefit programs were intended to increase workers' loyalty to the firm as well as to better their living conditions. In the post-War period, the "American Plan" with its greater emphasis on benefits, good labor relations and effective personnel management undermined further attempts at labor organization until the Depression. See Brody, *Workers in Industrial America*, pp. 9-14. The relationship between state and corporate welfare systems is described in Edward D. Berkowitz and Kim McQuaid, "Businessman and Bureaucrat: The Evolution of the American Social Welfare System, 1900-1940," *Journal of Economic History* 38 (March 1978), pp. 120-142.

33. Richard Hofstadter, *The Age of Reform: From Bryan to F. D. R.* (New York: Alfred A. Knopf and Random House, 1955), p. 122.

34. Hays, *The Response to Industrialism*, chap. 9.

35. This pool has been discussed in detail by P. W. MacAvoy, *The Economic Effects of Regulation — The Trunk Line Railroad Cartels and the Inter-State Commerce Commission Before 1900* (Cambridge, Mass.: M.I.T. Press, 1965).

36. Vanderbilt controlled the northern routes from New York to Chicago, and the Pennsylvania system held the routes from Pennsylvania and Maryland to the West. The Morgan interests were large in the southeast as were the Gould and Rock Island systems in the Mississippi Valley. Hill railroads dominated the northwest, and Harriman held large interests in central and southern transcontinental railroads. The seven major systems in reality collapsed to four, because there were significant financial interrelationships among the Morgan, Hill, Vanderbilt, and Pennsylvania systems.

37. An informative survey of the recent literature on regulation is Thomas K. McGraw, "Regulation in America: A Review Article," *Business History Review 49* (Summer 1975), pp. 159-183.

38. Gabriel Kolko, *Railroads and Regulation, 1877-1916* (Princeton: Princeton University Press, 1965).

39. Ibid., p. 5.

40. Ibid., p. 238.

41. Two excellent critiques are Albro Martin, "The Troubled Subject of Railroad Regulation in the Gilded Age — A Reappraisal," *Journal of American History* 61 (September 1976), pp. 339-371, and Robert W. Harbeson, "Railroads and Regulation, 1877-1916: Conspiracy or Public Interest?" *Journal of Economic History* 27 (June 1967), pp. 230-242. See also Ari and Olive Hoogenboom, *A History of the ICC: From Panacea to Palliative* (New York: W. W. Norton, 1976).

42. Harbeson, "Railroads and Regulation, 1877-1916," pp. 231-233.

43. On this point, see Albert Fishlow, "Productivity and Technological Change in the Railroad Sector, 1840-1910," in *Output, Employment, and Productivity in the United States After 1800,* N. B. E. R., Studies in Income and Wealth, vol. 30 (New York: Columbia University Press, 1966), pp. 583-646.

44. But an interesting theoretical exercise which suggests that price may approach the competitive level as the number of firms in an industry increases is presented by G. Warren Nutter, "Duopoly, Oligopoly, and Emerging Competition," *Southern Economic Journal* 30, no. 4 (April 1964), pp. 342-352.

45. Harbeson, "Railroads and Regulation, 1877-1916", pp. 236-241.

46. Kolko, *Railroads and Regulation, 1877-1916,* p. 216.

47. Ibid., p. 217.

48. Harbeson, "Railroads and Regulation, 1877-1916," p. 242.

49. George J. Stigler, "The Theory of Economic Regulation," *Bell Journal of Economics and Management Science* 2 (Spring 1971), pp. 3-21.

50. Stigler concludes that idealistic views of public regulation are no longer valid. Complaints about the ICC's pro-railroad policies are misdirected because they suggest that a "reformed" commission — one not subservient to the railroads and other carriers — could be obtained by instructing the commissioners or those who appoint them.

51. Robert M. Spann and Edward W. Erickson, "The Economics of Railroading: The Beginning of Cartelization and Regulation," *Bell Journal of Economics and Management Science* 1 (Autumn 1970), pp. 227-244.

52. See Harbeson, "Railroads and Regulation, 1877-1916," pp. 232-233. If fixed costs are a large proportion of total costs, then costs are largely independent of output and per unit costs are likely to be decreasing over a wide range of output.

53. Spann and Erickson, "The Economics of Railroading," pp. 231-234.

54. For example, the Delaware and Lackawanna Railroad was a small line which expanded and entered the cartel, then broke the agreement. If the smaller railroad had higher costs than the larger firms, in the ensuing price war losses would be incurred differentially by the high-cost, smaller firm. Ibid., p. 234.

55. Ibid., pp. 234-236. The interpretation of the cost and output data in

calculating average costs in this railroad sector is complicated by technological progress which biases the cost data to resemble decreasing per unit costs.

56. Ibid., pp. 236-238.

57. The increase in profits may have been coincidental with the introduction of federal legislation rather than "caused" by it.

58. Spann and Erickson, "The Economics of Railroading," pp. 238-242. See the correction of their results in the estimates presented by Richard O. Zerbe, Jr., "The Costs and Benefits of Early Regulation of the Railroads," *Bell Journal of Economics* 11, no. 1 (Spring 1980), pp. 343-350. The figures cited here are from p. 349.

59. A thorough consideration of these themes has not been attempted here. Useful literature surveys and bibliographical guides are presented in Hal Bridges, "The Robber Baron Concept in American History," *Business History Review* 32 (Spring 1958), pp. 1-13, and Gabriel Kolko, "The Premises of Business Revisionism," *Business History Review* 33 (Fall 1959), pp. 330-344. A developing revisionist interpretation has attempted to restore pride of place to the creative achievement of the great American capitalists, but the issue remains contentious.

8. The Market Economy: Prosperity and Prostration

1. For an excellent detailed discussion of the events of the 1920s see George Soule, *Prosperity Decade: From War to Depression, 1917-1929* (New York: Harper and Row, 1968) which, although originally published in 1947, remains the standard work. A useful recent treatment is Jim Potter's *The American Economy Between the World Wars* (New York: John Wiley and Sons, 1974), The best discussion of the chronology of the business cycle during the 1920s is Robert Aaron Gordon's *Economic Instability and Growth: The American Record* (New York: Harper and Row, 1974), chap. 2.

2. Recently, Peter Temin has attempted to assess the relative merits of the "spending" and "monetary" hypotheses as explanations of the Great Depression. According to Temin, the monetary explanation of the Depression focuses on changes in the financial sector and, in particular, the collapse of the banking system, whereas the spending hypothesis emphasizes declines in aggregate expenditures (consumption and/or investment). See Peter Temin, *Did Monetary Forces Cause the Great Depression*? (New York: W. W. Norton, 1976). Pages 7-12 provide a brief introduction to the two hypotheses, which are further elaborated in chaps. 1-3. We will return to the subject later in this chapter.

3. See, for example, Soule, *Prosperity Decade*, pp. 283-288, 332-335. He argues that from 1923-1930, there was a thirty percent increase in manufacturing output with little increase in employment and only an eight percent increase in average hourly earnings. In other words, lower labor costs benefited employers, and led to increased profit margins, dividends, and retained earnings. Corporate prosperity was the end result.

4. Robert P. Keller, "Factor Income Distribution in the United States During the 1920's: A Re-examination of Fact and Theory," *Journal of Economic History* 33 (March 1973), pp. 252-273.

5. Ibid., p. 258.

6. Charles F. Holt, "Who Benefited From the Prosperity of the 1920's?" *Explorations in Economic History* 14 (Summer 1977), pp. 277-289.

7. Kuznet's data for two variants — "economic" income and "disposable" income — are summarized in Holt, "Who Benefited," pp. 281-282.

8. Ibid., pp. 278-279.

9. Harold G. Vatter, "Has There Been a Twentieth-Century Consumer Durables Revolution?" *Journal of Economic History* 27 (March 1967), pp. 1-16.

10. Ibid., p. 5.

11. One can conceive of saturation in the broadest possible sense as involving a comparison of the current level of production of a particular good with the potential output of that good. But, to make the concept operational requires a meaningful definition of potential output. In fact, several possibilities exist. First, one may focus on static saturation, in which a state of saturation is reached when current new purchases are less than or equal to those of the previous period. Thus, a leveling off or decline in new purchases from one period to the next indicates saturation in the market for the good. In more widespread use is the notion of dynamic saturation, which involves the comparison of percentage changes in new purchases in the current period with percentage changes in the previous period. If percentage changes in new purchases are the same or lower in the more recent period, then a movement towards a state of saturation is indicated. For elaboration, see the discussion in Lloyd J. Mercer and W. Douglas Morgan, "Alternative Interpretations of Market Saturation: Evidence for the Automobile Market in the Late Twenties," *Explorations in Economic History* 9 (Spring 1972), pp. 272-278.

12. Ibid., p. 283, table 2.

13. Ibid., p. 284, table 3.

14. Peter J. George and E. H. Oksanen, "Saturation in the Automobile Market in the Late Twenties: Some Further Results," *Explorations in Economic History* 11 (Fall 1973), pp. 73-85.

15. Ben Bolch, Rendigs Fels, and Marshall McMahon, "Housing Surplus in the 1920's?" *Explorations in Economic History* 8 (Spring 1971), pp. 259-283.

16. Lloyd J. Mercer and W. Douglas Morgan, "Housing Surplus in the 1920's? Another Evaluation," *Explorations in Economic History* 10 (Summer 1973), pp. 295-303.

17. Two excellent monographs which study the Great Depression in fine detail are Broadus Mitchell, *Depression Decade: From New Era Through New Deal 1929-1941* (New York: Harper and Row, 1969), originally published in 1947, and Lester V. Chandler, *America's Greatest Depression, 1929-1941* (New York: Harper and Row, 1970). America's economic performance in the Depression is placed in its world-wide perspective by Charles P. Kindleberger in *The World in Depression 1929-1939* (Berkeley: University of California Press, 1973). For a business cycle chronology, see Gordon's *Economic Instability,* chap. 3.

18. See Milton Friedman and Anna Jacobson Schwartz, *The Great Contraction 1929-1933* (Princeton: University Press, 1965), which is chapter 7 of *A Monetary History of the United States, 1867-1960,* N. B. E. R. Studies in Business Cycles, no. 12 (Princeton: Princeton University Press, 1963). While the authors do allow for the possibility that nonmonetary factors initiated the con-

traction in 1929, they maintain that "the monetary collapse was. . . a largely independent factor which exerted a powerful influence on the course of events." *The Great Contraction*, p. 4.

19. Temin, *Did Monetary Forces*, p. 169.

20. Temin has many critics who claim he has not done justice to the monetary hypothesis. See, inter alia, Thomas Mayer, "Money and the Great Depression: A Critique of Temin," *Explorations in Economic History* 15 (April 1978), pp. 127-145.

21. Robert J. Gordon and James A. Wilcox, "Monetarist Interpretations of the Great Depression: An Evaluation and Critique," in Karl Brunner, ed., *The Great Depression Revisited* (Boston: Martinus Nijhoff, 1981), pp. 49-107.

22. Temin, *Did Monetary Forces,* pp. 170-178.

23. Ibid., especially pp. 62-83. Mayer is critical of Temin's consumption function, and his re-estimation of an improved consumption function fails to confirm Temin's contention that there was an unusually large decrease in consumption spending in 1930. Thomas Mayer, "Consumption in the Great Depression," *Journal of Political Economy* 86 (February 1978), pp. 139-145.

24. Frederic S. Mishkin, "The Household Balance Sheet and the Great Depression," *Journal of Economic History* 38 (December 1978), pp. 918-937.

25. The life-cycle hypothesis requires that the individual (or household) consider his lifetime resources in making his consumption decision.

26. Ibid., table 2, p. 921. Security losses were only one-quarter of liabilities in 1929, whereas mortgages constituted forty-five percent and consumer credit another fifteen percent.

27. Ibid., pp. 926-932, including table 4.

28. Temin, *Did Monetary Forces,* p. xi.

29. As cited in Mitchell, *Depression Decade*, p. 37.

30. The policy measures introduced by the Roosevelt administration during the New Deal are an often-told story, and are ably summarized in Mitchell, *Depression Decade,* passim, Chandler, *America's Greatest Depression,* passim, and William F. Leuchtenburg, *Franklin D. Roosevelt and the New Deal 1932-1940* (New York: Harper and Row, 1963). However, it's important to keep in mind that the policies of the New Deal did not constitute a coherent, consistent program, but represented an attempt to experiment and to innovate with new institutional and economic arrangements to find solutions to the many distinct problems comprising the Great Depression.

31. Not all of the Roosevelt adminstration's actions in this period were to have an expansionary effect. For example, during the campaign, Roosevelt castigated the Hoover Administration for its two years of budget deficits. This indictment must seem strange coming from a political leader who, in the popular mind, soon came to be identified with an innovative reliance on conscious deficit financing as a policy instrument. Although Roosevelt's Hundred Days are hailed for their positive measures, one must also recall that they began with the Economy Bill, which provided for an immediate reduction in federal government spending, partly at the expense of relief and partly at the expense of potential stim-

ulus to recovery. Moreover, Roosevelt and the Brains Trust viewed the deficits as "unfortunate" by-products of the Depression-induced revenue shortfall; they would have been glad to finance the New Deal out of tax revenues if they could have done so. Only a handful of economists were in favor of running deficits.

32. E. Cary Brown, "Fiscal Policy in the Thirties: A Reappraisal," *American Economic Review* 46 (December 1956), pp. 857-879, and John B. Kirkwood, "The Great Depression: A Structural Analysis," *Journal of Money, Credit and Banking* 4 (November 1972), pp. 811-837.

33. On the other hand, monetary policy was mildly expansionary until 1936, when the Federal Reserve introduced restrictive measures leading to the recession of 1937-38.

34. Brown may have exaggerated the expansionary effect of federal fiscal policy for 1933, and 1937-1939 because of his assumption of unit elasticity of total taxes with respect to GNP. But this finding does not jeopardize the conclusions reached below. See Larry Peppers, "Full Employment Surplus Analysis and Structural Change: The 1930's," *Explorations in Economic History* 10 (Winter 1973), pp. 197-210.

35. Alvin H. Hansen, "Was Fiscal Policy in the Thirties a Failure?" *Review of Economics and Statistics* 45 (August 1963), pp. 320-323.

36. Brown, "Fiscal Policy," p. 873.

37. Concern over the paucity of degrees of freedom associated with the use of small samples often leads to the use of additional observations. The "robustness" of regression coefficients to a varying sample size is therefore another criterion which might be used to assess the investment function.

38. To examine the implications of alternative terminal years, one can estimate the investment function sequentially through 1960, adding one year at a time (war years excluded). Some of the coefficients demonstrate appreciable instability. For example, until 1955, the coefficient of the accelerator term is not significant at the five percent level. In other words, the investment equation "works" only once an arbitrary decision is made to use 1955 or some subsequent year *to explain investment behavior during the Great Depression.*

39. Chandler, for one, is skeptical of the practicability in the early 1930s of government implementation of what now are taken for granted as "routine" economic policies. See Chandler, *America's Greatest Depression,* pp. 122-123.

40. George S. Murphy, "On Counterfactual Propositions," *Quantitative History and the Logic of the Social Sciences, History and Theory* 9, p. 36

41. Kirkwood, "The Great Depression," p. 830.

42. Now, in the 1980s, there is much debate about how these responsibilities are to be met, in the main because of a profound disagreement over the inherent stability of the market economy. Those who see the economy as highly unstable would have government use its fiscal powers and the Federal Reserve its monetary powers to dampen business fluctuations, whereas those who view the economy as intrinsically stable would drastically reduce the discretionary powers of fiscal and monetary authorities whose actions, they believe, worsen matters.

9. World War Two and its Aftermath The Ascending of the Mixed Economy

1. Musgrave and Musgrave, *Public Finance,* chap. 6 provides an excellent review of the growth of the public sector in the American economy. The data in this and following paragraphs are drawn from pp. 137, 640.

2. These figures tend to overstate the importance of federal expenditures with respect to actual purchases of goods and services, since there are substantial intergovernmental transfers from the federal to state governments. Actual purchases of goods and services by federal and state and local governments are approximately equal. See *Long Term Economic Growth*, ser. A34-36, pp. 186-187.

3. Harold G. Vatter, "Perspectives on the Forty-Sixth Anniversary of the U. S. Mixed Economy," *Explorations in Economic History,* 16 (July 1979), pp. 297-330.

4. For a detailed treatment of the development of these institutions, see Hugh S. Norton, *The Employment Act and the Council of Economic Advisers 1946-1976* (Columbia, S. C.: University of South Carolina Press, 1977).

5. A good review of the American business cycle from 1945 to 1970 is Robert Aaron Gordon, *Economic Instability and Growth: The American Record* (New York: Harper and Row, 1974), chaps. 4-6. For a comparison of prewar and postwar economic fluctuations, see Thomas Mayer, "A Comparison of Unemployment Rates and Income Fluctuations Prior to the Great Depression and in the Postwar Period," *Review of Economics and Statistics* 61 (February 1979), pp. 142-146. Mayer concludes that business cycle contractions and unemployment were more severe prior to 1930, thus providing some evidence that modern economic policies have been effective.

6. Vatter, "Perspectives on the Forty-Sixth Anniversary of the U. S. Mixed Economy," pp. 312-314.

7. An excellent survey is F. M. Scherer, *Industrial Market Structure and Economic Performance,* 2d ed. (Chicago: Rand McNally, 1980), chaps. 3, 4.

8. If, for example, one examines four-firm sales ratios (i.e., the percentage of total industry sales originating in the four largest firms), there is virtually no change from Nutter's figures for 1895-1904 to the present, aside from some cyclical variations. See Scherer, *Industrial Market Structure*, pp. 68-69.

9. The rise of Litton Industries is a case in point: from 249th on Fortune's list of industries in 1960, Litton rose to 35th in 1971 through some one hundred acquisitions of unrelated firms during the decade. Many other conglomerates followed a similar strategy, and the movement has persisted into the 1970s.

10. Walter Galenson and Robert S. Smith, "The United States," in John T. Dunlop and Walter Galenson, eds., *Labor in the Twentieth Century* (New York: Academic Press, 1978), pp. 30-31.

11. See, in particular, John Kenneth Galbraith, *American Capitalism: The Concept of Countervailing Power,* rev. ed. (Boston: Houghton Mifflin, 1956), and *The New Industrial State* (Boston: Houghton Mifflin, 1967) for his most recent position.

12. Galbraith's work has been velified by professional economists. For a critical

appraisal, see Milton Friedman, *Friedman on Galbraith* (Vancouver, B. C.: The Fraser Institute, 1977).

13. For example, the Civil Aeronautics Board ''prevents'' competition among airlines, the Federal Communications Commission ''prevents'' competition among television and radio stations, and so forth. This is the other side of the regulation coin, as was pointed out in chapter 7.

14. The phrase ''unholy trinity'' is Friedman's. See *Friedman on Galbriath*, p. 15.

Index

Library of Congress Cataloging in Publication Data

George, Peter James.

The emergence of industrial America.

Based on a series of lectures delivered at the University of Cambridge, England, during the Lent Term 1974.

Bibliography: p. 203

Includes index.

1. United States — Economic conditions.
2. United States — Industries — History. I. Title.

HC103.G4 1982 338.0973 82-5873

ISBN 0-87395-578-1 AACR2

ISBN 0-87395-579-X (pbk.)